LIVING LANGUAGE®

ADVANCED SPANISH

REVISED AND UPDATED

OTHER TITLES FROM LIVING LANGUAGE®

Complete Basic Courses: Whether you're just starting out or want a thorough review, the *Complete Basic Course* is the perfect choice. Developed by U.S. government experts, the building-block approach used here begins with simple words and phrases and progresses to more complex expressions. Just listen and repeat after the native speakers. English translations are provided in the coursebook. The lessons keep grammar to a minimum, but there's a full summary for easy reference. Includes three hours of recorded lessons in the target language, a coursebook, and a 15,000- to 20,000-word two-way dictionary. The dictionary includes thousands of phrases and idiomatic expressions to show how words are used in conversation.

Available in French, German, Italian, Japanese, Portuguese, Russian, Spanish, and English for Spanish speakers. Books available separately.

Skill Builders: Verbs: Mastering verb tenses is the key to real fluency in a foreign language. With this unique, award-winning program, you will learn conjugations in the context of useful phrases and dialogues and improve your conversational skills quickly, easily, and thoroughly. Four 60-minute bilingual cassettes, plus a 352-page manual. Verb charts are included for easy reference.

Available in French, German, Italian, and Spanish. Books available separately.

Ultimate Courses: Created for serious language learners, the *Ultimate* course is the equivalent of two years of college-level study. With refreshingly up-to-date conversations and vocabulary in each lesson, the *Ultimate* courses teach grammar, reading, writing, and culture along with conversational skills. The eight hours of recordings are separated into two sets. Listen to the first four recordings (Learn at Home) in the target language as you follow along in the manual. Then, with the second set of recordings (Learn on the Go), which are in both English and the target language, reinforce and build on the lessons in the first set of recordings. With these recordings, you're hearing conversations and speaking without the book—exactly as you would in real-life situations. Learn in the car, at the gym, or anywhere it's convenient.

Available in French, German, Italian, Japanese, Russian, Spanish, and English for Spanish speakers. Books available separately.

Adult/Child Activity Kits: Easy and fun, this activity kit for beginners introduces children ages 4–8 to a new language with 16 songs, games, and activities, centered around mealtime or car trips. Each *Adult/Child Activity Kit* includes a 60-minute bilingual cassette, a 48-page illustrated activity book that doubles as a scrapbook, and a full page of color stickers. Also included are tips on how to vary the activities for repeated use, making this a program parents and their children will turn to again and again.

Available in French, Italian, and Spanish.

Calendars: This amusing and informative day-by-day desk calendar introduces foreign phrases, cultural tidbits, and trivia. Each page includes the pronunciation and English translation of a French, Italian, Spanish, or Yiddish word or phrase. These calendars are ideal for beginners, as well as those who would like to brush up on the fun stuff! They make a perfect gift for students and teachers, co-workers, and family members with a love for foreign languages.

At bookstores everywhere, or call 1-800-733-3000. You can also reach us on the Web at www.livinglanguage.com or e-mail us at livinglanguage@randomhouse.com.

LIVING LANGUAGE®

ADVANCED SPANISH

REVISED AND UPDATED

Revised by
THE EDITORIAL STAFF OF LIVING LANGUAGE
AND
ANA SOFÍA RAMÍREZ-GELPÍ, PH.D.

Based on the original by
ROBERT E. HAMMARSTRAND, PH.D.,
HUNTER COLLEGE

Previously published as *Spanish 3*

Living Language, A Random House Company
New York

This work was previously published under the title *Living Language Conversation Manual, Spanish Advanced Course, Living Language Advanced Conversational Spanish,* and *Living Language Spanish 3* by Robert E. Hammarstrand, Ph.D.

Random House, Inc. New York, Toronto, London, Sydney, Auckland

www.livinglanguage.com

Published by Living Language, A Random House Company, 201 East 50th Street, New York, New York 10022. Member of the Crown Publishing Group.

Living Language is a registered trademark of Random House, Inc.

Printed in the United States of America

Library of Congress Cataloging-in-Publication Data is available on request.

ISBN 0-609-80450-2

10 9 8 7 6 5 4 3 2 1

1999 Updated Edition

CONTENTS

INTRODUCTION

Living Language® Advanced Spanish is a continuation of the beginner to intermediate level *Spanish Complete Course.* This program has been thoroughly revised and updated to reflect currect and idiomatic usage of Spanish. If you have already mastered the basics of Spanish in school, while traveling abroad, or with other Living Language courses, then *Advanced Spanish* is right for you.

The complete program includes this manual, along with four hours of recordings. However, if you are confident of your pronunciation, you can also use this manual on its own.

With *Advanced Spanish* you'll continue to learn how to speak and understand idiomatic Spanish. The program follows a Mexican couple visiting friends in Spain. While participating in their adventures you'll improve your proficiency to a level that allows you to take part in engaging conversations easily and comfortably.

COURSE MATERIALS

THE MANUAL

Living Language Advanced Spanish consists of 20 lessons. Every lesson includes a dialogue, notes, a grammar and usage section, and exercises.

DIALOGUE: Each lesson begins with a dialogue in standard, idiomatic Spanish presenting a realistic situation frequently encountered when traveling abroad. The dialogues feature Iberian and Latin American versions of Spanish, as they follow the adventures of a Mexican and a Spanish couple in Spain. All dialogues are translated into colloquial English.

NOTES: The notes refer to specific expressions and phrases in the dialogue. They'll allow you to see the grammar rules and vocabulary 'in action', and comment on the cultural and historical background of the particular expression. The notes are numbered according to the corresponding exchange in the dialogue, and the specific phrases covered are marked by the ° symbol.

GRAMMAR AND USAGE: This section reviews and expands upon basic Spanish grammar. You'll learn how to express yourself more accurately using advanced grammatical structures idiomatically.

EXERCISES: This section allows you to review the grammar and vocabulary covered in the lessons. With the ANSWER KEY in the back of the book you can check your progress. Note that the answers to the first exercise in each lesson do not appear in the ANSWER KEY, as this is primarily an oral and written drill.

The clear and concise SUMMARY OF SPANISH GRAMMAR, the easy-to-use VERB CHARTS, and the LETTER-WRITING section make this manual a valuable reference for future use.

THE RECORDINGS

The recordings include the complete dialogues of all 20 lessons in the manual plus a number of example sentences from the grammar and usage sections. The recorded material appears in **boldface** in your manual. Each dialogue is first read at normal conversational speed without interruption, and then a second time phrase by phrase with pauses for you to repeat after the native speakers. By listening to and imitating the native speakers you'll improve your pronunciation and comprehension while learning to use new phrases and structures.

INSTRUCTIONS

1. Look at page 1. The material in **boldface** type will appear on the recordings. Read each lesson through first, and pay careful attention to the vocabulary and grammar points emphasized in the Notes and Grammar and Usage sections. Examples of grammatical structures that appear on the recordings are in ***boldface italic*** type.

2. Then listen to the recordings as the dialogues are read at normal conversational speed. When the dialogues are read more slowly a second time, repeat after the native speakers in the pauses provided. Don't worry if your pronunciation is not perfect the first time around. Practice makes perfect. Study with the manual and listen to the recordings as often as you wish.

3. The exercises at the end of the lessons will help you to review the material covered in each lesson and will help you check your progress toward proficiency.

4. If you take breaks between lessons, it is always a good idea to review the previous lessons before you begin your studies again.

5. For future reference use the summary of Spanish grammar and the verb charts at the end of the manual.

LIVING LANGUAGE®

ADVANCED SPANISH

REVISED AND UPDATED

LESSON 1

UNA CITA EN UN CAFE
MEETING AT A CAFE

A. DIALOGUE

Se citan. They arrange to meet.

1. Miguel: **¿Diga?°**
   Hello.

2. Carlos: **Soy Carlos Andrade, de México.**
   This is Carlos Andrade, from Mexico.

3. Miguel: **¡Qué gusto!° ¿Dónde se encuentra?**
   What a pleasure! Where are you?

4. Carlos: **Estoy en el Hotel Plaza. *Acabamos de llegar,*° mi esposa y yo.°**
   At the Hotel Plaza. We have just arrived, my wife and I.

5. Miguel: **¡*Tengo ganas de verles* lo más pronto posible! ¿*Podemos vernos*° esta tarde? ¿Qué tal a las dos?**
   I'd like to see you as soon as possible! Can we get together this afternoon? How about two o'clock?

6. Carlos: **Claro que sí. ¿Dónde *podemos encontrarnos*?**
   Of course. Where can we meet?

7. Miguel: **En el Café Gijón.° Tome un taxi y vaya a la Castellana° cerca de la Cibeles.°**
   At the Café Gijón. Take a taxi and go to the Castellana near Cibeles Square.

8. Carlos: **Muy bien.° ¿Pero será posible encontrar una mesa a esa hora?**
All right. But will it be possible to get a table at that time?

9. Miguel: **Sin duda, hombre. Hasta luego, entonces.**
No doubt about it. (Of course.) See you in a little while, then.

10. Carlos: **Muy bien. Adiós.°**
Sounds good. So long.

Se encuentran en el café. They meet at the café.

11. Miguel: **Bueno, Carlos, por fin está usted aquí. ¡Bienvenido a Madrid!**
Well, Carlos, it's so good to see you. Welcome to Madrid!

12. Carlos: **Gracias, Miguel. Juana y yo estamos muy *contentos de estar* en Madrid finalmente.**
Thank you, Miguel. Juana and I are so happy to finally be in Madrid.

13. Miguel: **Pero . . . ¿dónde está Juana?**
But . . . where's Juana?

14. Carlos: **Ella se quedó en el hotel para desempacar las maletas. Además, fue un viaje largo y cansador.**
She stayed at the hotel to unpack. Besides, it was a long and tiring trip.

15. Miguel: **Ya veo. ¿Prefiere sentarse° adentro o afuera, al aire libre?**
I see. Do you prefer to sit in here or outside in the fresh air?

16. Carlos: **¡Al aire libre, claro!**
In the fresh air, of course!

17. Miguel: **¡Ah! Allí hay una mesa libre.**
Ah! There's an empty table.

18. Camarero: **¿Qué quieren tomar,° señores?**
Waiter: What would you like, gentlemen?

19. Miguel: **Una limonada, por favor. ¡Hace tanto calor!°**
A lemonade, please. It's so hot!

20. Carlos: **Y para mí, una cerveza.**
And for me, a beer.

21. Camerero: **En seguida,° señores.**
Right away, gentlemen.

22. Carlos: **¡Qué manera más *agradable de empezar* la estancia en Madrid! ¡Ah! Aquí está el camarero con las bebidas. ¡Salud!°**
What a pleasant way to begin my stay in Madrid! Ah! Here's the waiter with our drinks. Cheers!

23. Miguel: **¡Salud! ¡Y que ustedes lo pasen bien° en Madrid!**
Cheers! And I hope you'll have a good time in Madrid!

24. Carlos: **Se está° muy bien aquí. *Tengo ganas de*° quedarme aquí todo el día.°**
It's really nice here. I feel like staying here all day.

25. Miguel: **Uno puede quedarse en el café toda la tarde, si quiere.**
You can stay at the café all afternoon, if you want.

26. Carlos: **¿Y jamás hacen marcharse a° los clientes?**
Don't they ever ask the customers to leave?

27. Miguel: **¡Jamás! Y, si quiere,** ***puede leer el periódico,*** **escribir cartas, charlar con los amigos, o solamente observar a la gente que pasa.**
Never! And, if you want you can read the newspaper, write letters, chat with friends, or simply look at the people passing by.

28. Carlos: **En el mundo de los negocios, uno pierde fácilmente el arte de descansar.**
In the business world, one easily loses the art of relaxing.

29. Miguel: **Es cierto. Espero que hayan° tenido un buen viaje.**
True. I hope you had a good trip.

30. Carlos: **Sí, el vuelo estuvo bien.**
Yes, the flight was fine.

31. Miguel: **Bueno, si no tienen planes para mañana, tal vez podríamos pasear° un poco.**
Well, if you don't have any plans for tomorrow, perhaps we could do a little sightseeing.

32. Carlos: **¡Me parece bien!° Estoy seguro de que Juana querrá acompañarnos. Gracias.**
What a good idea! I'm sure Juana will want to come with us. Thank you.

33. Miguel: **Camarero, la cuenta, por favor. Pago la cuenta, y nos marchamos. . . . No, no, Carlos. Yo le invito, hombre, que es para celebrar su llegada a Madrid.**
Waiter! The check, please. I'm going to pay the bill, and we'll go. . . . No, no, Carlos. It's my treat, to celebrate your arrival in Madrid.

B. NOTES

1. *Diga:* In Spain, *Diga* or *Dígame* (imperative of *decir*) is the equivalent of the English "hello" when answering the telephone. There is considerable variety in other Spanish-speaking countries: *Bueno* in Mexico, *A ver* in Colombia, *Oigo* or *¿Qué hay?* in Cuba, *Holá* in Argentina, and *Aló* in most other countries.

3. *¡Qué gusto!:* Note the use of *qué* before nouns to express "What a . . ." in exclamations.

4. *acabamos de llegar:* Note the use of *acabar de* plus the infinitive to express "to have just."
mi esposa y yo: In Latin America, the possessive is preferred to the article. However in Spain, the article is more commonly used: *la esposa* (or *la mujer*) *y yo.*

5. *vernos:* Note the use of the reflexive pronoun to indicate mutual action: "to see each other" or "to meet one another." Compare *encontrarnos*, used later.

7. *Café Gijón:* Popular rendezvous for writers, directors, and actors on the long and beautiful, tree-lined boulevard *Avenida de la Castellana,* near the lovely fountain and statue of *Cibeles* in front of Madrid's main post office, *el Correo.*

8. *Muy bien:* Alright. OK; used to express agreement.

10. *Adiós:* Good-bye. *Adiós* is used in Mexico while *Hasta luego* is more common in Spain.

15. *sentarse:* to sit down. Note the use of the reflexive pronoun, attached here to the infinitive, and in sentence 14 placed before the form of the main verb in *Ella se quedó.*

18. *tomar:* to take; used in the sense of "to eat" or "to drink."

19. *¡Hace tanto calor!:* The verb *hacer* is generally used with expressions concerning weather conditions. Compare *hace frío* (it's cold); *hace fresco* (it's cool); *hace buen tiempo* (the weather is fine); *hace viento* (it's windy).

21. *En seguida:* Right away. Equivalents: *inmediatamente, ahora mismo.*

22. *¡Salud!:* Cheers! lit., "health." In toasting one another, Spanish-speaking people generally exchange this single word.

23. *Y que ustedes lo pasen bien:* In expressing a wish or desire, the verb "to hope" *(esperar)* is frequently omitted and the statement begins with the introductory *que,* with the following verb in the subjunctive. Equivalent to the English "(May you) have a good time." Compare *¡Que vivan mil años!* ("May they live a thousand years!") and *¡Que siga usted bien!* ("May you continue in good health!")

24. *Se está:* Note the use of the reflexive here for the impersonal "one feels."
tengo ganas de; me gustaría: I feel like,° I'd like to.
todo el día: all day. Note the use of the article in such expressions as *todo el año* (all year), *toda la tarde* (all afternoon), *toda la semana* (all week), *todo el verano* (all summer), etc.

26. *hacen marcharse a:* lit., "make go away."
Note the use of the personal *a* before *clientes.* Compare *observar a la gente* in sentence 27.

29. *hayan tenido:* Note the use of the subjunctive after the verb of emotion, "to hope."

31. *pasear:* to stroll, to walk around, to go sightseeing. This verb can also be used with *pasear en coche* (to drive around in a car), *pasear a caballo* (to ride around on horseback).

32. *¡Me parece bien!:* "What a good idea" or "That sounds good."

C. GRAMMAR AND USAGE

1. *Acabar de:* to have just

	acabar	*de*	Infinitive
a.	***Acabo***	***de***	***llegar.***
b. *Juan*	*acaba*	*de*	*llamar.*

a. I have just arrived.
b. Juan has just called.

2. *Tener ganas de:* to feel like

	tener	*ganas*	*de*	Infinitive	Complement
a.	***Tengo***	***ganas***	***de***	***comer***	***helado.***
b. *María*	*tiene*	*ganas*	*de*	*salir.*	
c. *Ellos*	*tendrán*	*ganas*	*de*	*acostarse.*	

a. I feel like eating ice cream.
b. María feels like leaving.
c. They will feel like going to bed.

Note:
- For forms of *tener,* see Summary of Grammar.

3. *Poder* + infinitive + complement: to be able to

	poder	Infinitive	Complement
a.	***Puedo***	***hacer***	***el trabajo.***
b. ***Juan***	***puede***	***estudiar***	***la lección mañana.***
c.	*Podemos*	*pasar*	*las vacaciones allí.*
d. *Ellos*	*pueden*	*ver*	*a María la semana que viene.*

a. I can do the work.
b. Juan can study the lesson tomorrow.
c. We can spend our vacation there.
d. They can see María next week.

Note:

- The *a* is used before nouns or pronouns referring to persons.
  He visto a papá. I have seen my dad.

		poder	Infinitive + Object pronoun
a.	***El***	***podía***	***hacerlo.***
b.	***Ellos***	***podrán***	***comerlo.***
c.	*Ella*	*puede*	*mandarlo.*

a. He was able to do it.
b. They will be able to eat it.
c. She can send it.

Note:

- The object pronoun may also precede the form of *poder*

  a. *Lo podía hacer.*

  b. *Ellos lo podrán comer.*

  c. *Ella lo puede mandar.*

- *Poder* generally implies physical ability to do something. When knowledge or learned skills are implied, *saber* is generally used.

  Compare:

  Puedo leerlo. ("I can read it" in the sense of having the ability to read it; i.e., in spite of the darkness, fog, bad script, etc.)

  Sé leerlo. ("I can read it" in the sense of knowing how to, as a language, a code, etc.)

4. Adjective + *de*

estar	Adjective	*de*	Infinitive + Object
a. ***Estoy***	***contenta***	***de***	***saberlo.***
b. *Estaba*	*sorprendido*	*de*	*verme.*
c. *Estarán*	*encantados*	*de*	*recibirnos.*

a. I'm happy to know it.
b. He was surprised to see me.
c. They will be happy to have us.

Note:

- Adjectives agree with the preceding subject.
  María está contenta. María is happy.
- Subject pronouns are generally omitted, as the verb form and the context clarify the subject.

EXERCISES

A. Substitute each of the words or expressions in parentheses for the underlined word or expression in the model sentence. Write each new sentence and say it aloud.

1. *Juan acaba de comer. (estudiar, entrar, salir, acostarse, lavarse)*

2. *Los hombres acaban de llegar. (verlo, escucharlo, hablar, telefonar)*

3. *Tengo ganas de ir al cine. (al concierto, a la biblioteca, al museo, al parque, al restaurante)*

4. *Tienen ganas de bailar. (cantar, leer, mirar la televisión, escuchar la radio, ir al cine)*

5. *Puedo hacer lo. (comer, beber, comprar, estudiar, ganar, aprender)*

6. *Los niños están contentos de estar aquí. (Los padres, Los hombres, Juan y José, Los profesores, María y Rafael)*

B. Convert these sentences to the plural. Write the complete sentence and translate.

1. *Acabo de llegar.*

2. *El niño tiene ganas de comer.*

3. *Usted puede hacerlo.*

4. *La muchacha está contenta de verlos.*

5. *Lo puedo hacer ahora.*

C. Translate the following sentences into Spanish, then say them aloud.

1. He has just come in.

2. She has just eaten.

3. We feel like going to thc movies.

4. I feel like dancing.

5. I can do it now.

6. We can see her tomorrow.

7. They'll be able to go there.

8. I am happy to see you.

9. We are surprised to hear it.

10. They are pleased to know it.

D. From among the three choices given, choose the best equivalent of the English given at the beginning of each sentence. Write the complete sentence and translate.

1. (Who) ¿__________ *habla?*
   (a) *Que*
   (b) *Cuál*
   (c) *Quién*

2. (What a) ¡ __________ *gusto!*
   (a) *Qué*
   (b) *Cuál*
   (c) *Cuál un*

3. (way) ¡Qué __________ *más agradable de empezar el día!*
   (a) *vía*
   (b) *manera*
   (c) *camino*

4. (had) *Espero que hayan* __________ *buen viaje.*
   (a) *habido*
   (b) *tenido*
   (c) *hecho*

5. (at) *Vimos a Miguel* __________ *el Café Gijón.*
   (a) *al*
   (b) *en*
   (c) *entre*

6. (all) *Estábamos aquí* __________ *el día.*
   (a) *todos*
   (b) *toda*
   (c) *todo*

7. (There are) __________ *muchos monumentos en Madrid.*
   (a) *Están*
   (b) *Allí son*
   (c) *Hay*

8. (sit down) *¿Quiere usted* __________ *aquí?*
   (a) *sentarte*
   (b) *sentarse*
   (c) *sentar*

9. (so much) *El señor tiene* __________ *dinero.*
   (a) *tan*
   (b) *tantas*
   (c) *tanto*

10. (arrived) *Acabamos de* __________ .
   (a) *llegado*
   (b) *llegar*
   (c) *llegamos*

LESSON 2

EL KIOSCO DE REVISTAS°
THE NEWSSTAND

A. DIALOGUE

1. Carlos: *(Al vendedor de periódicos)* **Acabamos de llegar de México, señor, y no *conozco*° los periódicos de España. ¿Podría usted ayudarme?**
(To the news vendor) We've just arrived from Mexico, sir, and I'm not familiar with Spanish newspapers. Could you help me?

2. Vendedor: **Con mucho gusto, señor. Para información política y noticias en general, tenemos varios periódicos en Madrid. Por ejemplo, aquí tenemos *El país,* que es muy bueno. También *hay* publicaciones literarias como *Indice,*° *Insula,*° *La estafeta literaria*°. . .**
With pleasure, sir. For politics and general news, we have several papers in Madrid. For example, here we have *El país,* which is very good. Also, there are literary publications like *Indice, Insula, La estafeta literaria . . .*

3. Juana: **Todas ésas son literarias, ¿verdad? ¿*Hay* una revista dedicada al teatro?**
Those are all literary, aren't they? Is there a magazine devoted to the theater?

4. Vendedor: **Sí, señora. *Hay* una muy buena que se llama *Primer acto.***
Yes, ma'am. There's a very good one called *Primer acto.*

5. Carlos: **Si no me equivoco, aquí veo unos siete u ocho° periódicos populares.**

If I'm not mistaken, I see about seven or eight popular papers here.

6. Juana: **Sí, ¿pero *cuál de* ellos es el mejor y el más extensamente leído?**
Yes, but which one is the best and the most widely read?

7. Vendedor: **Eso, señora, no es difícil contestarlo.° Es el *A B C,*° sin duda alguna. Tenga. ¿Quiere usted mirarlo?**
That, ma'am, is not difficult to answer. It's *A B C,* without any doubt. Here, would you like to look at it?

8. Carlos: **¡Pero parece una revista con este grabado en la portada! Y luego un artículo sobre la novela del siglo diecinueve.**
But it looks like a magazine with this picture on the cover! And then an article on the nineteenth-century novel.

9. Vendedor: **Pero, señor, aquí dentro hay todo lo que *le hace falta*:° noticias, teatro, programas de radio y televisión, modas, noticias de sociedad, deportes, hasta comentan las carreras de caballos y las corridas de toros.**
But, sir, there is everything here that you need: news, theater, radio and television programs, fashion, society news, sports . . . they even comment on horse racing and bullfights.

10. Carlos: **De todas formas, no parece muy serio . . . hay muchas fotos. ¿No tendría usted° algún otro con menos fotos, y un aspecto más serio?**
Still, it doesn't look very serious . . . there are a lot of pictures. Don't you have another with fewer pictures that is more serious?

11. Vendedor: **Bueno, entonces compre usted *Informaciones* o *Ya*.**
Well, then take *Informaciones* or *Ya*.

12. Carlos: **Bien, voy a empezar con *Informaciones*.**
OK. I will start with *Informaciones*.

13. Juana: **Veo que usted tiene revistas de todo el mundo—francesas, italianas, alemanas, inglesas, americanas, y japonesas.**
I see you have magazines from all over the world—French, Italian, German, English, American, and Japanese.

14. Vendedor: **Sí, señora, y de todas clases. Hay revistas semanales y mensuales y hasta hay otras que son quincenales.**
Yes, ma'am, and of all kinds. There are weekly and monthly magazines, and even some others that come out every other week.

15. Juana: **Aquellas son de interés general, ¿verdad? *Blanco y negro* y *Gaceta ilustrada*.**
Those over there are of general interest, aren't they? *Blanco y negro* and *Gaceta ilustrada*.

16. Vendedor: **Sí, y aquí en este lado tenemos revistas de modas, de cocina, y *¡Hola!* y *Arte y hogar*. . . .**
That's right, and on this side we have fashion and cooking magazines, and *¡Hola!* and *Arte y hogar*. . . .

17. Juana: **¿Me permite hojear° un poco este número de *¡Hola!*?**
May I look through this issue of *¡Hola!* for a moment?

18. Vendedor: **Por supuesto, señora. Es una buena revista.**
Of course, ma'am. It's a good magazine.

19. Carlos: **¿Tienen revistas sobre computadoras?**
Do you have any computer magazines?

20. Vendedor: **Claro que sí. Aquí tenemos *Informática plus* o el último número de *Mundo PC.* O si quiere algo menos específico, aquí está *Ciencia popular,* que también habla de computadoras.**
Of course. Here we have *Informática plus* or the latest issue of *Mundo PC.* Or if you want something less technical, here is *Ciencia popular,* which also discusses computers.

21. Carlos: **¿*Qué* más necesitamos? A ver.**
What else do we need? Let's see.

22. Vendedor: **¿Podría también recomendarles esta pequeña revista, *La Semana en Madrid*? Les da información sobre todos los espectáculos.**
May I also recommend this little magazine, *La Semana en Madrid*? It gives you information about all the shows.

23. Carlos: **Es exactamente lo que *nos hace falta,* señor. ¿Tiene también una guía de Madrid que indique los sitios de interés turístico?**
It's exactly what we need, sir. Would you also have a map of Madrid with all the points of interest marked?

24. Vendedor: **Claro. Esta es muy buena.**
Of course. This one is very good.

25. Juana: **Tenemos una guía de toda España, pero no tenemos una guía detallada de Madrid.**
We have a guidebook of all of Spain, but we don't have a detailed guide to Madrid.

26. Vendedor: **Este librito es exactamente lo que necesitan.**
This little book is exactly what you need.

27. Carlos: **Usted ha sido amable, señor. ¿Podría decirnos una tienda cerca de aquí donde vendan CDs y cintas magnetofónicas?**
You have been very kind, sir. Could you tell us if there's a store near here where they sell CDs and tapes?

28. Vendedor: **Hay una a cuatro pasos de aquí, en la esquina. Hasta luego, señores, y que les vaya bien.**
There's one nearby, at the corner. Good-bye, and all the best.

B. NOTES

Title: *kiosco de revistas:* newsstand. There are *kioscos* on street corners in Madrid, where one can buy newspapers, magazines, maps, guidebooks, etc.

1. *no conozco:* I don't know, in the sense "to not be familiar with" from *conocer.*

2. *Indice, Insula, La estafeta literaria:* literary magazines which include reviews of films, theater, art, television, as well as articles on political and economic topics.

5. *siete u ocho:* Note that *o* ("or") changes to *u* before a word beginning with *o.*

7. *contestarlo:* Notice that "it" is expressed in Spanish even though it is frequently omitted in similar English expressions.

9. *lo que le hace falta:* from *hacer falta,* to be lacking (to someone). Compare *Me hace falta un libro:* I need a book. *Nos hace falta más dinero:* We need more money.

10. *no tendría usted:* The conditional is sometimes used in polite expressions. See sentence 27.

17. *hojear:* from *hoja* (leaf), to "leaf through" or "glance over" the pages.

C. GRAMMAR AND USAGE

1. *Conocer/saber:* to know

conocer: to know, to be acquainted (familiar) with something or someone; to meet (a person)
saber: to know as a fact, to know how to

conocer

a. ***Conozco a los señores Hernández.***	a. I know Mr. and Mrs. Hernández.
b. *No conocemos el norte de España.*	b. We do not know (are not familiar with) the north of Spain.
c. *Ellos conocen bien el sistema.*	c. They know the system well.
d. *Conocí a María en Francia.*	d. I met María in France (i.e., we met for the first time, became acquainted).

saber

a. ***Sé que los señores Hernández están aquí.***	a. I know that Mr. and Mrs. Hernández are here.
b. *Todos sabemos la verdad.*	b. We all know the truth.
c. *Ella lo sabrá mañana.*	c. She will know it (i.e., some fact) tomorrow.
d. *El sabe cocinar.*	d. He knows how to cook.

2. *Hay:* these are, there are

a. ***Hay muchos libros sobre la mesa.***	a. There are many books on the table.
b. *Habrá un desfile mañana.*	b. There will be a parade tomorrow.
c. *Había mucha gente allí.*	c. There were many people there.

3. *¿Qué?:* What? *¿Cuál?:* Which? *¿Quién(es)?:* Who?

a. ***¿Qué sabe usted de la familia?***	a. What do you know about the family?
b. ***¿Cuál de los niños es amigo tuyo?***	b. Which of the children is a friend of yours?
c. ***¿Quién es aquel niño?***	c. Who is that child?

4. *Hacer falta:* to need (to lack)

Indirect object pronoun	*hacer falta*	Subject
a. ***Me***	***hace falta***	***más dinero.***
b. ***Te***	***hacen falta***	***tres pesetas.***
c. *Le*	*hará falta*	*(a él) mucha experiencia.*

a. I need more money.
b. You need three pesetas.
c. He will need a lot of experience.

EXERCISES

A. Substitute each of the words or expressions in parentheses for the underlined word or expression in the model sentence. Write each new sentence and say it aloud.

1. *Acaba de conocer a María. (a tu hermano, a los señores La Torre, a la señora de Aguirre, a la señorita Domenech, a los amigos de mi padre)*

2. *Ellos conocen a Juan. (María y yo, yo, Pepe, Francisco y Miguel, todo el mundo)*

3. *Ellos deben saber el número. (la dirección, la verdad, el precio, la fecha, el nombre, la palabra)*

4. *Hay muchas personas en el hotel. (una peluquería, varios salones, un comedor, algunas reuniones, un conserje)*

5. *Me hace(n) falta un libro. (unos discos, más información, un corte de pelo, más tiempo, los nombres)*

6. *¿Quién(es) es (son) aquel muchacho? (tu amigo, María Velarde, estos señores, el profesor, los alum nos)*

B. Convert these sentences to the plural. Write the complete sentence and translate.

1. *El sabe bailar.*
2. *Usted conocerá a los señores Pérez.*
3. *Hay una clase por la tarde.*
4. *Me hace falta una peseta.*
5. *¿Quién es el médico?*

C. Translate the following sentences into Spanish, then say them aloud.

1. Do you know the number?
2. They know how to dance.
3. There were many parades.

4. Which of these books do you want?

5. Who are the men on the corner?

6. What do you need?

7. Do they know the address?

8. Who knows María?

9. They need many classes.

10. We need more time.

D. From among the three choices given, choose the best equivalent of the English given at the beginning of each sentence. Write the complete sentence and translate.

1. (know) *Estoy seguro de que ellos* __________ *a María.*
   (a) *sepan*
   (b) *conocer*
   (c) *conocen*

2. (knew) *Me dijeron que ellos* __________ *el título del libro.*
   (a) *sabían*
   (b) *conocerán*
   (c) *conozco*

3. (need) *Me hace* __________ *un libro nuevo.*
   (a) *necesito*
   (b) *falta*
   (c) *faltas*

4. (good) *Hay una revista muy* __________ *que sale el lunes.*
   (a) *bueno*
   (b) *buenas*
   (c) *buena*

5. (which one) *No me dijo* __________ *de estas novelas es mejor.*
   (a) *qué*
   (b) *quién*
   (c) *cuál*

6. (there are) *En este lado* __________ *muchos periódicos extranjeros.*
   (a) *hay*
   (b) *estarán*
   (c) *habían*

7. (German) *Esta revista* __________ *es interesante.*
   (a) *alemanes*
   (b) *alemana*
   (c) *alemán*

8. (should be) *Este librito* __________ *lo que quieren ustedes.*
   (a) *debe ser*
   (b) *tiene que estar*
   (c) *son*

9. (feel like) *Ellos* __________ *de ir a la fiesta.*
   (a) *sienten como*
   (b) *tienen ganas*
   (c) *quieren*

10. (you) *Este libro* __________ *da a usted muchos informes.*
   (a) *le*
   (b) *os*
   (c) *les*

LESSON 3

AL TELEFONO
ON THE TELEPHONE

A. DIALOGUE

Una llamada de larga distancia. A long-distance call.

1. Carlos (*a una empleada en el mostrador del hotel*): **¿Puedo hacer una llamada de larga distancia° desde aquí, señorita?**
(to an employee at the hotel desk) May I make a long-distance call from here, miss?

2. Empleada: **¿A qué ciudad, señor?**
To what city, sir?

3. Carlos: **A Barcelona, pero no sé el número.**
Barcelona, but I don't know the number.

4. Empleada: **No es problema, señor. Puedo conseguirlo del servicio de información.**
That's no problem, sir. I can get it from Information.

5. Carlos: **No se moleste. Lo buscaré en la telefónica.**
Don't bother. I'll look it up in the telephone book.

6. Empleada: **Muy bien, señor. Encontrará la guía allí, a la derecha.**
Very well, sir. You'll find the directory over there, to the right.

7. Carlos: **Gracias, señorita.** ***Vamos a ver*** **. . . ¡Ah! Huerta, Felipe . . . cuarenta y ocho, sesenta y dos, cincuenta y siete.**

Thank you, miss. Let's see . . . Ah! Huerta, Felipe . . . forty-eight, sixty-two, fifty-seven.

8. Empleada: **¡Qué bueno que lo haya encontrado! Son ciento cincuenta pesetas por tres minutos.**
That's great—you found it. It's a hundred and fifty pesetas for three minutes.

9. Carlos: **Si es más de tres minutos, pago más, ¿no?**
And if it's more than three minutes, I pay more, don't I?

10. Empleada: **Sí, señor. ¿Puede usted esperar en la cabina número ocho? Le haré una señal en cuanto tenga su llamada.** *(Ella llama a la telefonista.)*
That's right, sir. Please wait in booth number eight. I'll signal you as soon as I have your call. *(She calls the operator.)*

11. Telefonista: **Número, por favor.**
Number, please.

12. Empleada: **Señorita, *póngame* con el cuatro cuarenta y ocho, sesenta y dos, cincuenta y siete, en Barcelona, por favor.**
Operator, connect me with four forty-eight, sixty-two, fifty-seven in Barcelona, please.

13. Telefonista: **Un momento, por favor. Aquí está la llamada.**
Just a minute, please. Here's your party.

14. Empleada: **Gracias, señorita.** *(Ella le hace una señal a Carlos.)*
Thank you, miss. *(She motions to Carlos.)*

15. Carlos: *(En la cabina número ocho)* **Bueno. ¿Podría hablar con el Sr. Huerta, por favor?**

(In booth number eight) Hello. May I speak to Mr. Huerta, please?

16. Criada: **¿De parte de quién, por favor?**
Who's calling, please?

17. Carlos: **Mi nombre es Carlos Andrade y llamo desde Madrid.**
This is Carlos Andrade, and I'm calling from Madrid.

18. Criada: **Voy a ver si el señor está. . . . No, señor, acaba de marcharse. *¿Quiere usted dejar un recado?***
I'll see if he's here. . . . No, sir, he's just left. Do you want to leave a message?

19. Carlos: ***Dígale* que le llamaré esta noche, por favor.**
Please tell him that I'll call him this evening.

20. Criada: **Muy bien, señor. Le daré el recado.**
Very well, sir. I'll give him your message.

21. Carlos: **Gracias. Adiós.**
Thank you. Good-bye.

Una llamada local. A local call.

22. Carlos: *(En la ventanilla°)* **Siento molestarla otra vez, señorita, pero . . .**
(At the service window) I'm sorry to bother you again, miss, but . . .

23. Empleada: **No es molestia, señor, en absoluto.**
It's no trouble at all, sir.

24. Carlos: **Es que no estoy acostumbrado a los teléfonos automáticos de aquí.**

It's just that I'm still not used to your dial phones.

25. Empleada: **No es muy complicado, señor. ¿Sabe usted el número?**
It's not very complicated, sir. Do you know the number?

26. Carlos: **Sí, esta vez es una llamada local, treinta y ocho, veinte y cinco, quince.**
Yes, this time it's a local call, thirty-eight, twenty-five, fifteen.

27. Empleada: **Le hace falta una moneda, señor. *Descuelgue*, *meta* la moneda, *espere* la señal, y *marque* el número.**
You need a coin, sir. Pick up the receiver, put the coin in, wait for the dial tone, and dial your number.

28. Carlos: **Bien . . . pero ¿qué son estos botones?**
Okay . . . but what are these buttons?

29. Empleada: **Bueno, usted oirá la señal, y cuando contesten, apriete el botón A.**
Well, you will hear the ring, and when they answer, press button A.

30. Carlos: **Pero, ¿y si no contestan? ¿O si la línea está ocupada? ¿O si me equivoco de número?**
But what if they don't answer? Or if the line is busy? Or if I get a wrong number?

31. Empleada: **Pues entonces, cuelgue. Espere un rato y vuelva a marcar.**
Well then, just hang up. Wait a while and dial again.

32. Carlos: **Gracias, señorita.**
Thank you, miss.

B. NOTES

1. *Larga distancia:* used in Mexico and other countries of Latin America to mean "long distance."

22. *ventanilla:* a small service-window such as is found in banks, post offices, and theaters.

C. GRAMMAR AND USAGE

1. *Ir a* + infinitive: going + infinitive

ir	*a*	Infinitive	Complement
a. ***Voy***	***a***	***estudiar***	***la lección.***
b. *Vamos*	*a*	*ir*	*a la tienda.*
c. *Van*	*a*	*hacer*	*una llamada.*

a. I'm going to study the lesson.
b. We're going to go to the store.
c. They're going to make a phone call.

2. *Más que (de:)* more than

más que

a. ***Juan tiene más libros que María.***	a. Juan has more books than María.
b. *Yo estudio más que Juan.*	b. I study more than Juan.
c. *Ellos viajan más que nadie.*	c. They travel more than anyone.

más de (used with numbers)

a. ***El vendió más de cien libros.***	a. He sold more than a hundred books.
b. *Ellos compraron más de cuatro casas.*	b. They bought more than four houses.
c. *Ustedes tienen más de tres horas.*	c. You have more than three hours.

Note:

- In the negative, *no más que* usually means "only" and *que* is used even before numbers.

No tengo más que cien pesetas.	I have only (I have no more than) a hundred pesetas.

3. Command or request forms:

POLITE FORMS

a. ***Ponga usted el libro allí.***	a. Put the book there.
b. *Vengan ustedes mañana.*	b. Come tomorrow.
c. *Vaya usted a verlo.*	c. Go (sing.) to see it.
d. *No fumen ustedes.*	d. Don't smoke.
e. *Entre usted.*	e. Come in (Enter).
f. *No coman ustedes tanto.*	f. Don't eat so much.

Note:

- The polite forms are the third person singular (for *usted*) and the third person plural (for *ustedes*) of the present subjunctive.

FAMILIAR SINGULAR

a. ***Mira. No mires.***	a. Look. Don't look.
b. *Esucha. No escuches.*	b. Listen. Don't listen.
c. *Come el helado. No comas el helado.*	c. Eat the ice cream. Don't eat the ice cream.
d. *Ven aquí en seguida. No vengas aquí.*	d. Come here at once. Don't come here.
e. *Ponte el sombrero. No te pongas el sombrero.*	e. Put on your hat. Don't put on your hat.
f. *Vete. No te vayas.*	f. Go away. Don't go away.

Note:

- The familiar singular affirmative command (*tú*) is usually the same as the third person singular of the present indicative. There are some irregular forms: *ten, pon, ven, ve, sal.*
- The negative uses the second person singular of the present subjunctive.
- The object pronouns (reflexive, indirect, and direct) are attached to both polite and familiar affirmative commands:

Dámelo.	Give it to me.
Póntelo.	Put it on.
Tráimelo.	Bring it to me.

but not to negative commands:

No me lo des.	Don't give it to me.
No te lo pongas.	Don't put it on.
No me lo traigas.	Don't bring it to me.

FAMILIAR PLURAL (VOSOTROS)

a. ***Hablad más alto. No habléis más alto.***	a. Speak louder. Don't speak louder.
b. *Escuchad. No escuchéis.*	b. Listen. Don't listen.
c. *Venid. No vengáis.*	c. Come. Don't come.
d. *Compradlo. No lo compréis.*	d. Buy it. Don't buy it.
e. *Traédmelo. No me lo traigáis.*	e. Bring it to me. Don't bring it to me.
f. *Dádnoslo. No nos lo deis.*	f. Give it to us. Don't give it to us.

Note:

- The affirmative familiar plural imperative is formed by changing the final *r* of the infinitive to *d.* The negative is the second person plural form of the present subjunctive. Note the position of pronouns.

- *Vosotros* forms, including these commands, are only used in Spain.

4. *querer* + infinitive: I want

a. ***Quiero llamarle ahora.***	a. I want to call him now.
b. *No queremos ir al cine.*	b. We don't want to go to the movies.
c. *Querían hablar con Pablo.*	c. They wanted to speak with Pablo.

EXERCISES

A. Substitute each of the words or expressions in the parentheses for the underlined word or expression in the model sentence. Write each new sentence and say it aloud.

1. *Van a comprar la casa. (los libros, el disco, un coche, dos entradas, el sombrero)*

2. *Voy a estudiar mañana. (escribir, comprarlo, salir, llamar, descansar)*

3. *Tengo más de tres clases. (libros, problemas, billetes, programas, pesetas)*

4. *Juan y María viajan más que yo. (el profesor, nadie, la Sra. Andrade, ella, nosotros)*

5. *No escuches la radio. (el programa, la música, las noticias, la broma, el cuento)*

6. *Ellos quieren cantar. (bailar, comer, comprarlo, irse, verlo)*

B. Change these commands to the negative. Write the complete sentence and translate.
Example: *Dámelo.—No me lo des.*

1. *Dígamelo.*

2. *Vete.*

3. *Póngaselo.*

4. *Quítatelo.*

5. *Cómpramelo.*

C. Translate the following sentences into Spanish, then say them aloud.

1. I work more than Juan.

2. They will travel more than three hours today.

3. We have more than ten pages to read *(que leer).*

4. They are going to buy a new car.

5. He is going to rest tomorrow.

6. We were going to sell the house.

7. Do you want to see the doctor?

8. He wants to give me the book.

9. Don't send it to him.

10. They don't want to leave.

D. From among the three choices given, choose the best equivalent of the English given at the beginning of each sentence. Write the complete sentence and translate.

1. (the telephone book) *Usted encontrará* __________ *allí.*
   (a) *la guía telefónica*
   (b) *el libro de teléfonos*
   (c) *la telefónica*

2. (than) *Tenemos más dinero* __________ *ellos.*
   (a) *de*
   (b) *que*
   (c) *el que*

3. (send to him) *Quieren* __________ *el libro.*
   (a) *mandarnos*
   (b) *mandarse*
   (c) *mandarle*

4. (go into) *Tenía que* __________ *la cabina.*
   (a) *ir a*
   (b) *entrar por*
   (c) *entrar en*

5. (Tell him) __________ *que estoy en Madrid.*
   (a) *Dale*
   (b) *Dígale*
   (c) *Dícele*

6. (make) *Puedo* __________ *una llamada de larga distancia a Madrid.*
   (a) *dar*
   (b) *poner*
   (c) *hacer*

7. (know) *¿* __________ *usted el número?*
   (a) *Sé*
   (b) *Sabe*
   (c) *Conozco*

8. Don't tell it to him.
   (a) *No dígaselo.*
   (b) *No le lo diga.*
   (c) *No se lo diga.*

9. (send it to us) __________ *usted mañana.*
   (a) *Mándelonos*
   (b) *Mándenoslo*
   (c) *Mándenoslos*

10. (to send them) *Ellos quieren* __________ *en seguida.*
   (a) *mandarle*
   (b) *mandarlos*
   (c) *mandarlo*

LESSON 4

TRANSPORTES URBANOS
CITY TRANSPORTATION

A. DIALOGUE

El metro.° The subway.

1. Carlos: **¿Cómo es que terminamos tan lejos del hotel? Tenemos bastante camino *para* regresar. Tal vez deberíamos pedir un taxi.**
   How did we end up so far from the hotel? We have quite a trip ahead of us to get back. Maybe we should take a taxi.

2. Juana: **¿Te has vuelto loco?° Un taxi nos costará un ojo de la cara.°**
   Have you gone crazy? A taxi will cost us a fortune.

3. Carlos: **¿Desde cuándo° piensas en ahorrar?**
   Since when did you start thinking of saving?

4. Juana: **Es que prefiero gastar el dinero en otras cosas.**
   It's just that I prefer to spend the money on other things.

5. Carlos: **Bueno, creo que podemos tomar el metro y luego el autobús *por* el resto del camino. Necesitaremos un taxi para el último trecho. Podremos llegar al hotel *por* poco dinero.**
   Well, I think we can take the subway and then the bus the rest of the way. We'll just need a taxi for the last part. We'll be able to get to the hotel for very little money.

6. Juana: **Muy bien. Compremos los boletos *para* el metro. Espero que eso no sea difícil.**
All right. Let's get our tickets for the subway. I hope it's not too difficult.

7. Carlos: **¿Cómo hacemos para ir a Correos?°**
How do we get to Correos (the Post Office)?

8. Empleada: **Es muy fácil. Es la cuarta parada en esta misma línea.**
It's very easy. It's the fourth stop on this very line.

9. Carlos: **¿Lo ves, Juana? Es facilísimo. Y tan rápido. Estaremos allí en pocos minutos.**
You see, Juana? It's very easy. And so fast. We'll be there in a few minutes.

10. Juana: **Si, ya veo . . . pero hay tanta gente y con el calor que hace . . .**
Yes, I see . . . but there are so many people and with the heat . . .

11. Carlos: **Bueno. Piensa en el dinero que estamos ahorrando. Y podemos bajarnos° dentro de poco.**
Well, think of the money we're saving. And we can get off in a little while.

12. Juana: **Gracias a Dios. Espero que los autobuses no vayan° tan llenos de gente.**
Thank God. I hope the buses aren't so crowded.

El autobús. The bus.

13. Juana: *(En la parada del autobús)* **¡Mira la gente que hay!**
(At the bus stop) Look at all the people!

14. Carlos: **Sí, desgraciadamente es la hora en que salen todos del trabajo.** ***Tendremos que*** **hacer cola.**
Yes, unfortunately it's the hour when everyone gets off work. We'll have to stand in line.

15. Juana: **¿Qué hacemos si no podemos subir?**
What do we do if we can't get on?

16. Carlos: **Hay muchos que van por La Castellana. Necesitamos un número veintidós.**
There are many that go up The Castellana. We need a number twenty-two (bus).

17. Juana: **Ya° viene uno. ¡Y está casi vacío! A ver si podemos subir.**
Here comes one already. And it's almost empty! Let's see if we can get on.

18. Carlos: **¿Estás contenta? Vamos sentados, cómodos, con una vista magnífica.**
Are you happy? We are seated, comfortable, and we have a magnificent view.

19. Juana: **Desde luego es muchísimo más cómodo que el metro, y La Castellana es preciosa . . . los árboles, la sombra. Me gusta ver a los niños jugando por aquí.**
Of course, it's much more comfortable than the subway, and The Castellana is beautiful . . . the trees, the shade. I like to see the children playing along here.

20. Carlos: **Estamos casi en la parada de Colón. Vamos a bajar allí.**
We're almost at the Colón stop. Let's get off there.

21. Juana: **¡Ah! ¡Qué día más hermoso! Podremos sentarnos° allí en la terraza, a la sombra, y tomar un refresco.**
Ah! What a beautiful day! We could sit down at the sidewalk café, in the shade, and have something to drink.

22. Carlos: **Claro, no estamos muy lejos del hotel ahora. Luego podemos tomar un taxi al hotel, echar una siesta . . .**
Sure, we're not far from the hotel now. Then we can take a taxi to the hotel, take a nap . . .

23. Juana: **¡Esa sí es una idea magnífica! Estoy un poco cansada.** *(Se bajan del autobús y van hacia el café.)*
Now that is a wonderful idea! I'm a little tired.

(They get off the bus and go to the sidewalk café.)

24. Carlos: **¡Camarero! Tráiganos un café helado y una limonada, por favor.**
Waiter! Bring us an iced coffee and a lemonade, please.

25. Camarero: **En seguida, señores.**
Right away.

26. Juana: **¡Ah, qué delicia! ¿Verdad que Madrid es agradable, Carlos?**
Ah, what a delight! Isn't Madrid pleasant, Carlos?

27. Carlos: **¡Ya lo creo!**
It certainly is!

El taxi. The taxi.

28. Carlos: **¡Taxi! ¡Taxi!**
Taxi! Taxi!

29. Juana: **Ese está ocupado. Es mejor que vayamos al otro lado de la calle. Allí está la parada de taxis.**
That one is taken. Let's go to the other side of the street. The taxi stand is there.

30. Carlos: *(En el taxi)* **¿Cuánto cuesta ir al Hotel Emperatriz?**
(In the taxi) How much is it to the Hotel Emperatriz?

31. Taxista: **Aproximadamente unas quienientas pesetas, pero depende del taxímetro.**
Approximately five hundred pesetas, but it depends on the taxi meter.

32. Carlos: **Muy bien. Tomemos el taxi de regreso.**
Very well. Let's take the taxi back.

33. Juana: **Perfecto. Ya me empezaban a doler los pies.**
Perfect. My feet were beginning to hurt.

34. Carlos: **¡Ya, ya! Cuando lleguemos al hotel, podremos descansar un rato, porque luego *tenemos que* arreglarnos para salir a cenar . . . y tal vez ir a una sala de fiestas° a bailar.**
OK, OK. When we get to the hotel, we'll rest awhile, because then we have to get ready to go out to dinner. . . and perhaps go to a nightclub and dance.

B. NOTES

First subtitle: *El metro:* Abbreviated form of *El metropolitano,* the name of the city subway system.

2. *¿Te has vuelto loco?: volverse loco* = to go crazy. *un ojo de la cara:* a fortune (lit., ''an eye from your face'').

3. *¿Desde cuándo?:* lit., "since when." Notice *pensar en.*

7. *Correos:* The Post Office. The central post office in Madrid is sometimes affectionately called *Nuestra Señora de Correos* ("Our Lady of the Mail") because of its Gothic, churchlike architecture.

11. *podemos bajarnos:* we can get off. *Subir* and *bajar* are used to express the idea of "getting into" and "getting out of" any vehicle.

12. *no vayan:* Note the use of the subjunctive after *esperar,* "to hope."

17. *ya:* already. Often used to preface an expression of pleasant surprise, the sense is often difficult to translate, as in *¡Ya lo creo!* ("I really *do* believe it!") Often equivalent to positive agreement: "You bet!"

21. Note the use of *sentarse* (to sit down); Compare: *sentirse* (to feel).

34. *sala de fiestas:* nightclub, in Spain. This expression is not used in Latin America, where the equivalents are *cabaret, club nocturno* (lit., "nightclub"), the French word "*boîte,*" or the English "nightclub."

C. GRAMMAR AND USAGE

1. *Por:* in exchange for, in place of, per

a. ***El me dio diez dólares por el libro.***	a. He gave me ten dollars for the book.
b. ***Ellos ganan tres mil pesetas por hora.***	b. They make (earn) three thousand pesetas an hour.
c. *Carlos vendió el coche por muy poco dinero.*	c. Carlos sold the car for very little money.

2. *Para:* to, in order to, for (directed toward)

a. ***El me dio un libro para leer.***	a. He gave me a book to read.
b. ***Trabajan mucho para ganarse la vida.***	b. They work hard in order to make (earn) a living.
c. *El regalo es para nuestro vecino.*	c. The gift is for our neighbor.
d. *Entraron aquí para buscar a Juan.*	d. They entered here to look for Juan.

3. *Tener que* + infinitive: to have to

a. ***Tenemos que ir temprano.***	a. We have to go early.
b. ***Ellos tendrán que comprar el libro.***	b. They'll have to buy the book.
c. *Tengo que quedarme aquí.*	c. I have to stay here.

4. *Estar* + present participle: denotes action in progress

a. ***Estoy esperando el autobús.***	a. I am waiting for the bus.
b. *Estaban durmiendo cuando sonó el timbre.*	b. They were sleeping when the bell rang.
c. *Estamos aprendiendo mucho.*	c. We are learning a lot.

EXERCISES

A. Substitute each of the words or expressions in the parentheses for the underlined word or expression in the model sentence. Write each new sentence and say it aloud.

1. *Juan lo compró por quinientas pesetas. (poco dinero, diez dólares, más de cien pesetas, un precio muy bajo, mucho menos dinero)*

2. *Juan lo compró para dárselo a su padre. (regalar, enviar, despachar, mandar, enseñar)*

3. *Tendremos que estudiar mucho. (aprender, trabajar, escribir, practicar, andar)*

4. *Estarán comiendo cuando lleguemos. (bailando, estudiando, leyendo, durmiendo, hablando)*

5. *Juan estaba leyendo el periódico cuando entré. (el libro, la lección, las noticias, la comedia, el primer acto)*

6. *María y Juana tienen que hacer el trabajo. (Los chicos, José y su hermano, Ellas, Todos, Los alumnos)*

B. Change these sentences to the plural. Write the complete sentence and translate it.

1. *El tiene que verlo mañana.*

2. *Yo tendré que levantarme temprano.*

3. *Ella está lavando los platos.*

4. *Tú tienes que leer la novela.*

5. *Usted me dio dos mil pesetas por el libro.*

C. Translate the following sentences into Spanish, then say them aloud.

1. Juan bought the car for his wife.
2. They paid two thousand pesetas for the tickets.
3. We have to leave at once.
4. They are writing letters now.
5. How much do you want for the suit?
6. You have to go through the park in order to get to the museum.
7. They gave him two hundred thousand pesetas in order to pay for the trip.
8. They were listening to the radio when I arrived.
9. In order to see well, you have to be in the front row.
10. Miguel has to buy a new book.

D. From among the three choices given, choose the best equivalent of the English given at the beginning of each sentence. Write the complete sentence and translate.

1. (to) *Juan cree que tenemos* __________ *ir al banco.*
   (a) *a*
   (b) *que*
   (c) __________
2. (for) *Paco pagó* __________ *el billete.*
   (a) __________
   (b) *por*
   (c) *para*

3. (per) *Hace cuarenta kilómetros* __________ *hora.*
   (a) *para*
   (b) *por*
   (c) *el*

4. (walking) *Los vimos* __________ *por la calle.*
   (a) *andando*
   (b) *andados*
   (c) *andandos*

5. (sitting) *Nosotros estábamos* __________ *en la terraza.*
   (a) *sentado*
   (b) *sentando*
   (c) *sentados*

6. (reading) *Juan está* __________ *el periódico.*
   (a) *lee*
   (b) *leyendo*
   (c) *leído*

7. (for) *Esta propina es* __________ *el camarero.*
   (a) *de*
   (b) *para*
   (c) *a*

8. (She has to) __________ *comprar el traje.*
   (a) *Ella hay que*
   (b) *Ella tiene que*
   (c) *Ella ha que*

9. (they want) *No sé lo que* __________.
   (a) *quieren*
   (b) *querer*
   (c) *queremos*

10. (we) *Ellos van a los mismos sitios que* __________.
    (a) *nosotros*
    (b) *ir*
    (c) *van*

LESSON 5

VAMOS A DAR UN PASEO
LET'S TAKE A WALK

A. DIALOGUE

Antes del paseo. Before the walk.

1. Juana: **¡Vamos a dar un paseo!° ¿Qué te parece? Los dos solos. Podríamos ir por La Castellana hasta el Museo del Prado.° ¿No tienes ganas de verlo? Yo, sí.**
   Let's take a walk! What do you think (of that)? Just the two of us. We could walk down The Castellana to the Prado Museum. Don't you feel like seeing it? I do.

2. Carlos: **¿Dar un paseo los dos? No sabría donde ir. *Hace tanto tiempo que* no salgo solo en Madrid.**
   Take a walk, the two of us? I wouldn't know where to go. It's such a long time since I've been out in Madrid by myself.

3. Juana: **Podemos preguntar *al hombre* en la recepción. El nos dirá donde debemos ir. Y si nos perdemos, podemos volver aquí en taxi.**
   We can ask the man at the reception desk. He will tell us where we should go. And if we get lost we can get back by taxi.

4. Carlos: **Bueno, ¡vámonos! Pero . . . como es un día tan espléndido, vamos a visitar la Plaza Mayor° y la parte antigua de la ciudad.**
   OK, let's go! But . . . since it's such a beautiful day, let's visit the Plaza Mayor and the old part of the city.

En la recepción. At the reception desk.

5. Carlos: **Dígame, señor, ¿cómo *se puede* ir a la Plaza Mayor?**
Tell me, sir, how does one get to the Plaza Mayor?

6. Empleado: **Pues, ustedes pueden tomar aquí en la esquina el autobús número . . .**
Well, here on the corner you can get bus number . . .

7. Carlos: **No, perdone. Yo quería decir a pie.**
No, I'm sorry. I meant on foot.

8. Empleado: **¡Ah! Bueno, pues, es bastante lejos para ir andando. Pero si ustedes quieren . . . Miren este plano de la ciudad. Nosotros estamos aquí, y ¿ven la Plaza Mayor, allí?**
Oh! Well, then, it's quite a distance to walk. But if you want to . . . Look at this map of the city. We are here, and . . . Do you see the Plaza Mayor there?

9. Juana: **Sí que es lejos. Pero tenemos muchas ganas de andar. Nos gusta mucho.**
It is a long way. But we really feel like walking. We enjoy it very much.

10. Empleado: **Bueno . . . Ustedes tendrán que seguir La Castellana hasta llegar a la Cibeles. *¿Se acuerdan?* Es la fuente frente a Correos. Allí, hay que doblar a la derecha y subir por la calle de Alcalá. Sigan hasta la Puerta del Sol . . .**
Well, you'll have to walk down The Castellana, to Cibeles. You remember? It's the fountain in front of the Post Office. There, you must turn right and go up Alcalá to the Puerta del Sol . . .

11. Juana: **Ah, sí, la Puerta del Sol. Me acuerdo de haber visto muchas fotos de ella.**
Oh yes, the Puerta del Sol. I remember having seen many pictures of it.

12. Empleado: **Sí, señora. Bueno, como iba diciendo . . . Doblen a la izquierda allí y suban por la calle de Carretas. ¿La ven ustedes?** (*indicando el plano*) **Al ver el Teatro Calderón en la esquina, doblen a la derecha otra vez y verán los arcos de la Plaza Mayor.**
Yes, ma'am. Well, as I was saying . . . Turn left there and go up Carretas Street. Do you see it (*pointing to the map*)? When you see the Teatro Calderón on the corner, turn to the right again and you will see the arches of the Plaza Mayor.

13. Carlos: **Gracias, señor. Parece muy claro y bastante fácil.**
Thank you, sir. It seems very clear and quite easy.

14. Empleado: **De nada, señores. Que lo pasen bien.**
You're welcome. I hope you enjoy it.

15. Juana: **¿Ves? Ya te lo había dicho . . . Es facilísimo.**
You see? I told you . . . it's very easy.

16. Carlos: **Pero será una caminata de media hora, por lo menos. ¿No te parece demasiado?**
But it will probably be a half-hour's walk, at least. Don't you think it's too much?

17. Juana: **Claro que no, querido. Ya verás. ¡Qué gusto!**
Of course not, darling. You'll see. What a pleasure!

Un cuarto de hora más tarde . . . Fifteen minutes later . . .

18. Carlos: **Nos falta muy poco para llegar a Cibeles. ¿No ves el Correo allá, con las torres?**
We have just a little way to go to Cibeles. Don't you see the Post Office there, with the towers?

19. Juana: **Sí, ya lo veo. Es donde hay que doblar a la derecha y subir por la calle de Alcalá, ¿verdad?**
Yes, I can see it. That's where we have to turn right and go up Alcalá, isn't it?

20. Carlos: **Eso es. Y si te parece, podemos sentarnos un rato en aquella terraza tan agradable y descansar un poco antes de seguir.**
That's right. And if you want to, we can sit down for a while at that nice sidewalk café and rest a bit before going on.

21. Juana: **Sí, pero, me parece que eres tú el que quiere descansar.**
Yes, but it seems to me that you're the one who wants to rest.

22. Carlos: (*Después del descanso*) **Creo que nos hemos equivocado. ¿Será ésta la calle de Alcalá? ¿Tienes la guía de la ciudad?**
(*After resting*) I think we've made a mistake. Can this be Alcalá? Do you have the map of the city?

23. Juana: **¡Ay! La dejé sobre la mesa en aquella terraza. No vale la pena volver a buscarla ahora. Pregúntale a esa señora si vamos bien.**
Oh! I left it on the table at the café. It's not worth the trouble to go back to look for it now. Ask that woman if we're on the right track.

24. Carlos: **Perdone, señora. ¿Vamos bien para llegar a la Puerta del Sol?**
Pardon me, ma'am. Are we going the right way to get to the Puerta del Sol?

25. Una Señora: **¿A la Puerta del Sol? No, no. Esta es la Gran Vía.° Ustedes tienen que volver atrás hasta el punto donde se separan la Gran Vía y la**

calle de Alcalá. Alcalá es la que sube a mano izquierda. ¿Ven aquel edificio grande, frente a la iglesia? Pues, es allí donde tienen que subir a la izquierda.
To the Puerta del Sol? No, no. This is the Gran Vía. You have to go back to the point where the Gran Vía and Alcalá separate. Alcalá is the one that goes up to the left. Do you see that big building opposite the church? Well, that's where you have to go up to the left.

26. Carlos: **Muchísimas gracias, señora. Vamos, Juana, o no llegamos nunca a la Plaza Mayor.**
Thank you very much, ma'am. Come on, Juana, or we'll never get to the Plaza Mayor.

27. Juana: **No me importa tanto. El paseo es agradable de todas maneras y estamos viendo cosas muy interesantes. Las tiendas por aquí son muy elegantes.**
It doesn't matter much to me. The walk is pleasant anyway and we're seeing interesting things. The shops along here are very elegant.

De vuelta en el hotel. Back at the hotel.

28. Empleado: **Buenas tardes, señores. ¿Les ha gustado la Plaza Mayor?**
Good afternoon. Did you like the Plaza Mayor?

29. Carlos: **No llegamos a verla. Nos equivocamos de camino varias veces y perdimos tanto tiempo con los escaparates de la Gran Vía que se hizo demasiado tarde para eso.**
We didn't even get to see it. We lost our way several times and wasted so much time with the shop windows of the Gran Vía that it got to be too late for that.

30. Juana: **Pero mañana iremos de compras,° y por la tarde iremos a la Plaza Mayor.**
But, tomorrow we'll go shopping, and in the afternoon we'll go to the Plaza Mayor.

B. NOTES

1. *dar un paseo:* to take a walk.
Museo del Prado: The famous Madrid museum that has one of the richest collections in the world.

4. *Plaza Mayor:* The old "Main Square" of Madrid. The center of the city's life in the sixteenth and seventeenth centuries.

25. *la Gran Vía:* The popular name for the Avenida de José Antonio Primo de Rivera, the main commercial artery in Madrid, which goes up from the Post Office to the Plaza de España.

30. *ir de compras:* to go shopping.

C. GRAMMAR AND USAGE

1. *Hacer* + time expression + *que:* for + time expression

a. ***Hace una semana que estoy aquí.***	a. I have been here for a week.
b. ***Hace dos horas que esperamos.***	b. We have been waiting for two hours.
c. *Hace un año que Carlo estudia español.*	c. Carlo has been studying Spanish for a year.

Note:

- *Hace* (without *que*) may go at the end of the sentence, as in *Estoy aquí hace una semana.*

- The present tense is used in this construction to indicate that an action has been, and still is, taking place.

2. Personal *a* + singular masculine definite article *(el): al*

a. ***Vamos a preguntar al hombre.***	a. Let's ask the man.
b. ***Tengo que ver al dentista.***	b. I have to see the dentist.
c. *Ellos llamaron al* ***médico.***	c. They called the doctor.
but:	but:
d. ***Hay que preguntar a los hombres.***	d. You must ask the men.
e. *Tengo que ver a la costurera.*	e. I have to see the dressmaker.
f. *Veo a María.*	f. I see María.

3. Impersonal *se*

a. ***¿Se puede fumar?***	a. Is smoking permitted? (May one smoke?)
b. ***Se tiene que ir de prisa.***	b. One has to go fast (hurry). You (impersonal) must go fast.
c. *Se come bien aquí.*	c. One eats well here. The food is good here.

4. *Acordarse de:* to remember

a. ***Me acuerdo muy bien de ella.***	a. I remember her very well.
b. *¿Se acuerda usted del accidente?*	b. Do you remember the accident?
c. *Nos acordamos frecuentemente de aquel viaje.*	c. We frequently remember that trip.

EXERCISES

A. Substitute each of the words or expressions in parentheses for the underlined word or expression in the model sentence. Write each new sentence and say it aloud.

1. *Hace una semana que vivo en Madrid. (un año, dos meses, mucho tiempo, varias semanas, muy poco [tiempo])*

2. *Hace tres horas que Juan trabaja. (viaja, estudia, duerme, escribe, lee)*

3. *Usted tiene que llamar al médico. (al dentista, al sereno, al oficial, al camarero, al agente)*

4. *Se come bien en Madrid. (duerme, bebe, está, habla, canta)*

5. *Nos acordamos mucho de España. (del viaje, de Madrid, de Teresa, de ustedes, del médico)*

6. *No me acuerdo de nada. (ella, María, Juan y Francisco, ellos, él)*

B. Change these sentences to the negative. Write the complete sentence and translate.

1. *Usted se acuerda de María.*

2. *Hace una semana que Juan está aquí.*

3. *Teresa tiene que llamar al médico.*

4. *Se come bien en este restaurante.*

5. *Ellos se acuerdan del viaje.*

C. Translate the following sentences into Spanish, then say them aloud.

1. They've been here for a month.
2. You have to call the doctor.
3. I remember you very well.
4. I have been sleeping for two hours.
5. You eat well in this restaurant.
6. I don't see María.
7. We can sit down to rest awhile.
8. We feel like walking.
9. You have to turn to the right.
10. Let's visit the museum.

D. From among the three choices given, choose the best equivalent of the English given at the beginning of each sentence. Write the complete sentence and translate.

1. (I have been) ________ *aquí hace dos años.*
   (a) *Estuve*
   (b) *He estado*
   (c) *Estoy*
2. (for three months) *Ellos viven en Madrid* ________.
   (a) *en tres meses*
   (b) *hace tres meses*
   (c) *de tres meses*

3. (have you been) *¿Cuánto tiempo hace que ________ aquí?*
   (a) *ha estado usted*
   (b) *está usted*
   (c) *usted estuve*
4. (is spoken) *Aquí ________ ruso.*
   (a) *hablamos*
   (b) *se habla*
   (c) *está hablando*
5. (One finds) ________ *muchos anuncios en el periódico.*
   (a) *Se encuentran*
   (b) *Se encuentra*
   (c) *Encontrar*
6. (remember) *Creo que ellos ________ la fecha.*
   (a) *se acuerda*
   (b) *se acuerdan de*
   (c) *acordarse*
7. (one meets) *Esta es una fiesta en la que ______ a mucha gente simpática.*
   (a) *se conoce*
   (b) *se conocen*
   (c) *se encuentran*
8. (my friend) *¿Conoce usted ________?*
   (a) *amigo mío*
   (b) *a mi amigo*
   (c) *mi amigo*
9. (they have been) *Hace tres años que ________ en Nueva York.*
   (a) *son*
   (b) *están*
   (c) *habían estado*
10. (for an hour) *Hace ________ que espero.*
    (a) *por una hora*
    (b) *una hora*
    (c) *un hora*

LESSON 6

EN UNA TIENDA
IN A STORE

A. DIALOGUE

En la sección de bolsas. In the handbag department.

1. Vendedora: **¿Puedo *servirle* en algo, señora?**
Can I help you with something, ma'am?

2. Juana: **Sí, por favor. Me gustaría una bolsa para uso corriente, como la mía pero de piel.°**
Yes, please. I'd like a handbag for everyday use, like mine but leather.

3. Vendedora: ***Las* tenemos de todas clases y colores. Aquí tiene usted unas preciosas, de gamuza.**
We have all kinds and colors. Here are some beautiful ones in suede.

4. Juana: **Sí, son muy bonitas. ¿*Las* tiene en negro?**
Yes, they're very pretty. Do you have them in black?

5. Vendedora: **No están aquí, pero tal vez *las* tenemos en el interior. Un momento, por favor.**
They're not here, but maybe we have them in the back room. Just a minute, please.

6. Juana: **Gracias.**
Thanks.

7. Vendedora: ***Aquí la tiene* usted. Es la última.**
Here you are. It's the last one.

8. Juana: **¡Qué suerte! ¡Cuánto cuesta?**
How lucky! How much is it?

9. Vendedora: **Son cinco mil pesetas, señora.**
It's five thousand pesetas, ma'am.

10. Juana: **Está bien. ¿*Me la puede* envolver?**
That's fine. Will you wrap it, please?

11. Vendedora: **Con mucho gusto, señora. *Aquí la tiene* usted. Muchas gracias.**
With pleasure, ma'am. Here you are. Thank you very much.

En la sección de vestidos de señoras. In the women's dress department.

12. Vendedora: **¿Necesita ayuda, señora?**
May I help you?

13. Juana: **Sí, estoy buscando un vestido de seda, verde claro, con mangas cortas.**
Yes, I'm looking for a light green silk dress, with short sleeves.

14. Vendedora: **Este vestido, señora, es de última moda, y una verdadera ganga a quince mil pesetas.**
This dress is the latest style and a real bargain at fifteen thousand pesetas.

15. Juana: **¡Ah! Es demasiado. ¿No tendría usted otro, menos caro?**
Oh, it's too much. Don't you have another, less expensive?

16. Vendedora: **Hay este otro a ocho mil pesetas. Vea que es un corte muy elegante. ¿Qué talla° lleva usted, señora?**

There's this one at eight thousand pesetas. Notice that it's a very elegant cut. What size do you wear, ma'am?

17. Juana: **Creo que trienta y seis.**
I think a thirty-six.

18. Vendedora: **Este vestido *le* va divinamente, señora. *Se lo* puede probar allí.**
This dress is perfect for you. You can try it on in there.

19. Juana: **Yo lo encuentro un poco ancho de espalda, y demasiado largo.**
I find it a little wide in the shoulders and too long.

20. Vendedora: **Desde luego, lo es. Probemos con una talla más pequeña entonces. ¡Ah! Ese le sienta a maravilla, señora. ¿Qué le parece?**
Of course, it is. Let's try a smaller size, then. Ah! It fits you marvelously. What do you think?

21. Juana: ***Me gusta* muchísimo.**
I like it very much.

22. Vendedora: **Venga por aquí. La acompaño a la caja.**
Come this way. I'll accompany you to the cashier.

23. Juana: (*En la caja*) **¿Aceptan Uds. cheques de viajero?**
(*At the cash register*) Do you accept traveler's checks?

24. Cajero: **Claro que sí, señora. Por favor, fírmelos.**
Certainly, ma'am. Please sign them.

En el mostrador de corbatas. At the tie counter.

25. Vendedor: **¿Le puedo ayudar, señor?**
May I help you, sir?

26. Carlos: **Sí. Busco una corbata para un amigo.**
Yes, I'm looking for a tie for a friend.

27. Vendedor: **Tenemos una selección muy grande. ¿Ve usted algo que le guste?**
We have a very large selection. Do you see something you like?

28. Carlos: **Sí, pero es difícil comprar para otra persona. No se sabe lo que le gusta.**
Yes, but it's difficult to shop for another person. You don't know what they like.

29. Vendedor: **Es cierto. Pero, siempre puede devolverla.**
That's true. But, he can always return it.

30. Carlos: **Estas de seda son muy elegantes.**
These silk ones are very elegant.

31. Vendedor: **Sí, pero son un poco más caras.**
Yes, but they're a little more expensive.

32. Carlos: **Mi amigo vale la pena. Estoy visitando de México y él ha sido muy amable. ¿Cuánto cuesta la roja?**
My friend is worth it. I'm visiting from Mexico and he has been very kind. How much is the red one?

33. Vendedor: **Son cuatro mil pesetas.**
It's four thousand pesetas.

34. Carlos: **Está bien.**
That's fine.

B. NOTES

2. *piel:* (lit., "skin") used for all kinds of cured and worked light leathers such as would be used in gloves, handbags, etc.
   cuero is the word for heavier varieties of leather.

16. *talla, tamaño:* used to refer to sizes of articles of clothing. *Talla* is generally used for suits and dresses (cf. *talle:* waist measurement).
   Número ("number") is frequently used for articles that are sized according to number. *¿Qué número lleva usted?* will be heard in reference to gloves and shoes.

C. GRAMMAR AND USAGE

1. Indirect and direct object pronouns may be:

attached to the complementary infinitive

	Infinitive + Indirect/Direct Object pronoun
a. ***Juan quiere***	***dárselo a él.***
b. ***María va a***	***mandármelo.***
c. ***Ellos tienen que***	***pagárnoslo.***

or placed before the main verb

a. ***Juan se lo quiere dar a él.***	a. Juan wants to give it to him.
b. ***María me lo va a mandar.***	b. María is going to send it to me.
c. *Ellos nos lo tienen que pagar.*	c. They have to pay us for it.

Note:

- Indirect *le* and *les* change to *se* before the third person (*lo, la,* etc.) direct object pronouns.

2. *Aquí* + (third person) direct object pronoun + *tener*

a. ***¿El libro? Aquí lo tiene usted.***	a. The book: Here it is. (Lit.: "Here you have it.")
b. *¿Los libros? Aquí los tiene usted.*	b. The books? Here they are.
c. *¿La novela? Aquí la tiene usted.*	c. The novel? Here it is.
d. *¿Las novelas? Aquí las tiene usted.*	d. The novels? Here they are.

3. The use of the verb *gustar*—to be pleasing, to like

Indirect Object	*gusta(n)*	Subject
a. ***Me***	***gusta***	***el vestido.***
b. *Me*	*gustan*	*los vestidos.*
c. *Nos*	*gusta*	*el hotel.*
d. *Nos*	*gustan*	*los hoteles.*

a. I like the dress.
b. I like the dresses.
c. We like the hotel.
d. We like the hotels.

EXERCISES

A. Substitute each of the words or expressions in the parentheses for the underlined word or expression in the model sentence. Write each new sentence and say it aloud.

1. *Mi padre quiere <u>dárselo</u> a él. (regalar, mandar, vender, pedir, preguntar)*

2. *Ellos me lo quieren comprar. (pueden, van a, desean, tienen que, podrán)*

3. *Me gusta comer. (bailar, cantar, beber, dormir, trabajar)*

4. *Nos gustan los viajes. (Te, Me, Le, Os, Les)*

5. *A él le gustan los vestidos. (los trajes, los libros, las películas, los barcos, los coches)*

6. *Aquí lo tiene usted. (tienes, tienen, tenéis, tenemos, tengo)*

B. Change the nouns to pronouns. Write the complete sentence and translate.

1. *María va a comprar el libro para Juan.*

2. *Ellos quieren mandarle el coche al señor Hernández.*

3. *Nosotros podemos regalarle los vestidos a tu madre.*

4. *Tú prefieres pedirle el dinero a su padre.*

5. *Tenéis que enviarle el paquete a mis padres.*

C. Translate the following sentences into Spanish, then say them aloud.

1. They want to give it (the gift) to me.

2. You will have to ask him for it.

3. We want to send it to them.

4. He will have to put it on.

5. We like to travel in Spain.

6. Here they (the books) are.

7. You (familiar singular) like ice cream.

8. I'm going to look for it (the hat) for you.

9. Do you want to carry the package?

10. We can send it to you, if you prefer.

D. From among the three choices given, choose the best equivalent of the English given at the beginning of each sentence. Write the complete sentence and translate.

1. (they are) *Aquí* __________ *usted.*
   (a) *lo tiene*
   (b) *los tiene*
   (c) *la tiene*
2. (them to me) *Quiere dár* __________ *ahora.*
   (a) *-losme*
   (b) *-melos*
   (c) *ellos me*
3. (Give it *[el libro]* to me.)
   (a) *Dámelo*
   (b) *Me lo das*
   (c) *Dámela*
4. (We have them *[guantes]*) __________ *de todas clases.*
   (a) *Tenémoslas*
   (b) *Los tenemos*
   (c) *Ellos tenemos*
5. (it *[el pasaporte]*) *Aquí* __________ *tiene usted.*
   (a) *los*
   (b) *lo*
   (c) *el*

6. (for you) *Voy a buscar* __________ *el paquete.*
   (a) *-le*
   (b) *-se*
   (c) *-los*

7. (silk dress) *Quiero comprar un* __________.
   (a) *vestido seda*
   (b) *seda vestido*
   (c) *vestido de seda*

8. (it is) *¿Es demasiado caro? Creo que sí* _________.
   (a) *está*
   (b) *lo es*
   (c) *el es*

9. (Here it is—Here you are.) __________.
   (a) *Aquí lo tiene usted.*
   (b) *Aquí lo está.*
   (c) *Aquí estamos.*

10. (send them *[las cartas]* to me) *¿Quiere usted* _____*?*
   (a) *mandárlasme*
   (b) *me las mandar*
   (c) *mandármelas*

LESSON 7

UN CORTE DE PELO
A HAIRCUT

A. DIALOGUE

En la barbería. In the barbershop.

1. Barbero: **Buenos días, señor. ¿En qué puedo servirle?**
Good morning, sir. What can I do for you?

2. Carlos: **Un corte de pelo, para empezar. Me parece que el pelo me crece como nunca en estos días.**
A haircut, to begin with. It seems to me that my hair is growing more than ever these days.

3. Barbero: ***Será* la buena vida que lleva usted, señor. *¿Se lo corto del mismo modo?***
It must be the good life you live, sir. Should I cut it in the same style?

4. Carlos: **Sí, por favor. Pero déjelo bastante llenito a los lados y detrás. Cuidado con la maquinilla. No quiero verme "pelado."**
Yes, please. But leave the sides and back fairly full. Careful with the clippers. I don't want to look "skinned."

5. Barbero: **Muy bien, señor. Tendré mucho cuidado. . . . ¡Listo! ¿Qué le parece, señor?**
Very well, sir. I'll be very careful. . . . It's done. What do you think of it, sir?

6. Carlos: **Muy bien. ¿Me permite usted el peine, un momento?**
Very good. Will you let me use the comb a minute?

7. Barbero: **¿Desea alguna otra cosa, señor?**
   Would you like anything else, sir?

8. Carlos: **Vamos a ver . . . Mi esposa está aquí al lado, en la peluquería.° Meintras yo la espero . . . Bueno, una afeitada, entonces. Pero tengo la barba bastante dura.**
   Let's see . . . My wife is right next door, at the beauty shop. While I'm waiting for her . . . Well, a shave then. But my beard is rather tough.

9. Barbero: **No se preocupe, señor.**
   Don't worry, sir.

10. Carlos: **¡Qué lujo! Es muy agradable hacerse afeitar de vez en cuando.**
    What a luxury! It's really nice to get a shave from time to time.

11. Barbero: **Bien, señor. ¿Le veremos otra vez?**
    OK, sir. Will we see you another time?

12. Carlos: **Espero que sí. Depende si tengo tiempo.**
    I hope so. It depends if I have time.

13. Barbero: **Usted puede tomar una tarjeta *al pagar* la cuenta, señor.**
    You can take a business card when you pay the bill, sir.

14. Carlos: **Muy bien. Muchas gracias. Tome usted** (*dándole una propina*).
    Very weil. Thank you. Here you are (*giving him a tip*).

15. Barbero: **Gracias, señor.**
    Thank you, sir.

En la calle. In the street.

16. Carlos: **¡Hola! ¡Ya estás!° Iba a buscarte.**
    Hi! You're ready. I was going to get you.

17. Juana: **Sí, ¡ya estoy! Parece que tú has tardado tanto como yo esta vez.**
Yes, I'm ready! It seems you took as long as I did this time.

18. Carlos: **¡Claro que tú has empezado antes que yo!**
Of course you began before I did!

19. Juana: **Pero, ¡qué guapo estás! ¡Te hacía falta un corte de pelo! Y ¡qué bien afeitado vas!**
But how handsome you look! You needed a haircut. And how nicely shaved you are!

20. Carlos: **Y tú. ¿Qué te has hecho?**
And you. What have you done?

21. Juana: **Un champú,° y un nuevo peinado. Es un poco más corto que de costumbre.**
A shampoo, and a new hairstyle. It's a little shorter than usual.

22. Carlos: **¡Vamos! Hay algo más. No me lo has contado todo.**
Come on! There's something else. You haven't told me everything.

23. Juana: **Bueno, *tienes razón.* Me he hecho aclarar un poco el pelo. ¿Te gusta?**
Well, you're right. I had my hair lightened a little. Do you like it?

24. Carlos: **¡Claro que sí! Es precioso. ¿Y la manicura?**
Of course! It's beautiful. And the manicure?

25. Juana: **Por supuesto. Me han pintado las uñas. ¿Te gusta el color? Va con el lápiz de labios.**
Of course. I had my nails done. Do you like the color? It goes with my lipstick.

26. Carlos: **¡Una maravilla! ¿Qué? Vamos a hacer algo especial esta noche.**
Marvelous! What do you say? Let's do something special tonight.

27. Juana: **Buena idea. ¿Qué podemos hacer?**
Good idea. What should we do?

28. Carlos: **Cenemos esta noche en el Pabellón.° Quiero que todo el mundo nos admire.**
Let's dine at the Pabellón tonight. I want everyone to admire us.

B. NOTES

8. *Barbería* = barbershop. *Peluquería* = beauty shop.

16. *¡Ya estás!*: A word such as *listo, lista* ("ready"), is understood in these expressions. See *¡Ya estoy!* in sentence 17.

21. *Un champú:* like the English "shampoo." One can also say *lavarse el pelo* ("to wash one's hair"). *Me he hecho lavar el pelo* = I had my hair washed.

28. *el Pabellón:* A club for dinner and dancing in Madrid.

C. GRAMMAR AND USAGE

1. Future of probability

a. ***¿Quién será?***	a. Who can it be?
b. ***Ellos habrán ido al cine.***	b. They must have gone (they probably went) to the movies.
c. *Estarán aquí en alguna parte.*	c. They must be (they probably are) here somewhere.

2. *Tener razón:* to be right

a. ***Usted tiene razón.***	a. You're right.
b. ***Ellos siempre creen tener razón.***	b. They always think they are right.
c. *Tenemos razón, como siempre.*	c. We are right, as usual.

3. Present tense with future meaning

a. ***¿Se lo corto del mismo modo?***	a. Shall I cut it in the same way?
b. *Qué haces esta tarde?*	b. What are you doing (will you do) this afternoon?
c. *Vuelvo en seguida.*	c. I'll come back right away.

4. *Al* + (infinitive): on, upon, when (doing something)

a. ***Usted lo puede hacer al pagar la cuenta.***	a. You can do it when you pay (on paying) the bill.
b. ***Al volver a casa, te llamo.***	b. Upon returning home (when I return home), I'll call you.
c. ***Me saludó al entrar.***	c. He greeted me on entering (when he entered).

EXERCISES

A. Substitute each of the words or expressions in the parentheses for the underlined word or expression in the model sentence. Write each new sentence and say it aloud.

1. *¿Dónde estará el libro? (el lápiz, la novela, Miguel, el profesor, el lápiz de labios)*

2. *¿Qué le habrá pasado a Teresa? (al Señor Andrade, a Miguel, al libro, a mis amigos, al profesor)*

3. *Los libros estarán en alguna parte. (Los señores, Juan y José, María y Juana, Ellas, Los jóvenes)*

4. *¿Se lo hago mañana? (digo, pregunto, pido, mando, pago)*

5. *Los chicos siempre tienen razón. (Las chicas, Los profesores, Juan y Francisco, Mis padres, Las hermanas)*

6. *Puedes hacerlo al entrar. (salir, pagar, acostarte, llegar, despertarte)*

B. Change these sentences to the present tense. Write the complete sentence and translate.

1. *Se lo diré al volver.*

2. *Juan me lo dará.*

3. *Usted tendrá razón.*

4. *Vendré por la mañana.*

5. *Ellos podrán dártelo.*

C. Translate the following sentences into Spanish, then say them aloud.

1. Where can the tickets be? (future of probability)

2. They must have gone home.

3. When he came in, he greeted us.

4. You can pay it when you leave.

5. I think he's right.

6. I'll give it (the book) to you tomorrow.

7. How handsome you are!

8. You need a haircut.

9. I was going to get you.

10. Do you like the color?

D. From among the three choices given, choose the best equivalent of the English given at the beginning of each sentence. Write the complete sentence and translate.

1. (It will be) __________ *difícil.*
   (a) *Será*
   (b) *Es*
   (c) *Sería*

2. (when you leave) *Usted puede dármelo* __________.
   (a) *cuando salir*
   (b) *al salir*
   (c) *en salir*

3. (you are right) *Creo que siempre* __________.
   (a) *está derecho*
   (b) *tienes razón*
   (c) *es razón*

4. (can it be) *¿Quién* __________ *?*
   (a) *lo puede ser*
   (b) *será*
   (c) *sea*

5. (next door) *La señora está aquí* __________ *en la peluquería.*
   (a) *próxima puerta*
   (b) *lado*
   (c) *al lado*

6. (I'm going) *Creo que* __________ *mañana.*
   (a) *va*
   (b) *voy*
   (c) *estoy yendo*

7. (before) *Claro que usted empezó* __________ *yo.*
   (a) *antes que*
   (b) *antes de*
   (c) *delante*

8. (to be right) *Le gusta* __________ *siempre.*
   (a) *ser derecho*
   (b) *tener razón*
   (c) *estar razón*

9. (upon arriving) *Nos saludamos* __________ *al hotel.*
   (a) *al llegar*
   (b) *en llegando*
   (c) *sobre llegar*

10. (else) *¿Hay algo* __________*?*
    (a) *otro*
    (b) *demás*
    (c) *más*

LESSON 8

EN EL TEATRO
AT THE THEATER

A. DIALOGUE

En la taquilla. At the ticket window.

1. Carlos: **¿Tiene usted cuatro entradas *para* esta noche? *Prefiero* butacas° de patio, si es posible.**
Do you have four seats for this evening? I prefer orchestra seats, if it's possible.

2. Empleada: **Vamos a ver . . . Podría darle unas localidades muy buenas, pero separadas. Me quedan cuatro juntas pero se *encuentran* bastante al costado. Tengo cuatro localidades excelentes en el centro de la primera fila del balcón, si le interesan.**
Let's see . . . I could give you some very good seats, but they're separated. I still have four together, but they are rather far over to the side. I have four excellent seats in the center of the first row of the balcony, if you're interested.

3. Carlos: **Está bien. Démelas, por favor.**
Fine. Give them to me, please.

4. Empleada: **Son diez mil pesetas, señor.**
That's ten thousand pesetas, sir.

5. Carlos: **¿A qué hora *empieza* la función, por favor?**
What time does the performance begin, please?

6. Empleada: **A las once,° señor.**
At eleven o'clock, sir.

En el Teatro Español. In the Teatro Español.

7. Carlos: **Mira, allí están Teresa y Miguel. Teresa, Miguel, *¡qué gusto* verlos otra vez!**
Look, there are Teresa and Miguel. Teresa, Miguel, what a pleasure to see you again!

8. Miguel: **Ustedes han sido muy amables al invitarnos esta noche. Es un verdadero placer *para* nosotros. Vamos al teatro muy de vez en cuando.**
You were so kind to invite us this evening. It's a real pleasure for us. We go to the theater very rarely.

9. Teresa: **¡Y es tan agradable!**
And it's so pleasant!

10. Juana: **Sí, es verdad!**
Yes that's right.

11. Miguel: **Bueno, vamos, ya que dentro de muy poco sube el telón.**
OK, let's go, the curtain will be going up in a little while.

12. Vendedora de programas: **¿Programas? ¿Programas, señores?**
Programs? Programs, ladies and gentlemen?

13. Miguel: **Permíteme, Carlos. Dos programas, por favor.**
Allow me, Carlos. Two programs, please.

14. Juana: **Me gusta tener estos programas especiales. Tienen tanta información, y los guardo como recuerdo de la noche.**
I like to have these special programs. They have so much information, and I keep them as a souvenir of the evening.

15. Acomodador: **Las entradas, señores. *Por* aquí, por favor. Primera fila, las cuatro primeras butacas.**
Usher Tickets, ladies and gentlemen. This way, please. First row, the first four seats.

16. Miguel: **¡Estas localidades son excelentes! Has tenido suerte, Carlos, porque al entrar esta noche, noté que habían puesto el anuncio "No hay localidades."**
These seats are excellent! You were lucky, Carlos, because when I came in this evening, I noticed that they had put up the sign "No seats available."

17. Teresa: **¡*Qué lleno* está! ¡No veo ni un sitio vacío!**
It's so full! I don't see a single empty seat!

18. Miguel: **Están bajando las luces. Ya va a empezar.**
The lights are going down. It's going to begin.

Durante el descanso. During intermission.

19. Teresa: **Por los aplausos, parece ser un gran éxito. A mí me ha gustado enormemente. El Español tiene siempre muy buenas companías. Son todos tan buenos actores. ¿No les parece?**
Judging by the applause, it seems to be a great success. I liked it very much. The Español always has very good companies. They are all such good actors. Don't you think so?

20. Juana: **Es muy dramático y tiene unos efectos escenográficos muy bien logrados.**
It's very dramatic and has some well done effects in the scenery.

21. Carlos: **La interpretación es estupenda. Se nota que la dirección es de primera calidad.**
The acting is terrific. You can see that the direction was the best.

22. Miguel: **No hay nadie como Carlos Saura.°**
There's no one like Carlos Saura.

23. Teresa: **Los decorados están muy bien hechos, y las luces, y el vestuario . . .**
The sets are very well done, and the lights and the costumes . . .

24. Carlos: **Y ¿qué dices de la sala? Es un público muy elegante, ¿verdad?**
And what do you say about the house? It's a very elegant audience, isn't it?

25. Teresa: **Sí, es verdad.**
Yes, it's true.

26. Miguel: **Oye, Carlos, ¿viste el programa cómico que pusieron anoche en televisíon?**
Listen, Carlos, did you see the funny program on television last night?

27. Carlos: **¿Cuál? Vi una película que fue muy divertida. Creo que se llamaba *Los secretos de Susana* o algo parecido.**
Which one? I saw a movie that was really funny. I think it was called *Los secretos de Susana* or something like that.

28. Miguel: **Sí. Me gustó mucho.**
Yes. I liked it a lot.

29. Teresa: **¿Les gusta la zarzuela?° Hay una obra buenísima ahora en el Teatro de la Zarzuela. No me acuerdo del título, pero tuvo muy buena crítica.**
Do you like zarzuela? There's a very good one now at the Teatro de la Zarzuela. I can't remember the title, but it's gotten very good reviews.

30. Juana: **Se llama *La verbena de la paloma.* Es preciosa. Una amiga mía fue a verla la semana pasada, y dice que la impresionó mucho. Tenemos que ir a verla.**
It's called *La verbena de la paloma.* It is beautiful. A friend of mine went to see it last week, and she says that it really impressed her. We should go see it.

31. Carlos: **Suenan las campanas. Va a empezar el segundo acto. Entremos.**
The bells are ringing. The second act is about to begin. Let's go in.

B. NOTES

1. *butaca:* lit., "armchair." *Butaca de patio* = Orchestra seat.

6. *A las once:* Spanish theater begins late by American standards. There is a "matinée" that begins at 7:30 P.M. and the evening performance begins at 10:45 P.M. or 11 P.M. The early show is called the *función de tarde* and the later one the *función de noche.*
Third subtitle: *descanso:* intermission. In Latin America it is more common to say *intermedio.*

22. *Carlos Saura:* Director of films and plays such as *Bodas de sangre.*

29. *Zarzuela:* A kind of short musical comedy, similar to the operetta, cultivated preeminently in the nineteenth century. The name comes from the Palace of the Zarzuela near Madrid, where these works were first performed. *La verbena de la paloma* (1893) by Tomás Bretón is one of the most beautiful and popular. The earliest varieties of the genre were written

by the Golden Age playwrights Lope de Vega and Calderón de la Barca.

C. GRAMMAR AND USAGE

1. *Por* and *para*

por: along, through, during (approximate time)

a. ***Le encontré andando por el parque.***	a. I met him walking through the park.
b. ***Vengan ustedes por aquí.***	b. Come this way (along here).
c. *Espero verle por la mañana.*	c. I hope to see him in the morning (anytime during the morning).
d. *Nos gusta andar por las calles céntricas.*	d. We like to walk along the streets downtown.

para: by (a certain time limit)
for (a definite purpose)

a. ***Usted lo tendrá para las ocho.***	a. You'll have it by eight o'clock.
b. ***Lo necesito para las once.***	b. I need it by eleven o'clock.
c. *¿Para qué necesita usted el dinero? Para pagar la cuenta.*	c. For what do you need the money? To pay the bill.

2. Stem-changing verbs

o⟶ue

a. ***No encuentro el número.***	a. I can't find the number.
b. *A ver si lo encuentras aquí.*	b. Let's see if you (familiar singular) find it here.
c. *Ella siempre lo encuentra.*	c. She always finds it.
d. *Ellos lo encuentran fácilmente.*	d. They find it easily.
e. *No lo encontramos nunca.*	e. We never find it.
f. *Vosotros lo encontráis allí.*	f. You (fam. pl.) find it there.

Note:

- In this type of stem-changing verb, the *o* of the stem changes to *ue* when it is stressed (that is, in the first, second, and third persons singular and the third person plural). (Similar *o* verbs⟶*ue* are: *poder, mover, contar, acostar, costar, acordar, probar, almorzar*)

e⟶ie

a. ***Lo entiendo.***	a. I understand it.
b. *¿Lo entiendes tú?*	b. Do you (familiar singular) understand it?
c. *Ella lo entiende.*	c. She understands it.
d. *Ellos lo entienden.*	d. They understand it.
e. *Nosotros lo entendemos.*	e. We understand it.
f. *Vosotros lo entendéis.*	f. You (fam. pl.) understand it.

Note:

- As with the change from *o* to *ue* (above), the *e* of the stem changes to *ie* under stress in the first, second, and third persons singular, and the third person plural forms. These changes occur in the present indicative and the present subjunctive. Like *entender* in this respect are: *sentar, cerrar, comenzar, despertar, empezar, pensar, perder, defender, querer.*

3. *¡Qué* + Noun! = What a __________!
   ¡Qué + Adjective! = How __________!

a. ***¡Qué día!***	a. What a day!
b. *¡Qué mujer!*	b. What a woman!
c. *¡Qué gusto!*	c. What a pleasure!

a. *¡Qué bonito!*	a. How pretty!
b. *¡Qué difícil!*	b. How difficult!
c. *¡Qué tonto!*	c. How silly!

Note:

- Some words may be used as either a noun or an adjective, depending on whether *ser* or *estar* is used:

  ¡Qué tonto eres! What a fool you are!
  ¡Qué tonto estás! How silly you are!

4. *Ser:* to be (permanent, fixed state, existence)
   Estar: to be (in a place, in a transitory or varying state)

a. ***Soy profesor.***	a. I am a teacher.
b. *Juan es estudiante.*	b. Juan is a student.
c. *La puerta es grande.*	c. The door is large.

a. ***Estoy en clase.***	a. I am in class.
b. *Juan está cansado.*	b. Juan is tired.
c. *La puerta está abierta.*	c. The door is open.

Note:

- Some adjectives may be used with *ser* to denote a permanent, unchanging state or condition.

Es viejo.	He's old (i.e., an old man).
Es aburrido.	He's dull (i.e., tiresome, a bore).
Es joven.	He's young.

Contrasted with:

Está viejo.	He looks old. (He may not really be old.)
Está aburrido.	He's bored.
Está joven.	He looks young. (He could actually be old.)

EXERCISES

A. Substitute each of the words or expressions in parentheses for the underlined word or expression in the model sentence. Write the new sentence and say it aloud.

1. *Le vi andando por <u>la calle</u>. (el centro, el parque, el pasillo, el campo, la carretera)*

2. *No tengo nada que hacer por <u>la mañana</u>. (la tarde, la noche, el día, esta semana, el verano)*

3. *Me lo tiene que entregar para <u>las ocho</u>. (el fin de semana, esta noche, esta tarde, mediodía, la semana que viene)*

4. *¡Qué <u>hermosa</u> está tu hermana hoy! (cansada, vieja, fea, bonita, ocupada)*

5. *¡Qué <u>placer</u>! (gusto, pena, lástima, horror, problema)*

6. *¿Cómo <u>va</u> tu hermano? (está, se siente, se encuentra)*

B. Change these sentences to the plural. Write the complete sentence and translate.

1. *Yo soy actor.*

2. *El está en los Estados Unidos.*

3. *Usted es de México.*

4. *Tú estás cansado.*

5. *Ella está en la sala.*

C. Translate the following sentences into Spanish, then say them aloud.

1. What time does the performance begin?

2. What a pleasure to see you again!

3. I just bought this dress.

4. It's a very amusing comedy.

5. I saw a movie last Wednesday.

6. I don't remember the title.

7. It's going to begin again.

8. A friend of mine went to see the comedy.

9. She liked it.

10. Let's go in right away.

D. From among the three choices given, choose the best equivalent of the English given at the beginning of each sentence. Write the complete sentence and translate it.

1. (How) ¡ __________ *hermosa es la vida!*
   (a) *Cómo*
   (b) *Qué*
   (c) *Como*

2. (find) *Usted* __________ *las cosas siempre.*
   (a) *encontra*
   (b) *encuentras*
   (c) *encuentra*

3. (can) *Ellos dicen que* __________ *ir mañana.*
   (a) *pueden*
   (b) *poden*
   (c) *puden*

4. (What a) ¡ __________ *día más agradable!*
   (a) *Qué un*
   (b) *Cómo*
   (c) *Qué*

5. (is) *Parece que él* __________ *un hombre muy importante.*
   (a) *es*
   (b) *está*
   (c) *ser*

6. (understand) *Yo lo* __________ *todo.*
   (a) *compriendo*
   (b) *entiendo*
   (c) *entendo*

7. (tells) *Juana les* __________ *una historia todos los días.*
   (a) *conta*
   (b) *cuentas*
   (c) *cuenta*

8. (can ________ be) *¿Dónde ________ el libro?*
   (a) *puede ser*
   (b) *estará*
   (c) *estar*

9. (was) *El hermano de Juan ________ el héroe.*
   (a) *estuvo*
   (b) *estaba*
   (c) *era*

10. (What a) ¡ ________ *placer me da verles aquí!*
   (a) *Qué*
   (b) *Que un*
   (c) *Cómo*

LESSON 9

EN EL MUSEO DEL PRADO
IN THE PRADO MUSEUM

A. DIALOGUE

1. Empleada: **Cuatrocientas pesetas, por favor.**
Four hundred pesetas, please.

2. Carlos: **Aquí tiene usted. Ochocientas por dos entradas.** (*A Juana*) ***Debimos*** **haber venido el martes. No cobran la entrada.**
Here you are. Eight hundred for two tickets. (*To Juana*) We should have come on Tuesday. They don't charge admission.

3. Juana: **Sí, pero hay *tanta* gente que no se puede ver nada.**
Yes, but there are so many people that you can't see anything.

4. Carlos: **Tienes razón. Quiero verlo todo con calma. Es una de las colecciones más fabulosas del mundo.**
You're right. I want to see it all, taking my time. It's one of the most fabulous collections in the world.

5. Guía: **¿Quieren una guía, señores? Yo les puedo dar detalles sobre todas las obras, y ayudarles a encontrar las que les interesan.**
Do you want a guide? I can give you details about all the works, and help you find the ones that interest you.

6. Juana: **No, gracias, pero tenemos unas preguntas.**
No, thank you, but we have a few questions.

7. Carlos: **Sí. Quiero aprender un poco porque me gusta pintar.**
Yes. I'd like to learn a little because I like to paint.

8. Guía: **Usted encontrará inspiración aquí. Hay obras de todas las épocas, de todos los estilos, de antiguos a modernos.**
You'll find inspiration here. There are works from every period, of every style, from ancient to modern.

9. Juana: **¿Dónde está la Dama de Elche?° Quiero verla primero. Se dice que es impresionante.**
Where is the Dama de Elche? I want to see her first. They say she's impressive.

10. Guía: **El hermoso busto de la Dama de Elche no se encuentra aquí en este museo, señora. Está en el Museo Arqueológico Nacional. ¿Sabe usted que dicen que es una falsificación?**
The beautiful bust of the Dama de Elche isn't here in this museum, ma'am. It's in the Museo Arqueológico Nacional. Do you know that they say it's a forgery?

11. Juana: **¡No! ¿De veras? No lo sabía.**
No, really? I didn't know that.

12. Carlos: **Interesante. Gracias, señora. Tenemos un plano del museo y sabemos lo que queremos ver hoy. Vamos, Juana.**
Interesting. Thank you, ma'am. We have a map of the museum, and we know what we want to see today. Let's go, Juana.

13. Carlos: **Vamos a subir aquí, por esta escalera, a los salones de la pintura española. Es lo que me interesa más.**

Let's go up this stairway here to the rooms with Spanish paintings. That's what interests me most.

14. Juana: **¡Ah! Aquí están las obras maestras de El Greco,° Velázquez,° Murillo,° Goya° . . . Quiero ver "Las Meninas," y "Las Lanzas," y "Los Borrachos" y . . .**
Oh! Here are the masterworks of El Greco, Velázquez, Murillo, Goya . . . I want to see "The Meninas," "The Lances," "The Drunkards" and . . .

15. Carlos: **¡Despacio! Espera un momento. No podemos verlo todo de un golpe. Vamos a empezar con este salón de las pinturas de El Greco.**
Slow down! Wait a minute. We can't see everything all at once. Let's begin with this room of paintings by El Greco.

16. Juana: **¡Ay sí! Mira, allí delante está "La Adoración de los Pastores." ¡Qué hermosa es la figura de la Virgen! ¿Verdad que todo en este cuadro es luminoso y espiritual?**
Oh, yes! Look, there in front of us is "The Adoration of the Shepherds." How beautiful the figure of the Virgin is! Isn't everything luminous and spiritual in this picture?

17. Carlos: **Fíjate qué alargadas parecen todas las figuras. Es como si se las mirase desde abajo. Todo tiende a subir.**
Notice how elongated the figures look. It's as if we were looking at them from below. Everything seems to be rising.

18. Juana: **¡Es verdaderamente una maravilla! Quiero ver el famoso cuadro "El Entierro del Conde Orgaz." ¿Dónde está? No lo veo por *ninguna* parte.**

It's really marvelous! I want to see the famous painting "The Burial of Count Orgaz." Where is it? I don't see it around here anywhere.

19. Carlos: **Es que no está aquí, Juana. Para eso tendremos que hacer un viaje a Toledo. Se encuentra en la Iglesia de Santo Tomé.**
That's because it's not here, Juana. For that, we'll have to take a trip to Toledo. It's in the Iglesia Santo Tomé.

20. Juana: **A ver si podemos ir a Toledo a verlo. Se dice que es una ciudad encantadora. Allí podemos visitar el museo de El Greco. Es la casa en que vivió el pintor. Está restaurada y se encuentra ahora en las mismas condiciones del siglo diecisiete. ¿Cuándo podremos hacerlo? ¡Me entusiasma la idea!**
Let's see if we can go to Toledo to see it. They say that it's a charming city. We can visit the El Greco Museum there. It's the house that the painter lived in. It's restored and is in the same condition as in the seventeenth century. When can we do it? I'm enthusiastic about the idea!

21. Carlos: **A mí también me gusta la idea. Miraremos nuestros planes para la semana que viene a ver si podemos organizarlo para algún día.**
I like the idea, too. We'll look at our plans for next week to see if we can arrange it for some day.

22. Juana: **¡Qué bien! Vamos a ver los cuadros de Velázquez. Quiero ver los famosos retratos del rey Felipe Cuarto y el del príncipe Don Baltasar Carlos.**
How wonderful! Let's see the paintings of Velázquez. I want to see the famous portraits of King Felipe IV and the one of Prince Baltasar Carlos.

23. Carlos: **Mira allí está "Las Meninas" con el famoso autorretrato. ¿Ves que el pintor está allí, a la izquierda, con el pincel en la mano como si estuviese pintando lo que tiene delante? Fíjate en la inocenia y belleza del retrato de la princesita.**
Look, there's "The Meninas" with the famous self-portrait. Do you see that the painter is there, on the left, with his brush in his hand as if he were painting what is before him? Notice the innocence and beauty of the portrait of the little princess.

24. Juana: **Velázquez era un maestro prodigioso. ¡Qué variedad de temas y estilos! No sé cuál de estos pintores me gusta más. ¡Todos me gustan *tanto*!**
Velázquez was a prodigious master. What a variety of themes and styles. I don't know which of these painters I like best. I like all of them so much.

25. Carlos: **Pues tendremos que volver para ver lo demás. Es casi la hora de cerrar, y todavía no hemos visto nada de Zurbarán,° ni de Murillo, ni de Goya, que te interesaba tanto. Las tres horas han pasado volando.**
We'll have to come back to see the rest. It's almost closing time, and we still haven't seen anything by Zurbarán, or Murillo, or Goya, that interested you so much. The three hours flew by.

26. Juana: **¡Qué lástima! ¡Cuando uno está pasándolo bien el tiempo sí que vuela!**
What a pity! Times flies when you're having fun!

B. NOTES

9. *la Dama de Elche:* A polychrome bust of an idol or goddess, so-called because it was found in Elche, a

small town on the Mediterranean coast south of Alicante. It dates from the fifth century B.C. and is considered one of the most important, as well as the most beautiful, of early Iberian artworks.

14. *El Greco:* Domenico Theotocopoulis, born in Crete, lived in Spain from approximately 1577 until his death in 1614. He is generally known by the name *El Greco* ("The Greek").
Velázquez: Painter, born in Seville in 1599; court painter for Felipe IV. He left a rich gallery of portraits of the royal family and retainers, as well as a justly famed variety of paintings of mythological and historical subjects.
Murillo: Painter, also from Seville (1617–1682), known as "the Spanish Correggio."
Goya: Born in a small town in Aragón, Fuendetodos, in 1746; died in Bordeaux in 1828. One of the giants of Spanish art, his influence is felt to the present day. He is considered a precursor to Expressionism.

25. *Zurbarán:* Born in Fuentes de Cantos, Extremadura, in 1598. Studied and painted in Seville. Known for his monochromatic portraits of monks and nuns, he was a master of perspective and effects of light.

C. GRAMMAR AND USAGE

1. *Deber* + infinitive: must, should, ought to

a. ***Juan debe tener las entradas.***	a. Juan must have the tickets.
b. *Deben estar por aquí.*	b. They must be around here.
c. *Debes estudiar la lección.*	c. You ought to study the lesson.

2. *Tanto* and *tan*

Tanto + noun: so much (sing.), so many (pl.)

a. ***Hay tanta gente en el teatro.***	a. There are so many people in the theater.
b. *Nunca he visto tantas joyas.*	b. I have never seen so many jewels.
c. *No sabía que tenía tanto dinero.*	c. I didn't know that he had so much money.

Tan + adjective (or adverb): so __________

a. ***Teresa está tan ocupada.***	a. Teresa is so busy.
b. *Estaban tan enfermos que no podían ir.*	b. They were so sick they couldn't go.
c. *Me parece tan fácil.*	c. It seems so easy to me.

a. ***Me habló tan lentamente que lo entendí todo.***	a. He spoke to me so slowly that I understood everything.
b. *Ella lo explicó tan claramente que todos lo entendieron.*	b. She explained it so clearly that everyone understood it.
c. *No debes hacerlo tan de prisa.*	c. You shouldn't do it so quickly.

Tanto is used by itself adverbially.

a. ***¡Las obras de Velázquez me gustan tanto!***	a. I like the works of Velázquez so (very) much!
b. *¡Todo me interesa tanto!*	b. Everything interests me so (very) much!
c. *¡He comido tanto!*	c. I ate so much!

3. *No, nunca, nadie, ninguno*

These double and triple negatives can express negative ideas.

a. ***No veo a nadie.***	a. I don't see anyone.
b. *No veo a nadie nunca.*	b. I never see anyone.
c. *No voy nunca a ninguna parte.*	c. I never go anywhere.

A negative word may be placed before the verb, replacing *no*. Compare:

a. ***No veo nunca a nadie. Nunca veo a nadie.***	a. I never see anyone.
b. *No me habla nadie. Nadie me habla.*	b. No one speaks to me.
c. *No voy nunca a ninguna parte. Nunca voy a ninguna parte.*	c. I never go anywhere.

EXERCISES

A. Substitute each of the words or expressions in parentheses for the underlined word or expression in the model sentence. Write each new sentence and say it aloud.

1. *Juan debe estar en la biblioteca. (el museo, la casa, la sala, el parque, el centro)*

2. *Ellos deben haber estudiado. (descansado, comido, ido, salido, terminado)*

3. *Juana y yo debemos empezar. (terminar, leer, practicar, hablar, salir)*

4. *Hay tanta gente en el museo. (tantos cuadros, tantas pinturas, tanto ruido, tantos niños, tantas señoras)*

5. *El lo hizo tan claramente. (lentamente, rápidamente, de prisa, fácilmente, bien)*

6. *Nunca he estado tan ocupado. (cansado, enfermo, perezoso, contento, equivocado)*

B. Rephrase the following sentences, placing *no* before the verb. Write the complete sentence and translate.

1. *Nunca escribo a nadie.*

2. *Nadie me escribe.*

3. *Nunca compramos nada.*

4. *Juan y José nunca van a ninguna parte.*

5. *Nunca he visto a tanta gente en el museo.*

C. Translate the following sentences into Spanish, then say them aloud.

1. There are so many people here.

2. He explained it so clearly that I understood everything.

3. I have never been so busy.

4. You must be tired.

5. Juan and María ought to study more.

6. I never want to see her.

7. How elongated all the figures look!

8. We have to take a trip to Toledo.

9. When can we do it?

10. I want to see the famous painting.

D. From among the three choices given, choose the best equivalent of the English given at the beginning of each sentence. Write the complete sentence and translate.

1. (so) *Es* __________ *difícil comprenderlo.*
   (a) *tanto*
   (b) *tanta*
   (c) *tan*

2. (ever) *No lo veo* __________.
   (a) *nunca*
   (b) *algo*
   (c) *algunas veces*

3. (everything that) *Creo* __________ *me dice Juan.*
   (a) *todo lo que*
   (b) *todos que*
   (c) *todas las*

4. (all the) *Juan ha comprado* __________ *libros que quería.*
   (a) *todos*
   (b) *todo el*
   (c) *todos los*

5. (so much) *¡Roberto tiene* __________ *tiempo libre!*
   (a) *tan mucho*
   (b) *tanto*
   (c) *tanto que*

6. (anything) *No quiero* __________ *ahora.*
   (a) *alguna cosa*
   (b) *nada*
   (c) *algo*

7. (ought to) *Me parece que yo* __________ *levantarme ahora.*
   (a) *debo*
   (b) *tengo que*
   (c) *hay que*

8. (so many) *No he tenido nunca* __________ *problemas.*
   (a) *tan muchos*
   (b) *tantos*
   (c) *tantas*

9. (anything) *No te debo* __________.
   (a) *algo*
   (b) *alguna cosa*
   (c) *nada*

10. (such) *Nunca ha leído libros* __________ *difíciles.*
   (a) *tan*
   (b) *tanto*
   (c) *tantos*

LESSON 10

LA ARTESANIA ESPAÑOLA
SPANISH HANDCRAFTS

A. DIALOGUE

Una visita al Rastro de Madrid. A visit to the Rastro (Flea Market) in Madrid.

1. Juana: **Nos han hablado° tanto del Rastro° que deberíamos visitarlo. Tiene que ser interesante. No sé exactamente lo que es.**
   People have talked to us so much about the Rastro that we should go to see it. It must be interesting. I don't know exactly what it is.

2. Carlos: **Seguramente es una sección de calles donde hay muchas tiendas de antigüedades, y vendedores de *toda* clase de cosas.**
   It must be a section of streets where there are many antique shops and vendors of all kinds of things.

3. Juana: **Seguro que es más divertido *los domingos*° por la mañana.**
   I bet it's more fun on Sunday mornings.

4. Carlos: **Es cuando *todo* el mundo va. ¿Quieres ir hoy, cuando hay menos gente?**
   It's when everyone goes. Do you want to go today, when there are fewer people?

5. Juana: **Sí, vamos. Miguel y Teresa me dijeron que querían ir también. Vamos a ver si pueden acompañarnos hoy. Como ellos lo conocen ya, pueden ayudarnos un poco.**
   Yes, let's go. Miguel and Teresa told me that they wanted to go, too. Let's see if they can come with us

today. Since they know it already, they can help us a little.

6. Carlos: (*en el teléfono*) **¿Miguel? Hola, ¿cómo estás? Bien, bien, me alegro. Juana y yo estábamos hablando, y pensábamos ir al Rastro esta mañana. Como Juana me ha dicho que ustedes habían hablado de ir, llamo a ver si quieren venir. Nos gustaría muchísimo. ¡Ah, sí! ¡Estupendo! Entonces, pasaremos a buscarles,° ya que están de camino. ¿Cuánto tiempo necesitan? ¿Una hora? Bien, Miguel, llegamos dentro de una hora. ¡Hasta pronto!**
   (*on the telephone*) Miguel? Hello, how are you? Fine, fine, I'm glad. Juana and I were talking, and we were thinking of going to the Rastro this morning. Juana told me that you had spoken of going, so I'm calling to find out if you want to come. We would like that very much. Oh, yes! Terrific! Then, we'll come by to pick you up, it's on the way. How much time do you need? An hour? Alright, Miguel, we'll be there in an hour. See you soon!

7. Juana: **¡Qué bien! Ellos vendrán con nosotros. Me alegro tanto. Teresa dice que hay que saber regatear, y ella ha prometido enseñarme la manera de hacerlo.**
   How nice! They're coming with us. I'm so pleased. Teresa says that you have to know how to bargain, and she promised to show me how to do it.

8. Carlos: **Eso es, hay que saber regatear. Y no debes dar la impresión de tener mucho dinero.**
   That's right, you have to know how to bargain. And you shouldn't give the impression of having a lot of money.

En el Rastro. At the Rastro.

9. Carlos: **Vamos a entrar en esta tienda. ¡Hay tantos artículos de loza! Vean aquellos platos y tazas. ¡Todo lo que hay aquí es hermoso! Dígame, señora, ¿dónde hacen esos platos?**
Let's go into this store. There is so much china! Look at those plates and cups. Everything that is here is beautiful! Tell me, ma'am, where are those plates made?

10. Vendedora: **Son de Valencia, señor, de una de las fábricas más conocidas. Se puede reconocer la producción de esa fábrica por la extraordinaria fineza del trabajo. Estos platos son todos del siglo pasado.**
They're from Valencia, sir, from one of the best-known factories. You can recognize the products of that factory by the extraordinary quality of the work. These plates are all from the last century.

11. Juana: **Son preciosos. Me imagino que serán carísimos. Me gustaría tener algunos de los más grandes para colgar en la pared del comedor.**
They're beautiful. I imagine they must be very expensive. I would like to have some of the larger ones to hang on the wall in the dining room.

12. Carlos: **¿Cuánto valen los grandes, señora? Especialmente estos, en azul y amarillo, con el diseño de pájaros.**
How much are the large ones, ma'am? Especially these in blue and yellow, with the bird design.

13. Vendedora: **Esos son precisamente los más caros. Están pintados a mano y son de un estilo que no se encuentra muy a menudo.**

Those are precisely the most expensive. They're painted by hand and in a style that isn't found very often.

14. Carlos: **Bueno, de acuerdo. Pero, ¿cuánto valen?**
Well, agreed. But how much do they cost?

15. Vendedora: **¿Cuántos quieren ustedes? Se los puedo dejar a muy buen precio.**
How many do you want? I could let you have them for a very good price.

16. Carlos: **Depende de lo que quiere decir "muy buen precio." Queremos cuatro o cinco, ¿no te parece, Juana?**
That depends on what "a very good price" means. We want four or five, don't you think, Juana?

17. Juana: **Sí. Y éstos son los que me gustan más. ¿Cuánto quiere usted por ellos?**
Yes. And these are the ones that I like best. How much do you want for them?

18. Vendedora: **Bueno, para ustedes, les hago precio especial. Les dejo cinco en veinticinco mil pesetas.**
Well, for you I'll make a special price. I'll let you have the five of them for twenty-five thousand pesetas.

19. Carlos: **Es demasiado. Por veinte mil, me los llevo.**
It's too much. For twenty thousand, I'll take them.

20. Vendedora: **Lo siento. Ya les he dado el mejor precio posible.**
I'm sorry. I've already given you the best possible price.

21. Juana: **¡Ay, y me gustan tanto! ¿Qué le parece veintidós mil?**
Oh, and I like them so much! What do you think of twenty-two thousand?

22. Vendedora: **Bueno, como ustedes me son muy simpáticos, se los dejo a ese precio.**
Well, since I like you, I'll let you have them for that price.

23. Carlos: **Bien, tome usted. Envuélvalos con cuidado y volveremos a buscarlos dentro de poco.**
Fine, here you are. Wrap them carefully and we'll come back for them in a little while.

24. Teresa: **Vamos a esa tienda de muebles antiguos. Tienen muchos arcones de madera labrada.**
Let's go to that antique furniture store. They have lots of chests of carved wood.

25. Juana: **¡Qué comedor! Mira esos sillones tan regios. ¿No los encuentras estupendos, Carlos?**
What a dining room set! Look at those big regal-looking chairs. Don't you think they're terrific, Carlos?

26. Carlos: **Desde luego. Pero ten en cuenta que no podemos cargar con cosas tan pesadas. Costaría una fortuna embalarlos y mandarlos.**
Of course. But bear in mind that we can't load ourselves down with such heavy things. It would cost a fortune to pack and send them.

27. Juana: **No te preocupes. Yo no estaba** ***pensando en*** **comprarlo.**
Don't worry. I wasn't thinking of buying it.

28. Teresa: **¿Qué les parece la idea de tomar algún refresco? Estoy cansada de andar.°**
What do you think of the idea of having something to drink? I am tired of walking.

29. Carlos: **¡Me parece muy bien! ¿Por qué no se sientan ustedes en la terraza de allí enfrente? Yo iré a buscar los platos. Los debe tener envueltos ya.°**
Sounds good. Why don't you sit down in that side-walk café across the street? I'll go get the plates. She ought to have them wrapped by now.

30. Juana: **¿Qué quieres tomar, Carlos? Te lo pido mientras tanto.**
What are you having, Carlos? I'll order it in the meantime.

31. Carlos: **Me gustaría una cerveza bien fría. Tengo mucha sed.**
I would like a cold beer. I'm very thirsty.

B. NOTES

1. *nos han hablado:* Note the third person plural (they) used impersonally.
El Rastro: an open-air market located in the old section of Madrid. There are restaurants and shops among the medieval-looking buildings of the neighborhood.

3. *los domingos:* "on Sundays"; the article is used with days of the week.

6. *buscarles: buscar,* to look for. This may also be used in the sense of "to stop by for someone," "to pick them up." See also sentence 23, *volveremos a buscarlos.*

28. *andar:* Notice the use of the infinitive as a noun here.

29. *ya:* Here, "already" means "by now" or "by this time." In this final position *ya* often has this meaning.

C. GRAMMAR AND USAGE

1. *Todo/a(s)*

Todos (as) + article: every, all

a. ***Tenemos todos los estilos.***	a. We have every style (all the styles).
b. *Hay pinturas de todas las épocas.*	b. There are paintings from every period (all the periods).
c. *Quiero ver todos las muebles.*	c. I want to see all the furniture.

Todo (a) + article: the whole, the entire

a. ***Me gusta toda la ciudad.***	a. I like the whole city.
b. *El ha viajado por todo el país.*	b. He has traveled through the entire country.
c. *Todo el mundo estaba allí.*	c. Everybody was there.

Note:

- *Todo el día*—all day (the entire day)
- *Todos los días*—every day (all the days)

2. Other expressions with *todo*

Todo lo que: everything (that)

a. ***Ella quiere comprar todo lo que ve.***	a. She wants to buy everything (that) she sees.
b. *Todo lo que hemos visto nos ha gustado.*	b. We have liked everything (that) we have seen.
c. *Juan comió todo lo que le pusieron delante.*	c. Juan ate everything (that) they put in front of him.

Lo + todo: everything

a. ***Quiero verlo todo.***	a. I want to see everything.
b. *Me lo explicó todo.*	b. He explained everything to me.
c. *Ellos querían comprarlo todo.*	c. They wanted to buy everything.

3. *El* and *los* + days of the week

a. ***Estoy menos ocupado los sábados.***	a. I am less busy (not so busy) on Saturdays.
b. ***Voy a verle el lunes.***	b. I am going to see him on Monday.
c. *Hay corridas (de toros) los domingos por la tarde.*	c. There are bullfights on Sundays in the afternoon.

4. *Pensar + en:* to think of, to think about

a. ***¿En qué piensa usted?***	a. What are you thinking about?
b. *Estaba pensando en todo lo que tengo que hacer.*	b. I was thinking about everything I have to do.
c. *Ellos piensan en las dificultades que tienen.*	c. They think about the difficulties they have.

EXERCISES

A. Substitute each of the words or expressions in the parentheses for the underlined word or expression in the model sentence. Write each new sentence and say it aloud.

1. *Juan quiere comprar todos los muebles. (libros, zapatos, coches, cuadros, ceniceros)*

2. *Ella ha visto todas las pinturas. (blusas, casas, obras de teatro, bolsas, medias)*

3. *Ellos han visto todo el país. (museo, pueblo, centro, mercado, teatro)*

4. *Lo vieron el martes. (compraron, vendieron, visitaron, hicieron, terminaron)*

5. *Me gusta descansar los domingos. (pasear, ir al cine, leer, dormir hasta la tarde, jugar)*

6. *Estaba pensando en el trabajo. (el viaje, el tiempo, la comedia, el museo, la música)*

B. Change these sentences to the negative. Write the complete sentence and translate.

1. *Siempre pienso en el viaje.*

2. *Vamos al museo el lunes.*

3. *Le gusta comprar todo lo que ve.*

4. *Los niños comieron todo el helado.*

5. *Es difícil comprenderlo.*

C. Translate the following sentences into Spanish, then say them aloud.

1. They have spoken to us so much about the museum.
2. It is said (*se dice*) that it's more amusing on Sundays.
3. We can go with you tomorrow.
4. You have to know how to bargain.
5. You shouldn't give the impression of being rich.
6. One can recognize all of the work of that factory by the style.
7. I can let you have it all at a very good price.
8. That depends on what you mean.
9. All the pictures are expensive.
10. He ought to have them (the plates) wrapped now.

D. From among the three choices given, choose the best equivalent of the English given at the beginning of each sentence. Write the complete sentence and translate.

1. (Every) *Le veo* __________ *martes.*
   (a) *todas las*
   (b) *todo el*
   (c) *todos los*
2. (all) *He pasado* __________ *tarde en la piscina.*
   (a) *todo el*
   (b) *toda la*
   (c) *toda*

3. (all day) *Juan estuvo leyendo* __________.
   (a) *todo el día*
   (b) *todo día*
   (c) *toda la día*

4. (on) *Voy a verle* __________ *domingo.*
   (a) *en*
   (b) *el*
   (c) *por*

5. (everything) *Usted cree* __________ *él le dice.*
   (a) *todos los que*
   (b) *todo el que*
   (c) *todo lo que*

6. (every) *Normalmente voy a visitarlo* __________ *sábados.*
   (a) *cada*
   (b) *todos los*
   (c) *algunos*

7. (on) __________ *miércoles vamos a ir de compras.*
   (a) *En*
   (b) *El*
   (c) *La*

8. (about her) *Nunca pienso* __________ *ahora.*
   (a) *en ella*
   (b) *sobre ella*
   (c) *de ellas*

9. (all the news) *Siempre oigo* __________ *por radio.*
   (a) *todo la noticia*
   (b) *todas las noticias*
   (c) *todas noticias*

10. (of) *Yo no estaba pensando* __________ *comprarlo.*
    (a) *en*
    (b) *sobre*
    (c) *a*

LESSON 11

SAQUEMOS FOTOGRAFIAS
LET'S TAKE PICTURES

A. DIALOGUE

En el hotel. At the hotel.

1. Carlos: **¿Recuerdas que hoy habíamos decidido volver a algunos de los sitios que nos gustaron más para sacar fotos?**
   Do you remember that today we had decided to go back to some of the places we liked best to take pictures?

2. Juana: **Claro que sí. ¿Has comprado película° para las cámeras?**
   Of course. Did you buy film for the cameras?

3. Carlos: **Sí. Tengo dos rollos para cada una, pero me gustaría ir a una tienda fotográfica a comprar más, y a hacer unas preguntas.**
   Yes. I have two rolls for each one, but I'd like to go to a photo shop to buy more and to ask some questions.

4. Juana: **Recuerda que queremos hacer algunas transparencias° y que nos hacen falta casetes para la cámara de video.**
   Remember that we want to make some slides and that we need tapes for the video camera.

5. Carlos: **¿Prefieres las películas en color o en blanco y negro?**
   Do you prefer color film or black and white?

6. Juana: **Deberíamos comprar por lo menos dos en color. Con el cielo tan claro que tenemos en Madrid *estos días,* las fotos en color deben salir preciosas.**

We ought to buy at least two in color. With the clear skies that we have in Madrid these days, the color photos ought to turn out beautiful.

7. Carlos: **Tienes razón. Quiero recuerdos de todo el colorido de algunos barrios de Madrid.**
You're right. I want memories of all the color of some districts of Madrid.

8. Juana: **Y *a mí* me gustaría tener un video y diapositivas de las plazas más hermosas, del Palacio Nacional y de muchos otros sitios.**
And I would like to have a video and slides of the prettiest squares, of the National Palace and of many other places.

En la tienda. In the shop.

9. Carlos: **¿Tiene usted película para *esta* cámara?**
Do you have film for this camera?

10. Empleado: **Permítame verla, por favor. ¿En blanco y negro o en color?**
Let me see it, please. In black and white or color?

11. Carlos: **Dos rollos de cada una, por favor.**
Two rolls of each, please.

12. Empleado: **Aquí los tiene. *Esa* que tiene usted es una cámara muy buena.**
Here you are. That's a very good camera that you have.

13. Carlos: **Gracias. He tenido bastante suerte con ella, aunque no soy experto. ¿Quiere usted darme dos rollos para *esta* otra cámára, por favor?**
Thanks. I have had good luck with it although I'm

no expert. Will you give me two rolls for this other camera, please?

14. Empleado: **¿De veinticuatro o de treinta y seis?** Twenty-four or thirty-six?

15. Carlos: **De treinta y seis, por favor. ¿Quiere usted revisar esta cámara, por favor? Hay algo que no funciona bien.** Thirty-six, please. Do you want to take a look at this camera? There's something that's not working well.

16. Empleado: **¿Qué es lo que no funciona?** What is it that isn't working?

17. Carlos: **A veces, cuando aprieto *este* botón, se queda enganchado.** Sometimes, when I press this button, it sticks.

18. Empleado: **Conozco bien *este* modelo. *Hay que* apretarlo rápidamente, sin dejarlo demasiado tiempo. Una presión rápida y ligera, levantando el dedo en seguida.** I know this model well. You must press it rapidly, without leaving it too long. A rapid and light pressure, lifting the finger immediately.

19. Carlos: **Muchas gracias. Quiero también unas pilas.** Thank you very much. I also want some batteries.

20. Empleado: **Muy bien, señor. ¿Desean ustedes algo más? Entonces voy a envolver todo *esto*. Buena suerte.** Very well, sir. Do you want anything else? Then I'll wrap all this. Good luck!

En la Plaza de España. At the Plaza de España.

21. Juana: **Ah, la Plaza de España.° Me gustariá tener una vista panorámica de toda la Plaza.** ***Hay tantas cosas que ver.*** **No te olvides de quitar la tapa del lente.**
Ah, the Plaza de España. I'd like to have a panoramic view of the square. There are so many things to see. Don't forget to take off the lens cap.

22. Carlos: **No te preocupes. Ponte delante de la estatua de Don Quijote. Así estarás en la foto.**
Don't worry. Stand in front of the statue of Don Quixote. That way you'll be in the picture.

23. Juana: **Pero si vas a sacarla de tan lejos, nadie podrá reconocerme.**
But if you're going to take it from so far away, no one will be able to recognize me.

24. Carlos: **Pero nosotros sabremos que estás allí, y se lo podremos decir a todos: "¿No ves** ***aquel*** **puntito azul al pie de la estatua de Don Quijote? Pues** ***ese*** **puntito es Juana."**
But we'll know that you're there, and we can tell everyone: "Don't you see that little blue dot at the foot of the statue of Don Quixote? Well, that little dot is Juana."

25. Juana: **¡Qué chistoso eres! ¿No quieres sacar alguna otra vista de la Torre de Madrid y del Edificio España?**
How funny you are! Don't you want to take some of another view of the Tower of Madrid and the España Building?

26. Carlos: **Sí, y luego vamos al otro lado de la plaza para sacar algunas de la Gran Vía.° A esta hora de la tarde es impresionante con todos los coches,**

el bullicio de la gente, las terrazas llenas y la luz tan fuerte.
Yes, and then let's go to the other side of the square to take some of the Gran Vía. At this time of the afternoon it's impressive with all the cars, the hubbub of people, the crowded sidewalk cafés and such strong light.

27. Juana: **Quiero sacarte una foto sentado en nuestra terraza preferida.**
I want to take a picture of you, sitting in our favorite café.

En la Plaza de Neptuno.° At the Plaza de Neptuno.

28. Carlos: **Desde aquí podemos sacar unas fotos de la fuente con el Museo del Prado al fondo.**
From here we can take some shots of the fountain with the Prado Museum in the background.

29. Juana: **Deberíamos tener algunas de la Castellana, con los árboles.**
We should have some of the Castellana, with the trees.

30. Carlos: **Espero que todas salgan bien. Tendremos una colección de fotos muy bonitas como recuerdo de nuestra visita a Madrid.**
I hope they all turn out well. We'll have a collection of very pretty pictures as a souvenir of our visit to Madrid.

31. Juana: **Saquemos unas de la Puerta de Alcalá° y del Retiro.**
Let's take some of the Gate of Alcalá and of Retiro Park.

32. Carlos: **Claro que sí. Vamos, y allá nos podremos sentar un rato a la sombra, cerca del estanque.**
Of course. Let's go and we can sit down there for a while in the shade, near the pool.

33. Juana: **Tenemos que sacar copias de las mejores para mandar a nuestros amigos.**
We'll have to make copies of the best ones to send to our friends.

34. Carlos: **Si es que salen bien.**
If they come out well.

35. Juana: **Tú eres buen fotógrafo, Carlos. Siempre te salen bien.**
You're a good photographer, Carlos. They always come out well for you.

B. NOTES

2. *película:* film. This word is also used for "movie" or "motion picture." *Mujeres al borde de un ataque de nervios es una buena película: Women on the Verge of a Nervous Breakdown* is a good movie.

4. *transparencia:* slide. Notice in sentence 8 that *diapositiva* is another Spanish word for the same.

21. *Plaza de España:* This square, at the foot of the Gran Vía, has statues of Don Quixote and Sancho Panza in the center. Madrid's "skyscrapers," the Tower of Madrid and the España Building, are also there.

26. *La Gran Vía:* Officially, the Avenida de José Antonio Promo de Rivera, but known to everyone as "The Gran Vía." It is a broad and beautiful commercial street in the center of Madrid that curves up

from the Post Office and ends at the Plaza de España. Many of Madrid's most elegant shops, movie theaters, and restaurants are found here.
Fourth subtitle: *La Plaza de Neptuno:* On Recoletos Street, it has a beautiful fountain of Neptune. It is between two of Madrid's finest hotels, The Ritz and the Palace.

31. *Puerta de Alcalá:* One of the beautiful baroque entrance gates to the city, just above the Post Office, on Alcalá Avenue.
El Retiro: Parque del Buen Retiro, the large and beautiful central park of Madrid.

C. GRAMMAR AND USAGE

1. The demonstrative adjectives, *este, ese,* and *aquel* in their various forms have a written accent to denote their use as pronouns.

éste/ésta(s): this (near the speaker)

a. ***¿El libro? No me gusta éste.***	a. The book? I don't like this one.
b. ***¿Los cuadros? Me gustan éstos.***	b. The pictures? I like these.
c. ***¿La máquina fotográfica? Quiero ver ésta.***	c. The camera? I want to see this one.
d. *¿Las pinturas? Podría venderle éstas.*	d. The paintings? I could sell you these.

ése/ésa(s): that (near the person spoken to)

a. ***Me gusta este libro pero no me gusta ése que estás leyendo.***	a. I like this book but I don't like that one you're reading.
b. ***Voy a llevar estos paquetes, y usted puede mandar ésos al hotel.***	b. I'm going to carry these packages and you can send those to the hotel.
c. ***Esta foto es preciosa pero ésa que miras no salió bien.***	c. This photograph is beautiful but that one you're looking at didn't turn out well.
d. *Estas blusas son preciosas pero ésas no me gustan.*	d. These blouses are pretty but I don't like those.

aquél/aquélla(s): that (removed from both speaker and person spoken to)

a. ***Ese disco que tiene usted en la mano es muy caro, pero es mejor que aquél que escuchamos ayer.***	a. That record (you have in your hand) is very expensive but it's better than that one we listened to yesterday.
b. ***Esos cuadernos son muy buenos, pero no tan buenos como aquéllos de la otra tienda.***	b. Those notebooks are very good, but they're not as good as those in the other store.
c. ***Esa mesa es demasiado grande, pero aquélla en el rincón es demasiado pequeña.***	c. That table is too large but that one in the corner is too small.
d. *Esas lámparas son muy prácticas pero aquéllas que vimos en Segovia son más bonitas.*	d. Those lamps are very practical but those that we saw in Segovia are prettier.

Note:

- The accent is not usually written on capital letters.

2. Special forms of the personal pronoun with prepositions for emphasis or clarification

a. ***A mí me gusta este helado. ¿Y a ti?***	a. I like this ice cream. Do you?
b. ***A mí también me gusta.***	b. I like it too.
c. ***A él no le gusta. ¿Y a ella?***	c. He doesn't like it. Does she?
d. *A ella le gusta mucho.*	d. She likes it very much.

Note:

- These forms are used with all prepositions with the exception of the forms *conmigo* and *contigo.*

a. ***Este regalo es para mí.***	a. This gift is for me.
b. ***Pablo lo ha hecho para ti.***	b. Pablo did it for you.
c. ***¿Quieres venir conmigo?***	c. Do you want to come with me?
d. *Juan hablará contigo mañana.*	d. Juan will speak with you tomorrow.
e. *Dice que estaba pensando en mí.*	e. She says she was thinking of me.
f. *Siempre pienso en ti.*	f. I always think of you.

But *entre tú y yo:* between you and me

3. *Hay que:* one must, you must (impersonal)

a. ***Al llegar a la esquina hay que doblar a la derecha.***	a. When you reach the corner, you must turn right.
b. ***Hay que estudiar mucho para comprenderlo.***	b. One must study a lot to understand it.
c. ***Hay que comprar las entradas en la taquilla.***	c. You must buy the tickets at the box office.

4. *Hay* + noun + *que* + infinitive: There are __________ to __________.

a. ***Hay muchos libros que leer.***	a. There are many books to read.
b. ***Hay unas películas interesantes que ver.***	b. There are some interesting movies to see.
c. ***Hay muchas cosas que comprar.***	c. There are many things to buy.

Compare:

Hay que comprar muchas cosas.	(One) You must buy many things.
Hay muchas cosas que comprar.	There are many things to buy.

EXERCISES

A. Substitute each of the words or expressions in parentheses for the underlined word or expression in the model sentence. Write each new sentence and say it aloud.

1. *Este cuadro es muy bonito pero no me gusta aquél. (edificio, mueble, libro, color, cenicero)*

2. *Aquellas pinturas que vimos ayer me gustaron. (obras, blusas, lámparas, mesas, camisas)*

3. *¿Dónde compraste esa camisa? (máquina, pluma, silla, papelera, chaqueta)*

4. *Hay que comprar el libro. (vender, leer, escribir, mandar, estudiar)*

5. *Se dice que hay muchas cosas que ver. (muchos cuadros, muchas estatuas, muchas fuentes, muchos monumentos, muchas pinturas)*

6. *Juan lo ha escrito para ti. (El poeta, El Señor Hernández, María, Mi amigo, Aquel señor)*

B. Change these sentences to the present tense. Write the complete sentence and translate.

1. *Lo compraste para él.*

2. *Los señores Andrade hicieron el viaje conmigo.*

3. *No le he visto jamás contigo.*

4. *Ellos me lo regalaron a mí.*

5. *El cuadro era para usted.*

C. Translate the following sentences into Spanish, then say them aloud.

1. I prefer to buy that camera in the other shop.

2. We ought to buy at least two rolls of color film.

3. We can take some wonderful pictures of that park.

4. Do you like the view with that building in the background?

5. They want to take a picture of you.

6. Don't forget to take off the lens cap.

7. We have to make copies for our friends.

8. They wanted to go to that museum on Sunday.

9. We have to buy more black-and-white film.

10. Do you think he likes that suit?

D. From among the three choices given, choose the best equivalent of the English given at the beginning of each sentence. Write the complete sentence and translate.

1. (with me) *Van a ir* __________ .
   (a) *con mí*
   (b) *conmigo*
   (c) *con me*

2. (to him) *Déselo* __________ .
   (a) *a ella*
   (b) *a él*
   (c) *a ello*

3. (these) *No me gustan aquellas lámparas. Déme dos de* __________ .
   (a) *éstos*
   (b) *éstas*
   (c) *estos*

4. (that one) *La novela que más me gusta es* ________ *que tienes en la mano.*
   (a) *eso*
   (b) *sea*
   (c) *ésa*

5. (that one) *Esta alfombra es muy bonita pero, ¿recuerdas ___________ que vimos ayer?*
   (a) *aquel*
   (b) *aquélla*
   (c) *ésa*

6. (one must) *Dicen que ___________ estudiar mucho.*
   (a) *debes*
   (b) *hay que*
   (c) *uno tiene*

7. (all these) *Tenemos que llevar ___________ papeles a casa.*
   (a) *estos todos*
   (b) *todos estos*
   (c) *todo esto*

8. (all that) *La historia es muy interesante. Pablo no me contó ___________ .*
   (a) *todo eso*
   (b) *todos esos*
   (c) *toda esa*

9. (many things) *Hay ___________ leer.*
   (a) *muchas cosas*
   (b) *muchas cosas que*
   (c) *mucha cosa*

10. (the whole) *Juan no me explicó ___________ problema.*
    (a) *toda la*
    (b) *todo el*
    (c) *el todo*

LESSON 12

LA AGENCIA DE VIAJES
THE TRAVEL AGENCY

A. DIALOGUE

En la agencia. In the agency.

1. Empleada: **Buenos días. ¿En qué puedo servirles?**
Good morning. How can I help you?

2. Carlos: **Nos gustaría viajar un poco por España, especialmente por los alrededores de Madrid. ¿Puede usted sugerirnos algunos itinerarios?**
We would like to travel a little through Spain, especially the area around Madrid. Could you suggest some itineraries?

3. Empleada: **Desde luego. Tenemos muchos viajes de un día a sitios de interés cerca de Madrid: a Toledo, al Escorial,° al Valle de los Caídos,° a Segovia° y muchos otros lugares de *gran* interés turístico. Los viajes son en autobús de lujo, con guía, a un precio fijo, con todos los gastos incluídos.**
Of course. We have many one-day trips to places of interest near Madrid: to Toledo, to the Escorial, to the Valle de los Caídos, to Segovia and many other places of great interest to tourists. The trips are by luxury bus, with a guide, at a set price with all costs included.

4. Carlos: **Queremos ver tantas cosas. ¿Qué piensa usted de la idea de alquilar un coche?**
We want to see so many things. What do you think of the idea of renting a car?

5. Empleada: **El coche les permite mucho más libertad de movimiento. Este folleto les da detalles sobre gastos y servicios.**
A car gives you much greater freedom of movement. This pamphlet gives you details on costs and services.

6. Carlos: **¿A qué hora salen los autobuses para Toledo?**
What time do the buses leave for Toledo?

7. Empleada: **Hay varias salidas todos los días. A las ocho, a las diez, y a la una.**
There are several departures every day. At eight, at ten, and at one o'clock.

8. Juana: **Carlos, ¿qué te parece la idea de ir mañana a Toledo? Tengo tantas ganas de verlo. Ya que hemos visto algunas obras de El Greco, quiero ver donde vivía y trabajaba.**
Carlos, what do you think of the idea of going to Toledo tomorrow? I really want to see it. Now that we've seen some of the works of El Greco, I want to see where he lived and worked.

9. Empleada: **Yo podría arreglarlo todo ahora, si quieren ustedes. Reservarles asientos en el autobús de las ocho. Claro que la comida en Toledo va incluida en el precio.**
I could arrange it all now, if you want. Reserve seats for you on the eight o'clock bus. Of course, your meal in Toledo is included in the price.

10. Carlos: **Bien. Eso es lo que haremos mañana. Ahora nos interesan también algunos informes sobre el sur de España. Queremos ir a Sevilla,° a Córdoba,° y a Jerez de la Frontera,° y tal vez podríamos hacer una breve visita a Gibraltar.**

Fine. That's what we'll do tomorrow. Now we're also interested in some information on the south of Spain. We want to go to Seville, Córdoba, Jerez de la Frontera, and perhaps we could make a brief visit to Gibraltar.

11. Empleada: **Todo eso es muy fácil de arreglar. Si quieren, les doy varios folletos, mapas, horarios de tren y de autobuses, y algunas sugerencias sobre posibles itinerarios.**
All of that is very easy to arrange. If you wish, I can give you several pamphlets, maps, train and bus timetables, and some suggestions on possible itineraries.

12. Carlos: **Perfecto. Así podremos pensarlo un poco esta noche y darle nuestra decisión mañana.**
Perfect. That way we can think about it a little tonight and give you our decision tomorrow.

13. Empleada: **Muy bien. Ahora les preparo una lista de todo lo que necesitan. Permítanme recomendarles el alquiler de un coche para visitar los sitios cerca de Madrid antes de hacer el viaje por el sur.**
Very well. Now I'm going to prepare a list of everything you need. Allow me to recommend renting a car to visit the places near Madrid before you make the trip through the south.

14. Carlos: **Me parece muy buena idea. Mañana podremos arreglarlo todo. ¿A qué hora dijo usted que sale el autobús para Toledo?**
That sounds like a very good idea to me. Tomorrow we can arrange everything. What time did you say the bus leaves for Toledo?

15. Empleada: **A las ocho en punto, señores. La agencia estará abierta a las siete y media.**

At eight o'clock sharp. The agency will be open at seven-thirty.

16. Carlos: **Bien. Así vendremos un poco antes de la hora de salida.**
Fine. So we'll come a little before the departure time.

Al día siguiente. The following day.

17. Empleada: **Muy buenos días, señores. ¿Qué han decidido ustedes?**
Good morning. What have you decided?

18. Carlos: **Pensamos ir a Segovia mañana y queremos ir en tren. Nos han dicho que es un viaje muy agradable. Así podemos ver el acueducto y el Alcázar.**
We intend to go to Segovia tomorrow and we want to go by train. We have heard it is a very pleasant trip. That way we can see the aqueduct and the Alcázar.

19. Empleada: **Muy bien. Yo les prepararé los billetes y los tendrán ustedes aquí al volver de Toledo esta tarde. Y les recomiendo *que coman* en el Mesón de Cándido, el Segoviano. Es famoso por el "tostón," el cochinillo asado, y tendrán a la vista el acueducto mientras están comiendo. ¿Quieren *que llame* para reservarles una mesa? Siempre está lleno.**
Very well. I'll prepare the tickets for you and you will have them here upon returning from Toledo this afternoon. And I recommend that you eat at the Mesón de Cándido, el Segoviano. It's famous for its roast suckling pig, and you will have a view of the aqueduct while you're eating. Do you want me to call and reserve a table for you? It's always full.

20. Juana: **Sí, por favor. Vamos a pasar un día espléndido en Toledo. Tendremos que hablar de hoteles y otros detalles del viaje por el sur, también.**
Yes, please. We're going to have a wonderful day in Toledo. We'll have to talk about hotels and other details of our trip through the south, too.

21. Empleada: **Desde luego. ¿Han decidido ustedes si quieren ir en tren, en autobús o en coche?**
Of course. Have you decided whether you want to go by train, by bus, or by car?

22. Carlos: **Por el momento habíamos pensado hacer el viaje de Madrid a Sevilla en tren, y luego ir en autobús de allí a Córdoba y a Jerez de la Frontera.**
For the moment we had thought about making the trip from Madrid to Seville by train, and then going by bus from there to Córdoba and Jerez de la Frontera.

23. Empleada: **Está bien. ¿Y luego?**
That's fine. And then?

24. Carlos: **Queríamos saber si podemos alquilar un coche en Cádiz° para seguir el viaje por la costa a Málaga° y luego, en Motril,° tomar la carretera que va a Granada.°**
We wanted to know if we could rent a car in Cádiz in order to continue the trip along the coast to Málaga and then, in Motril, take the highway that goes to Granada.

25. Empleada: **Sí, nuestra sucursal en Cádiz puede ayudarles. Pero necesitan fijar las fechas en cada sitio para la reserva de habitaciones. Me imagino que también querrán pasar unos días en Marbella° y Torremolinos,° ¿no?**

Yes, our branch in Cádiz can help you. But you have to fix the dates in each place for the room reservations. I imagine that you'll want to spend a few days in Marbella and Torremolinos too, won't you?

26. Carlos: **¡Claro que sí! Esa parte de la costa es muy bonita. Nos gustaría reservar habitaciones que dan a la playa en esos pueblos de la costa.**
By all means! That part of the coast is very pretty. We would like to reserve rooms that open on the beach in those coastal towns.

27. Empleada: **Podemos arreglarlo todo a su gusto. A su regreso podemos discutir el resto de los detalles. Espero *que sea* un buen viaje.**
We can arrange it all to your liking. Upon your return we can discuss the rest of the details. I hope it will be a good trip.

B. NOTES

3. *El Escorial:* Palace-pantheon-monastery built by order of Felipe II in El Escorial, north of Madrid. It is the masterwork of the architect Juan de Herrera, begun in 1563 and finished in 1584. It is an important treasury of art.
Valle de los Caídos (Valley of the Fallen): Grandiose and impressive monument to the dead in the Spanish Civil War in the Guardarrama Mountains, north of Madrid. It was also designated the burial place of the Spanish Chief of State, Francisco Franco.
Segovia: Capital of the province of Segovia, famed for its impressive Alcázar, one of the most beautiful of all of Spain's many castles, and the remains of a Roman aqueduct.

10. *Sevilla:* Heart of southern Spain's Andalusia. Its cathedral with the Moorish tower of La Giralda, its

Alcázar, its many treasures of art and architecture, its parks and statues, its Spring Fair (*La Feria de Sevilla*), and its famed Holy Week processions make it justly popular as a tourist center.
Córdoba: Another of the gems of Andalusia, capital of the province of the same name, it was the seat of a powerful Arabic Caliphate and has the beautiful *Mezquita* (Mosque) and other architectural souvenirs of the period of Arabic occupation of Spain.
Jerez de la Frontera: The heart of Spanish wine and olive country. From the earlier pronunciation of the name Jerez we get the English word "sherry."

24. *Cádiz:* Seaport on the southern coast, known as the *taza de plata* ("silver cup").
Málaga: Another of southern Spain's beautiful Mediterranean ports, north on the coast from Cádiz.
Motril: A small coastal town, sometimes called *la playa de Granada* ("the beach of Granada"). It is on the coast due east of that mountain-locked city.
Granada: The famed Moorish palace, the Alhambra, is there, along with other artistic and historic monuments.

25. *Marbella:* Another town, similar to Torremolinos, on Spain's *Costa del Sol*—Sunny Coast—which attracts international residents and tourists.
Torremolinos: A resort town on the coast, south of Málaga, it has grown from a small fishing village into an international tourist center, with enormous luxury hotels.

C. GRAMMAR AND USAGE

1. Certain adjectives have a shortened form before a masculine singular noun: *buen, mal, primer, tercer, ningún, algún.*

a. ***Hace muy buen tiempo.***	a. The weather is nice.
b. ***Hace mal tiempo.***	b. The weather is bad.
c. ***Es el primer libro.***	c. It's the first book.
d. ***Es el tercer capítulo.***	d. It's the third chapter.
e. ***Ningún libro lo dice.***	e. No book says it.
f. ***Algún amigo me lo ha dicho.***	f. Some friend told it to me.

In other positions these adjectives agree in the regular way.

a. ***Es un buen hombre. Es un hombre muy bueno.***	a. He's a good man. He's a very good man.
b. ***Es un mal hombre. Es un hombre muy malo.***	b. He's a bad man. He's a very bad man.
c. ***Es una buena película.***	c. It's a good movie.
d. *Las buenas novelas son pocas.*	d. The good novels are very few.
e. *La primera novela que leí fue muy mala.*	e. The first novel I read was very bad.

2. *Gran* and *cualquier* are used before either a masculine or a feminine singular noun.

a. ***Se me ha ocurrido una gran idea.***	a. I've had a great idea.
b. ***Es un gran hombre.***	b. He's a great man.
c. ***Cualquier libro es bueno.***	c. Any book is good.
d. *En cualquier tienda se encuentra eso.*	d. You find that in any store.

Note:

- *Gran* before the noun usually has the figurative meaning of "great." After the noun, it has its literal meaning of "large."

Compare:

Es un gran hombre.	He's a great man.
Es un hombre muy grande.	He's a very large man.

- *Cualquier* (used before either masculine or feminine singular nouns) has the singular form *cualquiera* and the plural form *cualesquiera* when used elsewhere.

a. ***No es un hombre cualquiera.***	a. He's not just any man.
b. ***No son mujeres cualesquiera.***	b. They are not just any women.
c. ***No son películas cualesquiera.***	c. They're not just any movies.

3. The subjunctive mood following verbs of emotion (when there is a change of subject).

a. ***Espero que ustedes hayan tenido buen viaje.***	a. I hope you have had a good trip.
b. ***Temo que se haya equivocado.***	b. I'm afraid you've made a mistake.
c. ***Me alegro de que te guste la habitación.***	c. I'm happy that you like the room.

4. Verbs of volition also take the subjunctive.

a. ***Quieren que lo hagamos ahora.***	a. They want us to do it now.
b. ***Juan prefiere que no lo leamos.***	b. Juan prefers that we not read it.
c. ***El recomienda que vayamos hoy al museo.***	c. He recommends that we go to the museum today.

EXERCISES

A. Substitute each of the words or expressions in parentheses for the underlined word or expression in the model sentence. Write each new sentence and say it aloud.

1. *Es un buen libro. (cuadro, hotel, hombre, parque, restaurante)*

2. *No me ha dado ningún regalo. (número, problema, horario, periódico, billete)*

3. *Me dijeron que es un(a) gran hombre. (poeta, idea, escritor, amigo, novela)*

4. *Espero que ellos estudien. (escriban, vengan, salgan, coman, lleguen)*

5. *Se alegran de que hayamos comido bien. (dormido, llegado, estudiado, oído, estado)*

6. *Los señores Fernández quieren que estudiemos. (descansemos, comamos, bebamos, nos vayamos, entremos)*

B. Change the sentences to the plural. Write each complete sentence and translate.

1. *El no quiere ningún coche.*

2. *Ella no ha comprado ningún regalo.*

3. *Espero que Juan llegue a tiempo.*

4. *Ella quiere que Teresa estudie esta noche.*

5. *Yo prefiero que usted se vaya.*

C. Translate the following sentences into Spanish, then say them aloud.

1. They want us to see the movie.
2. We hope you have a good trip.
3. Juan wants you to buy color film.
4. There isn't any money in this jacket.
5. It is said that it's a great hotel.
6. He was a great poet.
7. Don't give me just any book.
8. Do you want them to do it?
9. He was a great friend.
10. I'm afraid you can't go now.

D. From among the three choices given, choose the best equivalent of the English given at the beginning of each sentence. Write the complete sentence and translate.

1. (nice) *Me alegro de que haga tan* ________ *tiempo.*
   (a) *bueno*
   (b) *buen*
   (c) *buena*

2. (the first) *¿Ha terminado usted* __________ *capítulo?*
   (a) *la primera*
   (b) *el primer*
   (c) *los primeros*

3. (some) *Espero que nos veamos* __________ *día.*
   (a) *algún*
   (b) *alguna*
   (c) *algo*

4. (any) *Juan no tiene* __________ *dinero.*
   (a) *nada de*
   (b) *ninguna*
   (c) *ningún*

5. (good) *Es un hombre muy* __________ .
   (a) *bueno*
   (b) *buen*
   (c) *buenamente*

6. (any) *No me dé usted un libro* __________ .
   (a) *cualquier*
   (b) *cualquiera*
   (c) *cualesquiera*

7. (great) *Es una* __________ *idea.*
   (a) *grande*
   (b) *gran*
   (c) *grandes*

8. (like) *Espero que te* __________ *las habitaciones.*
   (a) *gustan*
   (b) *gusten*
   (c) *guste*

9. (do) *Prefieren que nosotros lo* __________ *ahora.*
   (a) *hacemos*
   (b) *hagamos*
   (c) *hacen*

10. (us to go) *Juan quiere* __________ .
   (a) *que vayamos*
   (b) *que vamos*
   (c) *para nosotros ir*

LESSON 13

ALQUILAR UN COCHE
RENTING A CAR

A. DIALOGUE

1. Empleado: **Buenos días, señores. ¿En qué puedo ayudarles?**
   Good morning. How can I help you?

2. Carlos: **Estábamos pensando en alquilar un coche. ¿Quiere usted decirme los precios y gastos? Me imagino que varían bastante, ¿verdad?**
   We were thinking of renting a car. Would you explain the prices and costs? I imagine that they vary a good deal, right?

3. Empleado: **Así es, señor. Depende del modelo que escojan. ¿Es para ustedes dos?**
   That's right, sir. It depends on the model that you choose. Is it for the two of you?

4. Carlos: **Sí, pero tenemos bastante equipaje también.**
   Yes, but we have quite a lot of baggage, too.

5. Empleado: **Me parece que el Seat 1500° sería ideal para ustedes. Hay sitio para cuatro *para que estén* cómodos, y tiene cuatro puertas.**
   I think the Seat 1500 would be ideal for you. There's room for four so that you'd be comfortable and it has four doors.

6. Carlos: **¿Se puede incluir un porta-equipajes sin cobrar extra?**
   Can a luggage rack be included without an extra charge?

7. Empleado: **No, señor, pero no cuestan mucho. Y *en cuanto al* alquiler, se necesite un depósito si no se usa una tarjeta de crédito.**
No, sir, but they don't cost much. And, as for the rates, a deposit is needed if you don't use a credit card.

8. Juana: **¿Qué se incluye en el precio?**
What's included in the price?

9. Empleado: **El aceite y el engrase, naturalmente, y los gastos normales. Y también los impuestos.**
The oil and the lubrication, naturally, and the normal expenses. And taxes, too.

10. Carlos: **¿Están incluidos la gasolina y el kilometraje°?**
Are gas and mileage included?

11. Empleado: **No hay límite en el kilometraje, señor. *En cuanto a* la gasolina, la Super sólo cuesta doscientas noventa y cinco pesetas el litro.°**
There's no limit on mileage, sir. As for gas, Super only costs two hundred and ninety-five pesetas a liter.

12. Juana: **¿Y cuántos litros necesita este coche por cien kilómetros?**
And how many liters does this car need per hundred kilometers?

13. Empleado: **Sólo siete, señora. Como ve, este coche es económico.**
Only seven, ma'am. As you see, this car is economical.

14. Carlos: **¿Pagamos al devolver el coche?**
Do we pay when we return the car?

15. Empleado: **No, señor. Se paga al llevarse el coche.**
No, sir. You pay when you take the car.

16. Carlos: **¿Cobran ustedes por entregar y recoger el coche?**
Do you charge to deliver and pick up the car?

17. Empleado: **Sí, señor,° si es aquí en Madrid, se lo podemos entregar en el hotel y mandar a alguien a buscarlo si ustedes nos llaman al volver.**
Yes, sir, if it is here in Madrid we can deliver it to your hotel and send someone to pick it up if you call us when you return.

18. Carlos: **Pero ¿qué pasa si decidimos dejarlo en otro sitio, por ejemplo en Málaga?**
But what happens if we decide to leave it somewhere else, for example in Malaga?

19. Empleado: **Si deciden dejarlo en una ciudad donde tengamos sucursal, lo pueden entregar en la sucursal sin pagar extra. En cambio, si quieren dejarlo en algun sitio donde no hay sucursal, tendrán que pagar los gastos para ir a recogerlo.**
If you decide to leave it in a city where we have a branch, you can deliver it to the branch office without paying anything extra. On the other hand, if you want to leave it in some place where there is no branch office, you will have to pay the expenses of going to pick it up.

20. Carlos: **¿Qué documentos necesitamos?**
What papers do we need?

21. Empleado: **Necesitan carnet de conductor y los pasaportes. Nosotros les daremos todos los documentos del coche.**
You need a driver's license and your passports. We will give you all the papers for the car.

Más tarde . . . Later . . .

22. Juana: **Pienso que es demasiado caro alquilar un coche para estos viajes cortos. ¿Qué piensas?**
I think it's too expensive to rent a car for these little trips. What do you think?

23. Carlos: **Estoy de acuerdo, pero ¿qué podemos hacer?**
I agree, but what can we do?

24. Juana: **Pues, Teresa dice que podemos pedir prestado su coche cuando queramos.**
Well, Teresa says we can borrow their car whenever we want.

25. Carlos: **¡Qué buenos amigos!**
What good friends!

B. NOTES

5. *Seat 1500:* The Seat is the Spanish-made model of the Italian Fiat. Other popular brands include Chrysler and the French-made Renault.

10. *kilometraje:* Distance is measured in kilometers. A kilometer is five-eights of a mile.

11. *litro:* liter, liquid measure. A little over a quart.

C. GRAMMAR AND USAGE

1. *A, en cuanto a:* as for, as far as ________ is concerned

a. ***En cuanto al alquiler, eso se puede arreglar mañana.***	a. As far as the rental is concerned, it can be arranged tomorrow.
b. ***En cuanto a la gasolina, no gasta mucho.***	b. As for the gasoline, it doesn't use much.
c. ***En cuanto a los precios, son económicos.***	c. As for the prices, they are economical.

2. *Cuando,* when it means "whenever" (i.e., in an indefinite or future time), takes the subjunctive.

a. ***Cuando lleguen, vamos a decírselo.***	a. When they arrive, we're going to tell them (it).
b. ***Usted puede marcharse cuando quiera.***	b. You can go whenever you want.
c. ***Lo haremos cuando venga el cartero.***	c. We'll do it when the mail carrier comes.

3. *Por* means "per" in the sense of "rate."

a. ***¿Cuánto cobra usted por sus cuadros?***	a. How much do you ask (charge) for your paintings?
b. ***¿Cuántos kilómetros hace por hora?***	b. How many kilometers per hour does it go?
c. ***El veinte por ciento de los problemas es imposible.***	c. Twenty percent of the problems are impossible.

4. *Para que* + subjunctive: in order that, so that

a. ***Se lo compro para que se ponga contenta.***	a. I'll buy it for her so that she'll be happy.
b. ***Se lo digo para que lo sepa.***	b. I'll tell you so (that) you'll know.
c. ***Hay que ayudarles para que terminen pronto.***	c. One must help them so (that) they'll finish soon.

EXERCISES

A. Substitute each of the words or expressions in parentheses for the underlined word or expression in the model sentence. Write each new sentence and say it aloud.

1. *En cuanto al <u>alquiler</u>, podemos arreglarlo. (precio, problema, viaje, hotel, coche)*

2. *Lo podemos hacer cuando vengan <u>los invitados.</u> (los señores Andrade, los estudiantes, nuestros amigos, María José)*

3. *No sé cuanto cobran por <u>hora</u>. (día, semana, mes, clase, cada viajero)*

4. *Voy a dárselo para que lo <u>tengan</u>. (estudien, lean, aprendan, envíen, envuelvan)*

5. *Hablaremos de eso cuando usted lo haya <u>terminado.</u> (visto, leído, mandado, comprado, arreglado)*

6. *En cuanto a <u>Juan</u>, puede pagar cuando quiera. (tu amigo, María, su peluquero, nuestro profesor, la empleada)*

B. Change these sentences to the present tense. Write the complete sentence and translate.

1. *Se lo pediremos cuando lleguen.*

2. *Me cobraron trescientas pesetas por hora.*

3. *Ellos me lo darán para que lo estudie.*

4. *No habrá fiesta mañana.*

5. *Juan lo compró para dármelo.*

C. Translate the following sentences into Spanish, then say them aloud.

1. I recommend that you go pick up the car at the factory.

2. As for the money, I'll give it to him when he comes.

3. When they arrive, Juan will tell them.

4. María may leave whenever she wishes.

5. They'll include a luggage rack.

6. How much does the gasoline cost per liter?

7. Take as many pamphlets as you want.

8. When you have chosen the model you want, go to the factory.

9. There are no taxes on factory prices, are there?

10. Do you want to meet a great friend of mine?

D. From among the three choices given, choose the best equivalent of the English given at the beginning of each sentence. Write the complete sentence and translate.

1. (As for) __________ *la gasolina, hay suficiente.*
   (a) *Como por*
   (b) *Cuanto*
   (c) *En cuanto a*

2. (they arrive) *Cuando* __________, *vamos a darles el regalo.*
   (a) *llegan*
   (b) *lleguen*
   (c) *llegaron*

3. (whenever you want) *Usted puede hacerlo* ________.
   (a) *cuando quieres*
   (b) *cuando quiera*
   (c) *como quiere*

4. (per hour) *Hace ciento viente kilómetros* ________.
   (a) *por hora*
   (b) *por la hora*
   (c) *para hora*

5. (he'll know) *Voy a decirle el número a Juan, para que lo* __________ .
   (a) *sabe*
   (b) *sepa*
   (c) *sabrá*

6. (tell it to them) *Hay que* __________ *para que vengan pronto.*
   (a) *decírleslo*
   (b) *les lo decir*
   (c) *decírselo*

7. (so that) *Escríbale los detalles* __________ *lo comprenda bien.*
   (a) *para que*
   (b) *para*
   (c) *porque*

8. (study) *Hay que anunciarles el examen para que* __________ .
   (a) *estudian*
   (b) *estudien*
   (c) *estudiaron*

9. (read) *Dásela a María para que la* __________ .
   (a) *lee*
   (b) *lea*
   (c) *leera*

10. (whenever they are) *Yo siempre les trato bien* __________ *aquí.*
    (a) *cuandoquiera sean*
    (b) *cuando están*
    (c) *cuando sean*

LESSON 14

EN LA ESTACION DE SERVICIO
AT THE SERVICE STATION

A. DIALOGUE

1. Empleado: **¿En que le puedo servir, señor?**
What can I do for you, sir?

2. Carlos: **No sé exactamente. Hay algo que no funciona bien. Al encender el coche oigo *unos* ruidos bastante raros en el motór. Me tienen preocupado. ¡Este es el coche de mi amigo!**
I don't know exactly. There's something that's not working well. When I turn the key I hear some rather strange noises in the engine. It has me worried. This is my friend's car!

3. Empleado: **¿No será que el tanque está vacío? ¿Lo ha mirado usted?**
Could it be that the tank is empty? Did you check it?

4. Carlos: **Creo que el tanque todavía está por la mitad.**
I think the tank is still half full.

5. Empleado: **¿Se lo lleno de todas maneras?**
Should I fill it up anyway?

6. Carlos: **Sí, llénelo, por favor. Y hágame el favor de llenar este bote° también, por si acaso. Vamos a hacer un viaje bastante largo.**
Yes, fill it up, please. And please fill this can too, just in case. We're going to take a rather long trip.

7. Empleado: **Es buena idea. A veces no se encuentran gasolineras.°**

It's a good idea. Sometimes you don't find gas stations.

8. Carlos: **¿Puede revisar las llantas? A ver si necesitan aire.**
Will you check the tires? To see if they need air.

9. Empleado: **Con mucho gusto. Pero, ¿qué es eso? Parece que éste de adelante tiene un pinchazo.**
Of course! But what's that? It looks as if this front tire has a puncture.

10. Carlos: **¿Qué dice? No puede ser.**
What are you saying? It can't be.

11. Empleado: **Habrá sido un clavo, o algo parecido. ¿No ha notado usted nada? ¿*Ningún* movimiento?**
It must have been a nail, or something similar. Didn't you notice anything? No movement?

12. Carlos: **Hace un momento, en la carretera, parecía patinar° un poco.**
A little while ago, on the highway, it seemed to skid a little.

13. Empleado: **Fue eso entonces. Voy a cambiárselo.**
That was it, then. I'm going to change it for you.

14. Carlos: **Hay una llanta de repuesto allí atrás.**
There's a spare tire back there.

15. Empleado: **Bien. Cambiaré la pinchada y luego la voy a reparar.**
Good. I'll change the flat tire and then I'm going to repair it.

16. Carlos: **Estupendo.**
Terrific.

17. Empleado: **Como hacen un viaje tan largo, hay que ver si las bujías y la batería están en buenas condiciones.**
Since you're taking such a long trip, we must see if the spark plugs and the battery are in good shape.

18. Carlos: **Por favor. Y échele un poco de agua al radiador. Hace poco se estaba calentando el motor.**
Please. And put a little water in the radiator. The engine was heating up a little while ago.

19. Empleado: **Muy bien, señor. ¿Quiere usted que lo engrase, o que le cambie el aceite?**
Very well, sir. Do you want me to do a lube job or change the oil?

20. Carlos: **No, gracias.**
No, thank you.

21. Empleado: **Veo *algunas* cosas que necesitan atención.**
I see some things that need attention.

22. Carlos: **¡Mi amigo no me dijo que tiene un cacharro!°**
My friend didn't tell me he has a piece of junk!

23. Empleado: **De *ningún* modo, señor. Estos problemas ocurren siempre. Más vale repararlos en seguida.**
Not at all, sir. These problems always happen. It's better to take care of them right away.

24. Carlos: **Tiene razón. ¿Tendré que dejarlo en el garaje?**
You're right. Will I have to leave it in the garage?

25. Empleado: **Por *lo menos* tres horas si quiere que lo deje en buenas condiciones.**
At least three hours if you want me to leave it in good shape.

26. Carlos: **Pero necesito el coche sin falta hoy mismo.**
But I need the car without fail today.

27. Empleado: **No se preocupe. Estoy seguro de que no hay que pedir piezas nuevas.**
Don't worry. I'm sure it won't be necessary to order any new parts.

28. Carlos: **Haga solamente *lo necesario.***
Do only what's necessary.

29. Empleado: **Bien. Si usted quiere volver a las cinco, todo estará listo.**
Good. If you want to come back at five o'clock, everything will be ready.

30. Carlos: **De acuerdo. Hasta las cinco, entonces.**
OK. Until five o'clock, then.

B. NOTES

6. *bote:* Here used as "can" or "container," this word is more commonly used for "boat." The word for "can" in Latin America is *lata.*

7. *gasolinera:* In most Latin American countries the term for "gas station" is *estación de gasolina.*

12. *patinar:* lit., "to skate," but it is often used to describe a motion such as skidding or slipping.

22. *cacharro:* lit., "an earthenware pot." Used often as a synonym for a worthless object.

C. GRAMMAR AND USAGE

1. *Unos, unas, algún*

unos, unas: some, a few

a. ***Oigo unos ruidos muy raros.***	a. I hear some very strange noises.
b. ***Hay unas tiendas muy buenas en esta calle.***	b. There are some very good stores on this street.

algún: some—singular and plural forms

a. ***Algún día vamos a visitarlo.***	a. Someday we're going to visit him.
b. ***Algunos amigos vinieron ayer.***	b. Some friends came yesterday.
c. ***Algunas personas no lo creen.***	c. Some people don't believe it.
d. ***Se lo ha dicho alguna chica.***	d. Some girl told him that.
e. ***Alguna señora lo ha dejado aquí.***	e. Some woman left it here.

Note:

- *Algunos* has a slightly more concrete, numeric meaning than *unos*.

2. *Ninguno* in negative sentences

a. ***No diría eso ningún amigo.*** (*or*) ***Ningún amigo diría eso.***	a. No friend would say that.
b. ***No quedaba ninguna mesa libre en el restaurante.***	b. There wasn't a free table in the restaurant.
c. ***No tengo ningún perjuicio.***	c. I don't have any prejudice.
d. ***¿Tiene usted alguna novela interesante? No, no tengo ninguna.***	d. Do you have an interesting novel? No, I don't have any.
e. ***¿Ha visto usted una parada de autobús por aquí? No, no he visto ninguna.***	e. Have you seen a bus stop along here? No, I haven't seen any.

3. *Unos cuantos:* some, an indefinite amount

a. ***¿Le gustan a usted estos dulces? Sí, déme unos cuantos por favor.***	a. Do you like these candies? Yes, give me some, please.
b. ***¿Le quedan algunas pesetas? Sí, aún me quedan unas cuantas.***	b. Do you have any pesetas left? Yes, I still have some left.

4. *Lo* + adjective = abstract noun

a. ***Lo difícil es hacerlo bien.***	a. The difficult thing (part) is to do it well.
b. ***Lo malo del caso es que no se comprenden.***	b. The bad part of the matter is that they don't understand each other.
c. ***Lo bueno es que vienen todos.***	c. The good part is that they're all coming.
d. ***Lo extraño es que el coche no funciona.***	d. The strange thing is that the car doesn't work.

Note:

- The adjectives may be in the superlative form.

lo más difícil	the most difficult thing
lo mejor	the best thing (part)
lo más extraño	the strangest thing

EXERCISES

A. Substitute the words or expressions in parentheses for the underlined word or expression in the model sentence. Write each new sentence and say it aloud.

1. *Me mandaron unos cuadros. (retratos, libros, sellos, folletos, lápices)*

2. *¿Tiene usted algunas pesetas? (novelas, amigas, casas, noticias, entradas, llantas)*

3. *No he visto ninguna película interesante. (co-media, ciudad, tienda, pintura, obra)*

4. *Juan ha comprado unos cuantos dulces. (libros, planos, pañuelos, sobres, sellos)*

5. *Lo bueno es comprenderlo bien. (Lo mejor, Lo interesante, Lo fácil, Lo difícil, Lo imposible)*

6. *¿Quiere usted mandarme unas revistas? (cartas, noticias, tarjetas, fotos, direcciones)*

B. Change these sentences to the negative. Write the complete sentence and translate.

1. *Me quedan algunas pesetas.*

2. *¿Quiere usted algunos periódicos?*

3. *Ellos tienen algunas dificultades.*

4. *Queríamos comprar algunas revistas.*

5. *Me dieron unos cuantos papeles.*

C. Translate the following sentences into Spanish, then say them aloud.

1. I think I left a few letters there.
2. He heard some strange noises.
3. Put a little water in the radiator.
4. I just bought some stamps.
5. Do you want to come back at five?
6. Do only what is necessary (the necessary thing).
7. We'll do everything we can.
8. The good thing is that we arrived early.
9. I'm sure you'll like the car.
10. The bad part of the matter is that they don't understand us.

D. From among the three choices given, choose the best equivalent of the English given at the beginning of each sentence. Write the complete sentence and translate.

1. (some) *Les voy a enviar* __________ *programas del concierto.*
   (a) *unas*
   (b) *algunas*
   (c) *unos*

2. (any) *No me ha dado* __________ *dinero.*
   (a) *ninguno*
   (b) *algún*
   (c) *nada de*

3. (any) *Me gustan las novelas románticas. Tiene usted ___________?*
   (a) *algunas*
   (b) *ninguna*
   (c) *ningunas*
4. (some) *Voy a decírselo* ___________ *día.*
   (a) *alguna*
   (b) *algún*
   (c) *algo*
5. (the impossible part) *Eso precisamente es* ________ *del caso.*
   (a) *lo imposible*
   (b) *los imposibles*
   (c) *imposible*
6. (none) *No se lo ha dicho a* ___________ *de sus amigos.*
   (a) *alguno*
   (b) *ninguno*
   (c) *ninguna*
7. (some) *Querían vender* ___________ *vestidos.*
   (a) *algunas*
   (b) *unos cuantos*
   (c) *unas*
8. (the best thing) *Me gustó la comedia. Las primeras escenas fueron* ___________ *de la obra.*
   (a) *la mejor*
   (b) *lo mejor*
   (c) *los mejores*
9. (any) *¿Le ha dado* ___________ *dinero?*
   (a) *alguno*
   (b) *algo de*
   (c) *ningúno*
10. (the most difficult part) *Les he explicado* _________.
   (a) *lo difícil*
   (b) *lo más difícil*
   (c) *los difíciles*

LESSON 15

LA FRONTERA
THE BORDER

A. DIALOGUE

Al acercarse a la frontera francesa. Approaching the French border.

1. Juana: **Mira, ¡qué cantidad de coches haciendo cola° delante de la Aduana!**
   Look. What a bunch of cars lined up before the customs station!

2. Carlos: **Lo esperaba. ¡Hay muchos turistas que pasan por Port Bou° desde la Costa Brava!**
   I expected it. There are so many tourists who go through Port Bou from the Costa Brava!

3. Juana: **¡Claro! Pero yo creía que los martes el tráfico sería mejor. Sin duda tendremos que esperar un poco.**
   Of course! But I thought on Tuesday traffic would be better. Undoubtedly, we will have to wait a little.

4. Carlos: **Dicen que por aquí pasan bastante rápido.**
   They say that here they go through rather fast.

5. Juana: **Bueno.**
   Good.

6. Carlos: **Mira, algunos coches, como *el azul* de allí, pasan muy *fácilmente*.**
   Look, some cars, like the blue one over there, go through really easily.

7. Juana: **Ya estamos en la frontera. ¡No puedo creerlo! ¡Van a pararnos! ¡Qué suerte que tenemos! Viene el inspector.**
   We are already at the border. I can't believe it! They're going to stop us! What luck we have! Here comes the inspector.

8. Inspector: **Buenos días, señores. ¿Piensan quedarse mucho tiempo en Francia?**
   Good morning. Do you intend to stay very long in France?

9. Carlos: **No, señor. Solamente el fin de la semana. Vamos a visitar Montecarlo y Cannes.**
   No, sir. Only the weekend. We're going to visit Monte Carlo and Cannes.

10. Inspector: **Permítame ver los documentos del coche y su carnet de conducir.**
    Let me see the documents for the car and your driver's license.

11. Carlos: **Aquí los tiene. Como ve, el coche tiene matrícula española.**
    Here you are. As you can see, the car has a Spanish license plate.

12. Inspector: **¿Y el carnet de conducir es mexicano?**
    And the driver's license is Mexican?

13. Carlos: **Sí, señor. Somos mexicanos.**
    Yes, sir. We're Mexican.

14. Inspector: **Entonces, ¿me permiten ustedes ver sus pasaportes, por favor?**
    Then may I see your passports, please?

15. Juana: **Ah, sí. Como no somos ciudadanos de la Comunidad Europea no podemos atraversar la frontera sin mostrar nuestros pasaportes. Pero,**

¿donde estarán? Los tenía en la bolsa, ¡pero ahora no los veo por ninguna parte°!
Oh, yes. Since we're not citizens of the European Community we can't cross the border without showing our passports. But, where did they go? I had them in this bag but now I don't see them anywhere!

16. Carlos: **Los sacaste *hace poco.* Deben de estar en el asiento.**
You took them out a little while ago. They must be on the seat.

17. Juana: ***Dile que espere* un momento. Deben haberse caído al suelo. ¡Ah! Los encontré. Se habían caído.**
Tell him to wait a minute. They must have fallen on the floor. Ah! I've found them. They had fallen.

18. Carlos: **Aquí los tiene, señor.**
Here you are, sir.

19. Inspector: **Muchas gracias. ¿Ustedes tienen algo que declarar?**
Thank you very much. Do you have anything to declare?

20. Carlos: **Nada que yo sepa.**
Nothing that I know of.

21. Inspector: **Muy bien. ¡Que tengan buen viaje!**
Very well. Have a good trip!

22. Carlos: **Gracias.**
Thank you.

23. Juana: **Ya estamos de camino a Montecarlo, donde podrás probar tu suerte en el casino.**
Now we're on our way to Monte Carlo, where you can try your luck in the casino.

B. NOTES

1. *hacer cola:* to get in line, to form a line, to wait in line.

2. Port Bou: the small Mediterranean town which is one of the entrances to France from the Spanish Costa Brava.

15. *no los veo por ninguna parte:* Notice the use of negative *ninguna* after a verb in the negative. The affirmative equivalent would be *alguna:* i.e., *¿Los ve usted por alguna parte?*

C. GRAMMAR AND USAGE

1. Preterite + *hace* + time expression = ago

a. ***Los sacaste hace poco.***	a. You took them out a while ago.
b. ***Ellos llegaron hace una semana.***	b. They arrived a week ago.
c. ***Juan salió hace una hora.***	c. Juan left an hour ago.

2. Use *decir* + *que* + subjunctive for indirect commands.

a. ***Dile que espere.***	a. Tell him to wait.
b. ***Les dijeron que vinieran en seguida.***	b. They told them to come at once.
c. ***Dígale a ella que saque su pasaporte.***	c. Tell her to take out her passport.

3. Add *-mente* to the feminine form of an adjective to form the adverb.

a. ***Se lo dije claramente.***	a. I told it to him clearly.
b. ***Le acusaron injustamente.***	b. They accused him unjustly.
c. ***Le preguntó amablemente.***	c. He asked him nicely.

Note:

- Adjectives that have only one singular form take the *-mente* ending without any other change. Adjectives with written accents retain them in the adverbial form.

a. ***Lo puedes hacer fácilmente.***	a. You can do it easily.
b. ***Normalmente, no lo hacemos así.***	b. Normally, we don't do it that way.
c. ***Posiblemente está aquí todavía.***	c. Possibly he's still here.

4. Nouns may be formed from adjectives by using the proper form of the article.

a. ***Estoy buscando un vestido azul. No me gusta el rojo.***	a. I'm looking for a blue dress. I don't like the red one.
b. ***Estos libros no valen nada. Los buenos están allí.***	b. These books aren't worth anything. The good ones are there.
c. ***Los malos siempre sufren.***	c. The bad always suffer.
d. ***Me gusta ayudar a los pobres.***	d. I like to help the poor.

EXERCISES

A. Substitute the words or expressions in parentheses for the underlined word or expression in the model sentence. Write each new sentence and say it aloud.

1. *Juan y José llegaron hace una semana. (una hora, un año, cuatro meses, mucho tiempo, poco)*

2. *Ellos lo compraron hace tres días. (vendieron, escribieron, hicieron, mandaron, recibieron)*

3. *Dígale a Juana que venga. (escriba, llame, entre, trabaje, coma)*

4. *Ya lo escribí claramente. (mala-, fácil-, difícil-, inútil-, inmediata-)*

5. *María es la rubia. (buena, morena, inteligente, fuerte, tímida)*

6. *Los buenos son siempre los primeros. (malos, inteligentes, perezosos, imposibles, interesantes)*

B. Rewrite these sentences following the example. Write the complete sentence and translate.

Example: *Juan llegó la semana pasada.*
Juan llegó hace una semana.

1. *Ellos vinieron el año pasado.*

2. *Ella me escribió el mes pasado.*

3. *Jorge se casó anteayer.*

4. *Hoy es el quince de agosto. María se marchó el doce.*

5. *Me mandaron el libro el año pasado.*

C. Translate the following sentences into Spanish, then say them aloud.

1. There are so many tourists that go through Port Bou.
2. Are you going to stay in France very long?
3. I thought it would be better on Tuesday.
4. You don't have to open the suitcases.
5. All the papers are in order.
6. Tell him to wait a minute.
7. I hope I see you on the return trip.
8. It was much quicker than the last time.
9. He came a year ago.
10. We're on our way to Monte Carlo.

D. From among the three choices given, choose the best equivalent of the English given at the beginning of each sentence. Write the complete sentence and translate.

1. (called) *Juan* __________ *hace una hora.*
   (a) *llama*
   (b) *llamó*
   (c) *llamaba*
2. (ago) *Nuestros amigos llegaron* __________ *unas horas.*
   (a) *hace*
   (b) *hacen*
   (c) *hizo*
3. (to wait) *Dígale que* __________.
   (a) *espera*
   (b) *espere*
   (c) *esperar*

4. (easily) *Él dice que lo puede hacer* __________.
   (a) *fácilmente*
   (b) *facilmente*
   (c) *fácil*

5. (did) *Lo* __________ *Juan hace mucho tiempo.*
   (a) *hace*
   (b) *hizo*
   (c) *haces*

6. (to come) *Dígales* __________.
   (a) *venir*
   (b) *vienen*
   (c) *que vengan*

7. (some days ago) *Los señores Andrade llegaron* __________.
   (a) *hizo unos días*
   (b) *hace unas días*
   (c) *hace unos días*

8. (clearly) *El jefe me lo dijo* __________.
   (a) *clara*
   (b) *claros*
   (c) *claramente*

9. (to write) *Dígale a María que* __________.
   (a) *escribe*
   (b) *escriba*
   (c) *escribir*

10. (to declare) *¿Tienen ustedes algo que* __________*?*
   (a) *declarar*
   (b) *declare*
   (c) *declaran*

LESSON 16

EN EL BANCO
AT THE BANK

A. DIALOGUE

En la ventanilla de cambio. At the foreign-exchange window.

1. Carlos: **¿Pueden cambiarme aquí un cheque de viajero?**
   Can you cash a traveler's check for me here?

2. Cajera: **Claro que sí. Usted lo tiene que firmar.**
   Of course. You'll have to sign it.

3. Carlos: **¿A cuánto está el cambio?**
   What's the exchange rate?

4. Cajera: **Ciento veintiocho pesetas por dólar, señor. Su pasaporte, por favor.**
   One hundred and twenty-eight pesetas to the dollar, sir. Your passport, please.

5. Carlos: **Ah, claro. Aquí lo tiene. Estamos hospedados en el Hotel Emperatriz, aquí en Madrid.**
   Of course. Here you are. We're staying at the Hotel Emperatriz, here in Madrid.

6. Cajera: **Voy a anotar su nombre, dirección y el número del pasaporte en su recibo, señor. ¿Cómo quiere usted el dinero?**
   I'll enter your name, address, and passport number on your receipt, sir. How would you like your money?

7. Carlos: **Déme cinco billetes de mil, ocho de cien, y doscientas pesetas en monedas, por favor.°**
Give me five one thousand peseta notes, eight one hundred, and two hundred pesetas in change, please.

8. Cajera: **Tome usted, señor. Le daré el recibo *tan pronto como la impresora termine.***
Here you are, sir. I'll give you the receipt as soon as the printer finishes.

9. Carlos: **Gracias. ¿Hay alguien *que pueda* ayudarme a mandar un giro postal?**
Thank you. Is there someone who can help me send a money order?

10. Cajera: **Yo le puedo ayudar con eso, señor.**
I can help you with that, sir.

11. Carlos: **Bueno. Necesito mandar un giro postal a un hotel en Barcelona. Quiero hacer una reservación.**
Good. I need to send a money order to a hotel in Barcelona. I want to make a reservation.

12. Cajera: **¿Cuánto necesita mandar?**
How much do you need to send?

13. Carlos: **A ver. Cuando hablamos por teléfono, la persona° en la recepción me dijo que serían diecisiete mil pesetas por una semana.**
Let's see. When we spoke on the phone, the person at the reception desk told me it would be seventeen thousand pesetas for a week.

14. Cajera: **Por favor, escriba el nombre y la dirección del hotel aquí, y eso es todo.**

Please write the name and address of the hotel here, and that's it.

15. Carlos: **Muchas gracias.**
Thank you very much.

B. NOTES

7. Pesetas come in bills of 1,000; 2,000; 5,000; and 10,000 and coins of 1, 5, 10, 25, 50, 100, 200, and 500. The 5-peseta coin is called a *duro.*

13. Note that *la persona* is always feminine, whether it refers to a man or a woman.

C. GRAMMAR AND USAGE

1. The subjunctive is used after verbs or expressions of disbelief, doubt, denial or impossibility.

a. ***Dudo que Juan esté aquí.***	a. I doubt that Juan is here.
b. ***Es imposible que María haga tal cosa.***	b. It's impossible that María would do such a thing.
c. ***Niego que sea verdad.***	c. I deny that it's true.
d. ***No creo que ellos vengan.***	d. I don't believe they'll come.

2. The subjunctive is used in an adjective clause when the noun or pronoun referred to is undetermined or nonexistent.

a. ***No conozco a nadie que pueda ayudarnos.***	a. I don't know anyone who can help us.
b. ***No tenemos nada que sea tan interesante.***	b. We have nothing that is so interesting.
c. ***Voy a buscar una agencia que tenga sucursal en Nueva York.***	c. I'm going to look for an agency that has a branch in New York.
d. ***¿Conoce usted a alguien que sepa el precio?***	d. Do you know anyone who knows the price?
e. ***No conocen a nadie que tenga este modelo.***	e. They don't know anyone who has this model.
f. ***¿Dónde puedo encontrar un guía que hable ruso?***	f. Where can I find a guide who speaks Russian?

3. Conjunctions referring to the future or an indeterminate time trigger the subjunctive.

a. ***Voy a esperar hasta que llegue Juan.***	a. I'm going to wait until Juan arrives.
b. ***Vamos a trabajar mucho mientras estemos aquí.***	b. We are going to work hard while we're here.
c. ***Se lo diré tan pronto como lleguen.***	c. I'll tell them as soon as they arrive.
d. ***En cuanto lo tenga, voy a mandártelo.***	d. As soon as I have it, I'm going to send it to you.

4. The reflexive is used for reciprocal actions: one another, each other.

a. ***Nos saludamos cada día.***	a. We greet each other every day.
b. ***Ellos se conocieron en Madrid.***	b. They met each other in Madrid.
c. ***No creo que nos veamos otra vez.***	c. I don't think we'll see each other again.
d. ***María y Teresa siempre se hablan.***	d. María and Teresa always talk to each other.

EXERCISES

A. Substitute each of the words or expressions in parentheses for the underlined word or expression in the model sentence. Write each new sentence and say it aloud.

1. *No creo que ellos lo sepan. (compren, vendan, escriban, manden, conozcan)*

2. *Es imposible que ellos lleguen ahora. (hablen, duerman, se levanten, vayan, entren)*

3. *Busco una casa que sea bastante grande. (cómoda, económica, pequeña, bonita, nueva)*

4. *No conocemos a nadie que hable ruso. (italiano, inglés, alemán, griego, árabe)*

5. *Vamos a esperar hasta que vengan. (llamen, lleguen, se levanten, escriban, coman)*

6. *En cuanto Juan lo compre, se lo dirá usted. (vea, venda, reciba, tenga, mande)*

B. Change the following sentences to the interrogative. Write the complete sentence and translate.

1. *Juan y José se saludan siempre que se ven.*

2. *Rafael está buscando una secretaria que hable inglés.*

3. *Ellos van a esperar hasta que lleguemos.*

4. *Usted conoce a alguien que trabaja rápidamente.*

5. *María lo dirá en cuanto lo sepa.*

C. Translate the following sentences into Spanish, then say them aloud.

1. I'm going to look for a book that I (will) like.
2. They don't know anyone who writes poetry.
3. Juan will wait until we arrive.
4. Do you always see each other in Paris?
5. Will you write to me when you arrive in New York?
6. I doubt that they are here.
7. We don't believe Juan knows it.
8. Juan doesn't think María will come.
9. He's looking for a bank that has a branch in Madrid.
10. As soon as I buy it, I will show it to you.

D. From among the three choices given, choose the best equivalent of the English given at the beginning of each sentence. Write the complete sentence and translate.

1. (is) *No creo que María* __________ *aquí.*
   (a) *está*
   (b) *esté*
   (c) *es*

2. (do) *Es imposible que ellos* __________ *tal cosa.*
   (a) *hacen*
   (b) *hagan*
   (c) *harán*

3. (can) *No hay ninguno que* __________ *hacerlo.*
   (a) *puede*
   (b) *pueda*
   (c) *podrá*
4. (has) *Quiero encontrar una casa que* __________. *siete habitaciones.*
   (a) *tiene*
   (b) *tener*
   (c) *tenga*
5. (believe) *Es imposible que ella* __________ *la historia.*
   (a) *cree*
   (b) *crea*
   (c) *creerá*
6. (it is) *Niegan que* __________ *verdad.*
   (a) *es*
   (b) *ser*
   (c) *sea*
7. (speaks) *Tenemos que esperar hasta que Juan* _____.
   (a) *habla*
   (b) *hable*
   (c) *hablará*
8. (have) *En cuanto ellos lo* __________ *se lo mandarán a usted.*
   (a) *tengan*
   (b) *tienen*
   (c) *tendrán*
9. (Each other) __________ *vemos todos los días.*
   (a) *Cada uno*
   (b) *Nos*
   (c) *Cada otro*
10. (is) *Busco una bolsa que* __________ *bastante grande.*
    (a) *sea*
    (b) *está*
    (c) *ser*

LESSON 17

EN LA OFICINA DE CORREOS
AT THE POST OFFICE

A. DIALOGUE

En la ventanilla de sellos. At the stamp window.

1. Carlos: **Perdone, señora. Quiero mandar estas tres cartas a México. ¿Cuánto cuesta, por favor?**
   Excuse me, ma'am. I want to send these three letters to Mexico. How much is it, please?

2. Empleada: **Tengo que pesarlas. Vamos a ver . . . son cien pesetas cada una, señor.**
   I have to weigh them. Let's see . . . they're one hundred pesetas each, sir.

3. Carlos: **Quiero mandar ésta urgente° también. ¿Cuánto es?**
   I want to send this one rush delivery too. How much is it?

4. Empleada: **Si es para Madrid, son solamente doscientas pesetas y será entregada esta tarde.**
   If it's for Madrid, it's only two hundred pesetas, and it will be delivered this afternoon.

5. Carlos: **Gracias. Tengo que ver si hay algo para mí en la lista de correos y mandar un paquete también. ¿Adónde hay que ir para mandar paquetes?**
   Thank you. I have to see if there's anything for me in general delivery and also send a package. Where do you have to go to mail a package?

6. Empleada: **Está en la sección de atrás. Pase por aquella puerta a la izquierda y la verá usted. También allí está la lista de correos.**
It's in the rear section. Go through that door on the left, and you'll see it. General delivery is there also.

En la ventanilla de la lista de correos. At the general delivery window.

7. Carlos: **¿Hay algo para mí? Me llamo Carlos Andrade Ramírez.**
Is there anything for me? My name is Carlos Andrade Ramírez.

8. Empleado: **A ver . . . Sí, señor. Hay varias postales, una carta certificada y un paquete pequeño. Tendrá que firmar el recibo aquí. ¿Me permite su pasaporte?**
Let's see . . . Yes, sir. There are several postcards, a registered letter, and a small package. You'll have to sign the receipt here. May I see your passport?

9. Carlos: **Por supuesto. ¿Dónde hay que firmar?**
Of course. Where do I have to sign?

10. Empleado: **En esta línea, por favor. Y por el paquete hay que pagar trescientas pesetas de aduana.**
On this line, please. And for the package, you'll have to pay three hundred pesetas of customs duties.

11. Carlos: **Gracias. ¿Qué será? No esperaba ningún paquete.**
Thank you. What can it be? I wasn't expecting any package.

En la ventanilla de telegramas. At the telegram window.

12. Carlos: **¿Dónde están los formularios para telegramas?**
Where are the telegram forms?

13. Empleada: **Los encontrará allí en el escritorio, señor. Puede escribir el telegrama y traérmelo.**
You'll find them there on the desk, sir. You can write the telegram and bring it to me.

14. Carlos: **¡Ya está!° ¿Cuánto es?**
It's finished. How much is it?

15. Empleada: **Contemos las palabras. Una, dos, tres, cuatro, cinco . . .**
Let's count the words. One, two, three, four, five . . .

16. Carlos: **¿Cuenta usted las palabras de la dirección también?**
Do you count the words in the address, too?

17. Empleada: **Sí, señor. Se cuentan todas.**
Yes, sir. All of them are counted.

18. Carlos: **Tengo que mandar este paquete también. ¿Dónde puedo hacerlo?**
I have to mail this package, too. Where can I do that?

19. Empleada: **Para eso hay que ir a aquella ventanilla de enfrente, la número veintiuno.**
For that, you'll have to go to that window opposite, number twenty-one.

En la ventanilla de paquetes. At the package window.

20. Carlos: **Quiero mandar este paquete a México.**
I want to send this package to Mexico.

21. Empleado: **A ver. Lo siento, señor, pero pesa demasiado para ir por correo. *Si quiere usted mandarlo, tendrá que hacerlo en la oficina de la RENFE,*° en la estación de Atocha.°**
Let's see. I'm sorry, sir, but it weighs too much to go by mail. If you want to send it, you'll have to do it at the offices of RENFE, at the Atocha station.

22. Carlos: **Pero va por barco, ¿no? ¿Por qué hay que ir a la RENFE?**
But it's going by ship, isn't it? Why must I go to the RENFE?

23. Empleado: **Bueno, señor, como usted sabe, tiene que llegar al puerto de embarque. Y para eso, va por tren.**
Well, sir, as you know, it has to get to the port of embarkment, and that's why it goes by train.

24. Carlos: **Sí, claro. *Si no pesara tanto, sería posible mandarlo por correo normal,* ¿verdad?**
Yes, of course. If it didn't weigh so much, it would be possible to send it by regular mail, wouldn't it?

25. Empleado: **Desde luego, señor. *Si quiere dividirlo en dos paquetes de no más de un kilo cada uno, usted podrá mandarlos desde aquí mismo.***
Certainly, sir. If you want to divide it into two packages of no more than one kilo each, you can send them right here.

26. Carlos: **No vale la pena. *No lo hagamos.* ¡Qué complicación! Bueno, ¿adónde hay que ir?**

It's not worth the trouble. Let's not do it. What a complication! Well, where do I have to go?

27. Empleado: **A la estación de Atocha, señor.**
To Atocha Station, sir.

En las oficinas de la RENFE. At the RENFE offices.

28. Carlos: **Quiero mandar este paquete a México.**
I want to send this package to Mexico.

29. Empleada: **Llene estas dos declaraciones para la aduana, por favor.**
Please fill out these two customs declarations.

30. Carlos: **Quiero asegurarlo también.**
I'd like to insure it, too.

31. Empleada: **¿Cuál es el valor, señor?**
What's the value, sir?

32. Carlos: **Yo diría que unas diez mil doscientas pesetas.**
I'd say about ten thousand two hundred pesetas.

33. Empleada: **Bueno. Pase usted a la caja con esto, y vuelva aquí por el recibo.**
All right. Go to the cashier with this, and come back here for your receipt.

B. NOTES

3. *urgente:* lit., "urgent." In Latin America it is more common to say *para entrega inmediata* or *por mensajero especial* ("for immediate delivery" or "by special messenger").

14. *¡Ya está!* In an exclamation of this kind, some idea such as *hecho* ("done," "finished"), or *listo* ("ready"), is understood, as in *¡Ya estoy!* "I'm ready!"

21. *RENFE: la Red Nacional de Ferrocarriles Españoles*—the Spanish National Railroad, almost always referred to by the abbreviation *la RENFE.*
Atocha: One of the large train stations of Madrid. Atocha generally serves Andalusia and all points south.

C. GRAMMAR AND USAGE

1. Contrary-to-fact conditions
When "if" introduces a contrary-to-fact condition, the verb is in the imperfect subjunctive, and the result is expressed by the conditional.

a. ***Si yo fuera rico, viajaría mucho.***	a. If I were rich, I would travel a lot.
b. ***Si los señores Andrade estuvieran aquí, podríamos decírselo.***	b. If Mr. and Mrs. Andrade were here, we could tell them (*it*).
c. ***Si estuviéramos en Londres ahora, podríamos ver la comedia.***	c. If we were in London now, we could see the comedy.
d. ***Si trabajara más, usted ganaría más dinero.***	d. If you worked harder, you would earn more money.

2. "If" with the indicative
When "if" introduces a possible condition, the indicative can follow it.

a. ***Si puedo encontrarlo, te lo daré.***	a. If I can find it, I'll give it to you.
b. ***Si ellos me lo dicen, lo creo.***	b. If they tell me (it), I'll believe it.
c. ***Si llueve, no salgo.***	c. If it rains, I'm not going out.
d. ***Si ella llega a tiempo, podemos ir.***	d. If she arrives on time, we can go.

3. "Let's" is expressed by *vamos a* + the infinitive or by the first person plural of the present subjunctive.

a. ***Vamos a hablar del viaje.*** ***Hablemos del viaje.***	a. Let's talk about the trip.
b. ***Vamos a acostarnos temprano esta noche.*** ***Acostémonos temprano esta noche.***	b. Let's go to bed early tonight.
c. ***Vamos a salir en seguida.*** ***Salgamos en seguida.***	c. Let's leave at once.
d. ***Vamos a comprarlo.*** ***Comprémoslo.***	d. Let's buy it.
e. ***Vamos a levantarnos a las siete.*** ***Levantémonos a las siete.***	e. Let's get up at seven o'clock.

Note:

- When the reflexive *-nos* is added to the first person plural form, the final *s* of the verb form is dropped.

Levantémonos.	Let's get up.
Sentémonos.	Let's sit down.

- *ss* is reduced to *s:*

Comprémoselo.
Let's buy it for him.

4. In the negative "Let's not," the pronoun is not attached to the verb.

a. ***No los compremos.***	a. Let's not buy it.
b. ***No nos levantemos.***	b. Let's not get up.
c. ***No se lo compremos.***	c. Let's not buy it for him.

EXERCISES

A. Substitute each of the words or expressions in parentheses for the underlined word or expression in the model sentence. Write each new sentence and say it aloud.

1. *Si Juan fuera rico, lo podría hacer. (norteamericano, dentista, médico, profesor, millonario)*

2. *Si tuviéramos el libro, lo (la) podríamos leer. (el diccionario, la revista, el periódico, la novela, la carta)*

3. *Si veo a Juan, se lo digo. (María, los señores Andrade, tu amigo, los estudiantes, mi hermano)*

4. *Si llegan hoy, yo voy a verlos. (mañana, la semana que viene, el martes, esta mañana, pronto)*

5. *Compremos las entradas. (el libro, los periódicos, la revista, el billete, los guantes)*

6. *Levantémonos pronto. (a las ocho, más tarde, en seguida, ahora, después)*

B. Rewrite these sentences following the example. Write the complete sentence and translate.

Example: *Vamos a decírselo.*
Digámoselo.

1. *Vamos a acostarnos.*
2. *Vamos a comprarlo.*
3. *No vamos a decirlo.*
4. *Vamos a llegar a tiempo.*
5. *Vamos a estudiarlo.*

C. Translate the following sentences into Spanish, then say them aloud.

1. If Juan were here, I would give him the book.
2. If they had the time, they would go to Barcelona.
3. If María were in Paris, she would buy the dress.
4. If it rains, we won't go to the theater.
5. If they see us, we'll talk to them.
6. If you had your car, we would arrive on time.
7. Let's go to the store.
8. Let's not get up early tomorrow.
9. Let's look for the book next week.
10. Let's not give it (the book) to Juan.

D. From among the three choices given, choose the best equivalent of the English given at the beginning of each sentence. Write the complete sentence and translate.

1. (were) *Si yo* __________ *usted, no lo haría.*
   (a) *fuí*
   (b) *fuera*
   (c) *estuve*

2. (worked) *Juan ganaría mucho más si* ________ *más.*
   (a) *trabajará*
   (b) *trabajó*
   (c) *trabajara*

3. (were) *Yo se lo daría a los señores Andrade si* __________ *aquí.*
   (a) *estuvieron*
   (b) *estuvieran*
   (c) *estan*

4. (read) *Si ellos* __________ *el periódico sabrían lo que ha pasado.*
   (a) *leen*
   (b) *lean*
   (c) *leyeran*

5. (Let's get up) __________ *temprano mañana.*
   (a) *Vamos a levantar*
   (b) *Levantémonos*
   (c) *Levantémosnos*

6. (Let's not read) __________ *el periódico esta mañana.*
   (a) *No leemos*
   (b) *No leamos*
   (c) *No leeremos*

7. (arrive) *No les decimos nada si ________ tarde.*
   (a) *lleguen*
   (b) *llegan*
   (c) *llegaran*

8. (rains) *No queremos ir al campo si ________.*
   (a) *llueva*
   (b) *lloverá*
   (c) *llueve*

9. (Let's talk) ________ *de lo que tenemos que hacer.*
   (a) *Hablamos*
   (b) *Hablemos*
   (c) *Hablaremos*

10. (Let me) ________ *contar las palabras.*
   (a) *Permítame*
   (b) *Permitamos*
   (c) *Me permitamos*

LESSON 18

LA LAVANDERIA DEL HOTEL Y LA TINTORERIA
THE HOTEL LAUNDRY AND THE DRY CLEANER

A. DIALOGUE

1. Empleada: **Buenos días, señora. Veo que tiene muchas cosas para lavar.**
   Good morning, ma'am. I see you have a lot of things to wash.

2. Juana: **Buenos días. Sí, tengo una lista bastante larga. Para empezar, estas cinco camisas de mi marido.**
   Good morning. Yes, I have a rather long list. To begin with, these five shirts of my husband's.

3. Empleada: **¿Las quiere almidonadas?**
   Does he want them starched?

4. Juana: **No, mejor no.**
   No, I'd better not.

5. Empleada: **Muy bien.**
   Very well.

6. Juana: **Este botón se ha caído también. ¿Puede usted coserlo?**
   Also, this button fell off. Can you sew it on?

7. Empleada: **Claro que sí, señora. Siempre miro si están todos los botones.**
   Of course, miss. I always look to see if all the buttons are on.

8. Juana: **Aquí hay unos pijamas, una combinación, una falda, varios calzoncillos, y calcetines.**
Here there are some pajamas, a slip, a skirt, several shorts, and socks.

9. Empleada: **Muy bien. ¿Lo quiere todo planchado?**
Very well. Would you like everything ironed?

10. Juana: **Las camisas, por favor. ¿Para cuándo estará listo?**
The shirts, please. When will it be ready?

11. Empleada: **Mañana por la tarde.**
Tomorrow afternoon.

12. Juana: **Perfecto. Me gustaría lavar en seco algunas cosas. ¿Puede usted recomendarme una buena tintorería?**
Perfect. I'd like to have some things dry cleaned. Can you recommend a good dry cleaner?

13. Empleada: **Hay una aquí mismo en la esquina de General Goded y la Castellana. Dicen que trabajan bien. Creo que es *la mejor*. Si no es *mejor* que las otras, por lo menos es tan buena como ellas, y es *más rápida*. No sé si será *más cara* pero . . .**
There's one right here at the corner of General Goded and the Castellana. They say that they do good work. I think it's the best. If it's not better, it's at least as good as the others, and it's faster. I don't know if it's more expensive but . . .

14. Juana: **Bueno, gracias.**
Alright, thank you.

En la tintorería. At the dry cleaner's.

15. Juana: **Hola, tengo un vestido de seda, un traje, unos pantalones y una chaqueta° para lavar.**
    Hi, I have a silk dress, a suit, some pants, and a jacket to be cleaned.

16. Empleado: **Bueno, llene este boleto, por favor.**
    OK, fill out this claim ticket, please.

17. Juana: **Por favor, tenga mucho cuidado con el vestido. La tela es muy delicada.**
    Please be very careful with the dress. The material is very delicate.

18. Empleado: **Seguramente, señora. No debería tomar *más de* dos días.**
    Certainly, ma'am. It shouldn't be more than two days.

19. Juana: **Gracias.**
    Thanks.

B. NOTES

15. *la chaqueta:* In Spain, the sports coat is generally called *la americana.* In other parts of the Spanish-speaking world, it is called *el saco* or *la chaqueta.*

C. GRAMMAR AND USAGE

1. The comparative and superlative with *más* (more) or *menos* (less) used with nouns, verbs, adjectives, or adverbs

a. ***No puedo andar más.***	a. I can't walk (any) more.
b. ***Tengo más tiempo.***	b. I have more time.
c. ***Juan está menos cansado.***	c. Juan is less tired.
d. ***Este libro es más interesante.***	d. This book is more interesting.
e. ***Ellos hablan más fuerte.***	e. They speak louder.
f. ***Ella vendrá más tarde.***	f. She will come later.

2. Comparatives not formed with *más* or *menos:*

mejor = better, best
peor = worse, worst
mayor = older, oldest; greater, greatest; bigger, biggest
menor = younger, youngest; smaller, smallest; lesser, least

a. ***Mis hermanos escriben mejor.***	a. My brothers write better.
b. ***Este vestido es mejor.***	b. This dress is better.
c. ***Es la mejor chaqueta.***	c. It's the best jacket.
d. ***Yo soy el hermano menor.***	d. I'm the younger (youngest) brother.
e. ***El es mi hermano mayor.***	e. He is my older (oldest) brother.

Note:

- *Más grande* and *más pequeño* are used when physical size is emphasized.

3. To distinguish adequately between the comparative and superlative in Spanish, the article and a following prepositional phrase or adjective clause may be added.

a. ***Pedro es mejor que usted.***	a. Pedro is better than you.
Pedro es el mejor del mundo.	Pedro is the best in the world.
b. ***Ella es más bonita que Juana.***	b. She's prettier than Juana.
Ella es la más bonita de la ciudad.	She's the prettiest in the city.
c. ***Esta lección es más difícil.***	c. This lesson is more difficult.
Es la lección más difícil del libro.	It's the most difficult lesson in the book.
d. ***Roberto es más fuerte que Juan.***	d. Roberto is stronger than Juan.
Roberto es el más fuerte del equipo.	Roberto is the strongest on the team.
e. *Este libro es más interesante.*	e. This book is more interesting.
Es el libro más interesante que jamás he leído.	It's the most interesting book that I've ever read.
f. *Ella es más inteligente.*	f. She's more intelligent.
Ella es más inteligente que nadie.	She's more intelligent than anyone.

4. "Than" is translated by *de* with numbers or degrees in comparisons.

a. ***Hay más de veinte alumnos.***	a. There are more than twenty students.
b. ***El tiene más de cuarenta dólares.***	b. He has more than forty dollars.
c. ***Ellos vieron más de cien aviones.***	c. They saw more than a hundred airplanes.

Note:

- In the negative, *que* is used before numbers to mean "no more than," or "only."

No tengo más que veinte dólares.	I have only twenty dollars.

EXERCISES

A. Substitute the word or expression in parentheses for the underlined word or expression in the model sentence. Write each new sentence and say it aloud.

1. *Roberto es más fuerte que tú. (ambicioso, inteligente, pobre, rico, lento)*
2. *Ellos tienen el restaurante más típico de Madrid. (caro, económico, bonito, divertido, antiguo)*
3. *Lo siento. No puedo andar más. (estudiar, hablar, escribir, mandar, pedir)*
4. *Mi hermano menor canta mejor que yo. (baila, escribe, juega, lee, contesta)*
5. *Es el coche más moderno del mundo. (caro, peligroso, rápido, bonito, pequeño)*
6. *Ellos me dieron más de cuarenta libros. (dólares, números, folletos, sellos, nombres)*

B. Rewrite these sentences in the negative. Write the complete sentence and translate.

1. *Tengo más de tres hermanos.*
2. *Me cobraron más de cien pesetas.*
3. *Hay más de cinco sastres.*
4. *Compraron más de cinco maletas.*
5. *Murieron más de veinte soldados.*

C. Translate the following sentences into Spanish, then say them aloud.

1. They have a better car.

2. We are older than they.

3. This dress is more expensive.

4. This soap washes better.

5. The cloth that I bought is softer.

6. Juana is the prettiest girl in the class.

7. He is my youngest son.

8. It's the best magazine in the world.

9. I can't write (any) more.

10. He is more intelligent than his older brother.

D. From among the three choices given, choose the best equivalent of the English given at the beginning of each sentence. Write the complete sentence and translate.

1. (any more) *No quiero estudiar* __________ .
   (a) *alguna más*
   (b) *más*
   (c) *algo más*

2. (stronger) *Juan es mucho* __________ *que José.*
   (a) *mas fuerte*
   (b) *más fuerte*
   (c) *fuerte*

3. (bigger) *Este edificio es bastante* __________ .
   (a) *grande*
   (b) *más*
   (c) *más grande*

4. (biggest) *Es el edificio* __________ *de la ciudad.*
   (a) *menos grande*
   (b) *más grande*
   (c) *mas grande*

5. (than) *No creo que tenga más* __________ *veinte pesetas.*
   (a) *que*
   (b) *de*
   (c) *de los*

6. (than) *No me dieron más* __________ *treinta dólares.*
   (a) *de*
   (b) *que*
   (c) *de las*

7. (easier than) *Esta lección es* __________ *la otra.*
   (a) *más fácil de*
   (b) *menos fácil*
   (c) *más fácil que*

8. (than her sister) *Ella es más inteligente* __________ .
   (a) *de su hermana*
   (b) *que su hermana*
   (c) *su hermana*

9. (louder) *El profesor les dijo que hablaran* ________ .
   (a) *alto*
   (b) *fuerte*
   (c) *más fuerte*

10. (younger) *Es mi hermana* __________ .
   (a) *menor*
   (b) *más menor*
   (c) *la menor*

LESSON 19

LA DENTISTA, EL MEDICO Y EL FARMACEUTICO
THE DENTIST, THE DOCTOR, AND THE PHARMACIST

A. *La dentista.* The dentist.

1. Recepcionista: **Buenos días. ¿En qué puedo servirle, señora?**
   Good morning. What can I do for you, ma'am?

2. Juana: **Tengo un dolor de muelas terrible. Es un dolor punzante. ¿Puedo ver a la dentista?**
   I have a terrible toothache. It's a very sharp pain. Could I see the dentist?

3. Recepcionista: **Claro. Un momento, por favor.**
   Of course. Just a minute, please.

4. Dentista: **A ver, señora. ¿Quiere sentarse? Muy bien. ¿Qué es lo que le pasa?**
   Let's see, ma'am. Would you like to sit down? Okay. What is the matter?

5. Juana: **La encía está un poco hinchada y hasta sangra a veces.**
   The gum is a little swollen and it even bleeds at times.

6. Dentista: **Más vale tomar una radiografía. Eche usted la cabeza un poco para atrás. Y abra la boca, por favor. Muerda esto.**
   Better take an X-ray. Tilt your head back a little. And open your mouth, please. Bite on this.

7. Juana: **¿Tardará mucho?**
Will it take very long?

8. Dentista: **No. La radiografía estará en seguida. Mientras tanto, déjeme examinarle el diente.**
No. The X-ray will be ready right away. Meanwhile, let me examine the tooth.

9. Juana: **¡Ay! ¡Cómo me duele!**
Ouch! How painful!

10. Dentista: **Tendré que ponerle una injección.**
I'll have to give you an injection.

11. Juana: **Sí, por favor. No aguanto el dolor.**
Yes, please. I can't stand this pain.

12. Dentista: **Ya veo lo que es. Tiene una caries en la muela aquí a la izquierda. No me parece muy serio el asunto.**
Now I see what it is. You have a cavity in the molar on the left. It doesn't look very serious.

13. Juana: **Menos mal. Espero que no tenga usted que sacármela.**
Good. I hope you don't have to pull it.

14. Dentista: **Vamos a ver la radiografía. No, no hay que sacarla, pero hay que reparar esa caries.**
Let's look at the X-ray. No, it won't have to come out, but I have to fill the cavity.

15. Juana: **¿Me lo puede arreglar, entonces?**
You can fix it for me, then?

16. Dentista: **Será cosa de unos minutos y no sentirá nada, señora. No se preocupe.**
It will be a matter of a few minutes, and you won't feel anything. Don't worry.

El médico. The doctor.

17. Carlos: **Juana, no estoy nada bien. Tengo dolores por todo el cuerpo. Me duele la cabeza, el estómago, hasta me duele la garganta.**
I'm not well at all, Juana. I have aches all over my body. My head aches, my stomach aches, even my throat is sore.

18. Juana: **Desde luego, tienes mal aspecto. Voy a llamar al médico. Teresa me recomendó el suyo. Mientras tanto, acuéstate.** (*Llama.*)
You sure don't look well. I'm going to call the doctor. Teresa recommended hers. Meanwhile, go to bed. (*She calls.*)

19. Médico: (*Más tarde*) **A ver, señor, ¿qué le pasa? Abra la boca, por favor. Tosa . . . usted tiene fiebre y la garganta está bastante irritada.**
(*Later*) Let's see, sir. What seems to be the problem? Open your mouth, please. Cough . . . You have a fever and your throat is quite irritated.

20. Juana: **¿Qué hay que hacer?**
What should we do?

21. Médico: **Su marido tendrá que guardar cama° dos o tres días, señora, hasta que le pase la fiebre.**
Your husband will have to stay in bed for two or three days, ma'am, until the fever goes away.

22. Juana: **¿Puede comer de todo?**
Can he eat everything?

23. Médico: **No, señora. Sopa o caldos. Bastante líquido. Zumos de frutas,° cosas parecidas, y debe tomar estas píldoras que le voy a recetar. Déle**

una cada cuatro horas hasta que le baje la temperatura. Si no mejora esta noche, vuelva a llamarme.
No, ma'am. Soups or broths. A lot of liquids. Fruit juices, similar things, and he ought to take these pills that I'm going to prescribe. Give him one every four hours until his temperature goes down. If he doesn't get better by tonight, call me again.

24. Carlos: **¡Qué lástima! Ahora tenemos que aplazar el viaje al sur.**
What a shame! Now we have to postpone the trip south.

25. Médico: **Ya lo creo. Tendrá que descansar.**
I certainly think so. He'll have to rest.

26. Juana: (*La mañana siguiente*) **¿Cómo te sientes hoy, querido? ¿Has dormido bien?**
(*The following day*) How do you feel today, dear? Did you sleep well?

27. Carlos: **Mucho mejor, gracias. Me parece que no tengo tanta fiebre como antes. Y no me duele tanto la garganta.**
Much better, thank you. I don't think I have as much of a fever as before. And my throat isn't so sore.

28. Juana: **Me alegro. Creo que es *la misma enfermedad que* yo tenía el mes pasado. Aquí está el periódico de hoy, si lo quieres leer. Voy a la farmacia. Vuelvo en seguida.**
I'm glad. I think it's the same illness that I had last month. Here's today's paper if you want to read it. I'm going to the pharmacy. I'll be right back.

En la farmacia. At the pharmacy.

29. Juana: **Por favor, ¿quiere prepararme esta receta del doctor Menéndez?**
Will you prepare this prescription from Dr. Menéndez, please?

30. Farmacéutico: **No se preocupe, señora. Estará dentro de un momento. ¿Quiere alguna otra cosa?**
Druggist: Don't worry, ma'am. It will be ready in a moment. Do you want anything else?

31. Juana: **Ah, sí. Por poco se me olvida.° ¿Tiene usted una buena crema para la piel delicada?**
Oh, yes. I almost forgot. Do you have a good cream for sensitive skin?

32. Farmacéutico: **Sí, no hay *ninguna* tan buena como *la nuestra.***
Yes, there isn't any (cream) that's as good as ours.

33. Juana: **Voy a probarla ¿Dónde están las hojas de afeitar y la crema dentífrica?**
I'm going to try it. Where are the razor blades and the toothpaste?

B. NOTES

21. *guardar cama:* to stay in bed.

23. *Zumos de frutas: Jugos* is more common in Latin America.

31. *Por poco se me olvida:* Notice the present tense for an idea that is usually expressed by the past tense in English. "I almost forgot." *Por poco* is used in this manner quite frequently. *Por poco se me cae el planto.* ("I almost dropped the plate.") *Por poco se pierde Juan.* ("Juan almost got lost.")

C. GRAMMAR AND USAGE

1. *el mismo que:* the same as

a. ***Rafael tiene el mismo disco que yo.***	a. Rafael has the same record as I.
b. ***Ellos estudian los mismos libros que nosotros.***	b. They are studying the same books as we are.
c. ***Teresa lleva la misma blusa que ayer.***	c. Teresa is wearing the same blouse as yesterday.
d. ***Todos tienen las mismas preocupaciones que él.***	d. They all have the same worries as he does.

2. To form the possessive pronoun, use the appropriate form of the article and the long form of the possessive adjective.

a. ***Juan dice que este coche es mejor que el suyo.***	a. Juan says this car is better than his.
b. ***Aquí está tu pluma. ¿Dónde está la mía?***	b. Here's your pen. Where's mine?
c. ***La clase de Rafael empieza a las cuatro. ¿Cuándo empieza la nuestra?***	c. Rafael's class begins at four o'clock. When does ours begin?
d. ***Los zapatos de María son nuevos. Me gustan tanto como los tuyos.***	d. Maria's shoes are new. I like them as much as yours.
e. ***Préstame tu libro, por favor. He perdido el mío.***	e. Lend me your book, please. I lost mine.
f. ***¿Las maletas? Las mías están aquí.***	f. The suitcases? Mine are here.

g. ***¿Los abrigos? El mío está allí y éste es el tuyo.***	g. The coats? Mine is there and this one is yours.
h. ***¿El de Juan? Dile que el suyo está aquí también.***	h. Juan's? Tell him that his is here, too.

3. You can use *poco, mucho, otro, alguno,* and *ninguno* as nouns.

a. ***¿Flores? Me quedan muy pocas.***	a. Flowers? I have very few left.
b. ***¿Botones? ¿Quiere usted muchos?***	b. Buttons? Do you want many?
c. ***Sí, quiero algunos grandes.***	c. Yes, I want some big ones.
d. ***No tengo ninguno.***	d. I don't have any.
e. ***¿Tiene usted otro más barato?***	e. Do you have another cheaper one?

EXERCISES

A. Substitute the words or expressions in parentheses for the underlined word or expression in the model sentence. Write each new sentence and say it aloud.

1. *Margarita ha comprado el mismo modelo que yo. (coche, abrigo, sombrero, vestido, traje)*

2. *Ella siempre compra los mismos libros que su amiga. (zapatos, vestidos, periódicos, cuadernos, cigarillos)*

3. *Creo que esta casa es más bonita que la mía. (blusa, máquina, lámpara, mesa, revista)*

4. *¿Cuadros? Tenemos unos más bonitos. (algunos, pocos, muchos, otros)*

5. *¿Máquina de coser? ¿Quiere usted ver una portátil? (nueva, barata, bonita, práctica, moderna, alemana)*

6. *No veo mis zapatos pero aquí están los tuyos. (libros, lápices, papeles, cuadernos, guantes)*

B. Change these sentences to the present tense. Write the complete sentence and translate.

1. *Ellos siempre mandaron los mismos periódicos.*

2. *El compró la misma crema de afeitar que Juan.*

3. *Tú recibiste el mismo premio que yo.*

4. *Cuando mi padre recibió su máquina de escribir nueva, me dio la vieja.*

5. *Juan no escuchó el mismo programa que yo.*

C. Translate the following sentences into Spanish, then say them aloud.

1. I like your car but mine is better.

2. We bought the same record as María.

3. Juan always goes to the same school as his brother.

4. When he lost his book, I gave him mine.

5. They bought tickets in the same row as ours.

6. Juan and I went to the same theater as you.

7. I had my umbrella but Juan lost his.

8. I bought some candy. Do you want some?

9. Will you give me a few pesetas?

10. Where are yours (pesetas)?

D. From among the three choices given, choose the best equivalent of the English given at the beginning of each sentence. Write the complete sentence and translate.

1. (the same) *Estos discos son* __________ *que tengo yo.*
   (a) *los mismos*
   (b) *la misma*
   (c) *mismos*

2. (mine) *Me gusta este coche más que* __________ .
   (a) *la mía*
   (b) *el mío*
   (c) *míos*

3. (yours) *Esta es mi pluma. ¿Dónde está* __________ *?*
   (a) *el tuyo*
   (b) *los tuyos*
   (c) *la tuya*

4. (ours) *Me gusta esta casa.* __________ *es más pequeña.*
   (a) *La nuestra*
   (b) *Las nuestras*
   (c) *El nuestro*

5. (his) *Me pidió el libro porque había perdido* __________.
   (a) *la suya*
   (b) *lo suyo*
   (c) *el suyo*

6. (few) *Puedes llevar estos lápices aunque me quedan muy* __________ .
   (a) *pocas*
   (b) *pocos*
   (c) *unos pocos*

7. (some) *Veo que hay muchas revistas. Voy a comprar* __________ .
   (a) *alguno*
   (b) *algunas*
   (c) *algunos*

8. (the same) *Tengo* __________ *preocupaciones que tú.*
   (a) *el mismo*
   (b) *los mismos*
   (c) *las mismas*

9. (yours) *Aquí están mis maletas. ¿Dónde están* __________ *?*
   (a) *el tuyo*
   (b) *las tuyas*
   (c) *la tuya*

10. (hers) *Tu sombrero es muy bonito y me gusta* __________ *también.*
   (a) *la suya*
   (b) *el suyo*
   (c) *las suyas*

LESSON 20

LA RELIGION
RELIGION

A. DIALOGUE

Servicios religiosos. Religious services.

1. Carlos: **¿Hay una iglesia católica cerca del hotel? Queremos oír la misa.°**
   Is there a Catholic church near the hotel? We want to attend mass.

2. Recepcionista: **La catedral es impresionante. Hay misas los domingos desde las siete de la mañana. Pueden ustedes escoger la hora que prefieran.**
   The cathedral is impressive. There are masses on Sundays from seven in the morning. You can choose the time that you prefer.

3. Juana: **¿Y hay una iglesia protestante? Queremos asistir el domingo.**
   And is there a Protestant Church? We want to attend on Sunday.

4. Recepcionista: **En Madrid hay una iglesia protestante. Creo que es la de San Jorge.**
   In Madrid there is a Protestant church. I think it's San Jorge.

5. Juana: **¿A qué hora empiezan los servicios?**
   At what time do the services start?

6. Recepcionista: **No estoy segura. Pero creo que a las once. Si quiere usted, puedo averiguar y se lo dejo dicho.**
   I'm not sure. But I think that it's at eleven. If you would like, I can find out and let you know.

7. Carlos: **Gracias. Usted es muy amable. ¿Podemos ir andando? Si sigue este tiempo, sería agradable ir a pie.**
Thank you. You're very kind. Can we walk there? If this weather continues it would be nice to go there on foot.

8. Recepcionista: **Sí. Está en la esquina de Calle Hermosilla y Calle Nuñez de Balboa. Son unas seis u° ocho cuadras.**
Yes. It's on the corner of Calle Hermosilla and Calle Nuñez de Balboa. It's only six or eight blocks.

9. Carlos: **Me gustaría visitar una sinagoga también. ¿Qué te parece, Juana?**
I would also like to attend a synagogue. What do you think, Juana?

10. Juana: **Me encantaría. ¿Hay una sinagoga aquí en Madrid?**
I'd like to very much. Is there a synagogue here in Madrid?

11. Recepcionista: **Conozco una sinagoga en Toledo. Se llama la Sinagoga del Tránsito, y el interior es muy hermoso. Hay tambien un museo de la cultura judía en España.**
I know a synagogue in Toledo. It's called the Tránsito Synagogue, and the interior is very beautiful. There is also a museum of Jewish culture in Spain.

12. Juana: **¡Sería muy interesante! Quieres visitarla?**
That would be very interesting! Do you want to visit it?

13. Carlos: **Claro que sí. Me intereso mucho en la arquitectura religiosa. Hacemos un viaje por el sur. ¿Usted sabe si hay una mezquita que podemos visitar?**

Of course. I'm very interested in religious architecture. We're taking a trip through the south. Do you know if there is a mosque that we can visit?

14. Recepcionista: **¡Ah, sí! En Córdoba hay la mezquita la más famosa del país. Y hay muchos ejemplos de la arquitectura mora.**
Oh, yes! In Córdoba there is the most famous mosque in the country. And there are many examples of Moorish architecture.

15. Carlos: **¡Estupendo! Tendrémos que visitar la Mezquita en Córdoba.**
Great! We'll have to visit the Mezquita in Córdoba.

Invitación a una boda. Invitation to a wedding.

16. Juana: **Mira, Carlos, hemos recibido una invitación a una boda. Se casa el sobrino de Miguel.**
Look, Carlos, we've received an invitation to a wedding. Miguel's nephew is getting married.

17. Carlos: **¡Ah, sí! Ahora me acuerdo que habían hablado de eso.** ***Esperaban que pasara.***
Oh, yes! Now I remember they had talked about that. They hoped this would happen.

18. Juana: (*Leyendo*) **"El señor y la señora González Ballester tienen el placer de anunciar el enlace de su hija María Mercedes con el señor Rafael Herrero Hernández.**
"Los novios y los padres se complacen en invitarles a la ceremonia religiosa que tendrá lugar en la iglesia de San Gerónimo el día dieciséis de julio."
Voy a llamar a Teresa a ver cómo va a ir vestida. Tengo que pensar en lo que voy a ponerme.

(*Reading*) "Mr. and Mrs. González Ballester have the pleasure of announcing the marriage of their daughter María Mercedes to Mr. Rafael Herrero Hernández.

"The bride, the groom, and their parents take pleasure in inviting you to attend the religious ceremony which will take place at San Gerónimo's church on July sixteenth."

I'm going to call Teresa to see what she's wearing. I have to think about what I'll wear.

19. Carlos: **Yo también. Es muy divertido vestirse de etiqueta. Espero que conozcamos algunos de *los invitados.***
Me too. It's fun to get dressed up. I hope we know some of the guests.

20. Juana: **Miguel y Teresa estarán allí. Necesitamos comprar un regalo, también. ¡*Ojalá que tuviéramos* más tiempo! Me gustan tanto las bodas, como a mi madre, que en paz descanse.**
Miguel and Teresa will be there. We need to buy a gift, too. If only we had more time! I love weddings, like my mother did, may she rest in peace.

B. NOTES

1. *oír la misa* or *oír misa:* generally used for the idea of attending mass.

8. *u ocho:* Notice that *o* ("or") changes to *u* before a word beginning with *o*.

C. GRAMMAR AND USAGE

1. The past participle used as a noun:

a. ***El invitado fue muy simpático.***	a. The guest was very nice.
b. ***Los heridos fueron muchos.***	b. The wounded were many.
c. ***Los más avanzados llegaron.***	c. The most advanced arrived.
d. ***El Valle de los Caídos es impresionante.***	d. The Valley of the Fallen is impressive.
e. ***La más informada nos habló del asunto.***	e. The most informed (one) spoke to us about the matter.
f. ***Juan es el menos preparado para el trabajo.***	f. Juan is the one least prepared for the job.
g. ***El preferido fue un hombre mayor.***	g. The preferred one was an older man.
h. ***La casada no habló.***	h. The married one didn't speak.
i. ***El más conocido era Don Juan Satrústegui.***	i. The best known one was Don Juan Satrústegui.

2. Indirect commands/wishes are formed using the subjunctive: *Que él lo haga.* Let (have) him do it.

a. ***Que ellos lo compren.***	a. Have them buy it.
b. ***Que él lo diga.***	b. Let him say it.
c. ***Que ella lo mande.***	c. Have her send it.

Note:

- In these indirect commands, the subject, if expressed, may precede or follow the verb form.

a. *Que lo diga Juan.*	a. Let Juan say it.
b. *Que lo hagan ellos.*	b. Have them do it.

3. Sequence of tenses with subjunctive: the past tense and the imperfect subjunctive.

a. ***Me dijo que fuera a misa.***	a. He told me to go to Mass.
b. ***Querían que él lo hiciera.***	b. They wanted him to do it.
c. ***Fue imposible que ellos llegaran tan temprano.***	c. It was impossible for them to arrive so early.
d. ***Esperaban que Juan los invitara.***	d. They hoped that Juan would invite them.
e. ***Pidió que nosotros mandáramos los paquetes.***	e. He asked us to send the packages.
f. ***Era necesario que ustedes lo leyeran.***	f. It was necessary for you to read it.
g. ***El jefe sentía que ella tuviera que marcharse.***	g. The boss was sorry that she had to leave.
h. ***Ella se alegró de que no oyéramos las noticias.***	h. She was happy that we didn't hear the news.

4. *Ojalá* + imperfect subjunctive:

a. ***Ojalá que estuvieran aquí.***	a. If only [I wish that] they were here!
b. ***Ojalá que lo encontrara usted.***	b. If only [I wish that] you would find it!
c. ***Ojalá que ella lo supiera.***	c. If only [I wish that] she knew it!

Note:

- *Ojalá* may be used alone in exclamation.

a. *¿Qué yo soy muy rico? ¡Ojalá!*	a. Am I very rich? I wish I were!
b. *¿Se casó ella? ¡Ojalá!*	b. Did she get married? I wish she had!

EXERCISES

A. Substitute the words or expressions in parentheses for the underlined word or expression in the model sentence. Write each new sentence and say it aloud.

1. *El desconocido llegó muy tarde. (La casada, El conocido, La acusada, El herido, La más querida)*

2. *Que él lo haga. (diga, compre, mande, escriba, lea)*

3. *Ojalá que ellos lo supieran. (vendieran, vieran, sintieran, dudaran, dijeran)*

4. *Era imposible que yo llegara a las seis y treinta. (saliera, viniera, me levantara, hablara, llamara)*

5. *Era difícil que ellos me creyeran. (imposible, increíble, necesario, fantástico, probable)*

6. *El jefe dijo que mandáramos las cartas en seguida. (rogó, mandó, pidió, se alegró de, quiso)*

B. Change these sentences to the past tense. Write the complete sentence and translate.

1. *Es posible que vengan Juan y José.*

2. *Lo dice para que lo sepamos.*

3. *Espero que lo hagan inmediatamente.*

4. *Dudo que Juan lo oiga.*

5. *María siente que ellos lo crean.*

C. Translate the following sentences into Spanish, then say them aloud.

1. I'm sorry he's here.
2. He was sorry that I did it.
3. If only he were here!
4. Let them do it!
5. The best informed (one) spoke to us.
6. They said it so that he would know (it).
7. It's impossible for them to believe it.
8. He doubted that we knew it.
9. They wanted us to buy the book.
10. The boss told me to do it.

D. From among the three choices given, choose the best equivalent of the English given at the beginning of each sentence. Write the complete sentence and translate.

1. (the best-informed girl) *Me gustaría hablar con* ________.
   (a) *el más informado*
   (b) *la más informada*
   (c) *las más informadas*
2. (the wounded) *Tenían que ayudar* ________.
   (a) *los heridos*
   (b) *herido*
   (c) *a los heridos*
3. (Have) ________ *él lo escriba.*
   (a) *Tenga*
   (b) *Que*
   (c) *Dígale*

4. (sell) *Fue imposible que ellos* __________ *el coche.*
   (a) *vendiera*
   (b) *vendieron*
   (c) *vendieran*

5. (couldn't) *Sentía que Juan* __________ *venir a la boda.*
   (a) *no puede*
   (b) *no podrá*
   (c) *no pudiera*

6. (go) *Quería que ellos* __________ *al cine.*
   (a) *van*
   (b) *fueran*
   (c) *fueron*

7. (do) *Que lo* __________ *Juan.*
   (a) *haga*
   (b) *hace*
   (c) *hagan*

8. (the preferred man) *De todos los empleados, Rafael es* __________.
   (a) *el preferido*
   (b) *lo preferido*
   (c) *la preferida*

9. (say) *Querían que el jefe lo* __________.
   (a) *dice*
   (b) *dijera*
   (c) *dijo*

10. (I wish I were) *Dicen que soy muy inteligente. ¡* __________ *!*
   (a) *Quiero estar*
   (b) *Quería*
   (c) *Ojalá*

SUMMARY OF SPANISH GRAMMAR

1. THE ALPHABET

Letter	Name	Letter	Name	Letter	Name
a	a	*j*	jota	*r*	ere
b	be	*k*	ka	*rr*	erre
c	ce	*l*	ele	*s*	ese
ch	che	*ll*	elle	*t*	te
d	de	*m*	eme	*u*	u
e	e	*n*	ene	*v*	ve/uve
f	efe	*ñ*	eñe	*w*	doble ve/ uve doble
g	ge	*o*	o	*x*	equis
h	hache	*p*	pe	*y*	i griega
i	i	*q*	cu	*z*	zeta

2. PRONUNCIATION

SIMPLE VOWELS

a [a] as in *ah* or *father.*
e [e] as in *day.*
i [i] as in *machine.*
o [o] as in *open.*
u [u] as in *rule.*

VOWEL COMBINATIONS

ai, *ay* [ai] *ai* in *aisle.*

au [av] *ou* in *out.*

ei, *ey* [ej] *aý-ee.*

ie [ie] *ye* in *yes.*

io [io] *yo* in *yoke.*

ua [ua] *wah.*

ou [ou] *o-oo.*

eu [eu] *áy-oo.*

iu [iu] *you.*

oi / ***oy*** [oi] *oy* in *boy.*

ui / ***uy*** [ui] *óo-ee.*

ia [ia] *ya* in *yard.*

CONSONANTS

Notice the following points:

b, v have the same sound. After a pause and after *m* or *n,* both are like *b* in *boy.* When the sound occurs between vowels you bring the upper and lower lips together and blow between them (the upper teeth may touch the inside of the lower lip, as well).

c before *o, a,* and *u,* and before consonants, is like *c* in *cut.*

c before *e* and *i* is pronounced in Spain like *th* in *thin.* In Latin America, it is pronounced like *s* in *see.*

ch as in *church.*

d after a pause or *n* and *l,* like *d* but touching the inside of the upper teeth. When it occurs between vowels, like *th* in *that.*

g before *a, o,* and *u,* before consonants, and after *n,* like *g* in *go.*

g before *e* and *i* is a strong rasping *h* (like the sound of a cat hissing).

h is not pronounced.

j is always like *g* before *e* and *i* (see above.)

ll is pronounced in Spain like *lli* in *million;* in many countries of Latin America like *y* in yes; in Argentina it is pronounced like *s* in *pleasure.*

ñ	is like *ni* in *onion* or *ny* in *canyon*.
qu	is like *k*.
r	is pronounced by tapping the tip of the tongue against the gum ridge in back of the upper teeth.
rr	is trilled several times.
s	as in *see*.
x	before a consonant and between vowels, like *x* (*ks*) in *extra* (and occasionally like the *x* (*gs*) in *examine*). It may also be like the Spanish *j* at times.
y	when it begins a word or syllable, like *y* in *yes*.
y	when it serves as a vowel, like *i*.
z	is pronounced the same as the Spanish *c* before *e* and *i* (see above).

3. STRESS

1. Stress the last syllable if the word ends in a consonant other than *n* or *s*.
   ciudad city

2. Stress the next to the last syllable if the word ends in a vowel or *n* or *s*.
   amigo friend
   hablan they speak

3. Otherwise stress the syllable that has the accent (ʹ).
   inglés English
   teléfono telephone

4. PUNCTUATION

There are several differences between Spanish and English.

1. Exclamation and question marks precede as well as follow the sentence:

¿Adónde va usted?	Where are you going?
¡Hombre!	Man!
¡Venga!	Come!
¡Qué hermoso día!	What a beautiful day!

2. The question mark is placed before the question part of the sentence:

Juan, ¿adónde vas?	Juan, where are you going?
Usted conoce al Sr. Díaz, ¿no es verdad?	You know Mr. Díaz, don't you?

3. Dashes are often used instead of quotation marks:

Muchas gracias—dijo.	"Thanks a lot," he said.
Esta mañana—dijo—, fui al centro.	"This morning," he said, "I went downtown."
—¿Cómo está usted?	"How are you?"
—Muy bien, gracias.	"Very well, thank you."

4. Capitals are not used as frequently as in English. They are only used at the beginning of sentences and with proper nouns. *Yo* "I," adjectives of nationality, the days of the week, and the months are not capitalized:

Somos americanos.	We're Americans.
El no es francés sino inglés.	He's not French but English.
Vendré el martes o el miércoles.	I'll come Tuesday or Wednesday.
Hoy es el primero de febrero.	Today is the first of February.

5. Suspension points (. . .) are used more frequently than in English to indicate interruption, hesitation, etc.

5. SOME ORTHOGRAPHIC SIGNS

1. The tilde (˜) is used over the letter *n* to indicate the sound of *ni* in *onion* or *ny* in *canyon.*

2. The diaeresis (¨) is used over *u* in the combination *gu* before the vowels *e* and *i* when it is pronounced *gw.*

vergüenza	shame
pingüino	penguin

6. THE DEFINITE ARTICLE

	SINGULAR	PLURAL
Masculine	*el*	*los*
Feminine	*la*	*las*

SINGULAR

el muchacho	the boy
la muchacha	the girl

PLURAL

los muchachos	the boys
las muchachas	the girls

1. *El* is used before a feminine noun beginning with stressed *a* (or *ha*):

el agua	the water
But—	
las aguas	the waters
el hacha	the axe
But—	
las hachas	the axes

2. The neuter article *lo* is used before parts of speech other than nouns when they are used as nouns:

lo malo	what is bad, the bad part of it
lo hecho	what is done
lo dicho	what is said
lo útil	the useful
lo difícil	the difficult
lo posible	the possible
lo necesario	the necessary

3. The definite article is used:

a. with abstract nouns:

La verdad vale más que las riquezas.	Truth is worth more than riches.

b. with nouns referring to a class:

los soldados	soldiers
los generales	generals

c. with names of languages (except immediately after *hablar* or *en*):

Escribo el español.	I write Spanish.
Habla bien el español.	He or she speaks Spanish well.

But—

Dígalo Ud. en inglés.	Say it in English.
Hablo español.	I speak Spanish.

d. in expressions of time:

la una	one o'clock
las dos	two o'clock
las diez	ten o'clock

e. for days of the week:

Abren los domingos a las dos y media.	They open Sundays at 2:30.
el lunes próximo	next Monday

f. for the year, seasons, etc.

el año 1945	the year 1945
Vino el año pasado.	He came last year.
la primavera	spring
En el invierno hace frío.	It's cold in winter.

g. with certain geographical names:

El Brasil	Brazil
El Canadá	Canada
El Perú	Peru
El Uruguay	Uruguay
El Ecuador	Ecuador
El Japón	Japan
La Argentina	Argentina

h. with parts of the body and articles of clothing:

Me duele la cabeza.	My head hurts.
Quítese el abrigo.	Take off your coat.

7. THE INDEFINITE ARTICLE

	SINGULAR	PLURAL
Masculine	*un*	*unos*
Feminine	*una*	*unas*

SINGULAR	
un hombre	a man
una mujer	a woman

PLURAL

unos hombres	men, some (a few) men
unas mujeres	women, some (a few) women

1. *Unos* (*unas*) is often used where we use "some" or "a few" in English:
   unos días — a few days

2. The indefinite article is omitted:

   a. before rank, profession, trade, nationality, etc.:

Soy capitán.	I'm a captain.
Soy médico.	I'm a doctor.
Soy abogado.	I'm a lawyer.
Es profesor.	He's a teacher.
Ella es española.	She's Spanish.

   b. before *ciento* (or *cien*) "hundred," *cierto* "certain," *mil* "thousand":

cien hombres	a hundred men
cierto hombre	a certain man
mil hombres	a thousand men

   c. in various idiomatic expressions, such as:

Salió sin sombrero.	He left without a hat.

8. CONTRACTIONS

1. *de + el = del*	of (from) the
del hermano	from (of) the brother
2. *a + el = al*	to the
al padre	to the father

9. THE DAYS OF THE WEEK

The days of the week are masculine and are not capitalized. The article is usually necessary, except after *ser:*

el domingo	Sunday
el lunes	Monday
el martes	Tuesday
el miércoles	Wednesday
el jueves	Thursday
el viernes	Friday
el sábado	Saturday
El domingo es el primer día de la semana.	Sunday is the first day of the week.
Van a visitarlos el domingo.	They're going to pay them a visit on Sunday.
La veo los lunes.	I see her every Monday.
Mañana es sábado.	Tomorrow is Saturday.

Notice that "on Sunday," "on Monday," etc., are *el domingo, el lunes,* etc.

10. THE NAMES OF THE MONTHS

The names of the months are masculine and are not capitalized. They are usually used without the definite article:

enero	January
febrero	February
marzo	March
abril	April
mayo	May
junio	June
julio	July
agosto	August

septiembre	September
octubre	October
noviembre	November
diciembre	December

11. THE NAMES OF THE SEASONS

el invierno	winter
la primavera	spring
el verano	summer
el otoño	fall

The names of seasons are not capitalized. They are preceded by the definite article but after *de* and *en* the article may or may not be used:

Hace frío en (el) invierno.	It's cold in (the) winter.
Trabajo durante los meses de verano.	I work during the summer months.

12. MASCULINE AND FEMININE GENDER

Nouns referring to males are masculine; nouns referring to females are feminine:

el padre	the father	*la madre*	the mother
el hijo	the son	*la hija*	the daughter
el hombre	the man	*la mujer*	the woman
el toro	the bull	*la vaca*	the cow
el gato	the tomcat	*la gata*	the she-cat

The masculine plural of certain nouns stands for both genders:

los padres	the parents, the father and mother
los reyes	the king and queen
mis hermanos	my brothers and sisters

Masculine nouns and adjectives usually end in *-o*, and feminine nouns and adjectives in *-a*.

MASCULINE NOUNS

1. Nouns ending in *-o* are usually masculine:

el cuerpo	the body
el cielo	the sky
el dinero	the money

Common exceptions:

la mano	the hand
la radio	the radio

2. Nouns ending in *r, n,* and *l* are generally masculine:

el calor	the heat
el pan	the bread
el sol	the sun

3. Names of trees, days of the week, months, oceans, rivers, mountains, and other parts of speech used as nouns are generally masculine:

el álamo	the poplar
el martes	Tuesday
el Atlántico	the Atlantic Ocean
el Tajo	the Tagus River
los Andes	the Andes
el ser joven	being young, the fact of being young

FEMININE NOUNS

1. Nouns ending in *-a* (also *-dad, -tad, -tud, -ción, -sión, -ez, -umbre, -ie*) are usually feminine:

la cabeza	the head
la ciudad	the city
la cantidad	the quantity
la libertad	the liberty
la virtud	the virtue
la condición	the condition
la tensión	the tension
la madurez	the maturity
la costumbre	the custom
la serie	the series

Common exceptions:

el día	the day
el mapa	the map
el drama	the drama
el clima	the climate
el problema	the problem
el poeta	the poet

2. Names of cities and towns are feminine:

Barcelona es muy bonita.	Barcelona is very nice.

Note:

- Certain nouns differ in meaning depending on whether they take *el* or *la:*

el orden	the order (arrangement)
el capital	the capital (money)
el cura	the priest

But—

la orden	the order (command)
la capital	the capital (city)
la cura	the cure

13. THE PLURAL

1. Nouns ending in an unstressed vowel add *-s:*

el libro	the book	*los libros*	the books

2. Nouns ending in a consonant add *-es:*

el avión	the airplane
los aviones	the airplanes

3. Nouns ending in *-z* change the *z* to *c* and then add *es:*

la luz	the light	*las luces*	the lights
el lápiz	the pencil	*los lápices*	the pencils

4. Some nouns are unchanged in the plural:

los martes	Tuesdays
los Martínez	the Martínez family

14. THE POSSESSIVE

English -'s or -s' is translated by *de* "of":

el libro de Juan	Juan's book ("the book of Juan")
los libros de los niños	the boys' books ("the books of the boys")

15. ADJECTIVES

1. Singular and plural

SINGULAR	
un muchacho alto	a tall boy
una muchacha alta	a tall girl
PLURAL	
dos muchachos altos	two tall boys
dos muchachas altas	two tall girls

Notice that the adjective comes after the noun and is masculine if the noun is masculine, plural if the noun is plural, etc.

2. Feminine endings

a. If the ending is *-o*, it becomes *-a:*

MASCULINE		FEMININE	
alto	tall	*alta*	tall
rico	rich	*rica*	rich
bajo	low	*baja*	low

b. In other cases there is no change:

MASCULINE	FEMININE	
grande	*grande*	big, large
azul	*azul*	blue
cortés	*cortés*	polite
útil	*útil*	useful
triste	*triste*	sad

Examples:

una cosa útil	a useful thing
una mujer triste	a sad woman
una muchacha cortés	a polite girl

c. Adjectives of nationality add *-a* or change *o* to *a:*

MASCULINE	FEMININE	
español	*española*	Spanish
francés	*francesa*	French
inglés	*inglesa*	English
americano	*americana*	American

Examples:

una señora inglesa	an English woman
la lengua española	the Spanish language

d. Adjectives ending in *-án, -ón*[1] and *-ador:*

MASCULINE	FEMININE	
holgazán	*holgazana*	lazy
burlón	*burlona*	jesting
preguntón	*preguntona*	inquisitive
encantador	*encantadora*	charming
trabajador	*trabajadora*	hard-working

3. The following adjectives drop the final *-o* when they come before a masculine singular noun:

uno	one
bueno	good
malo	bad
alguno	some
ninguno	no (none)
primero	first
tercero	third

Examples:

un buen amigo	a good friend
ningún hombre	no man
el mal tiempo	the bad weather
el primer día	the first day

4. *Grande* becomes *gran* when it comes before any singular noun:

una gran amiga	a great friend
un gran poeta	a great poet
un gran hombre	a great (important) man

1. Notice that the accent is dropped in the feminine.

But—

un hombre grande	a large (tall) man

5. *Santo* becomes *San* when it comes before a noun (except those beginning in *To-* and *Do-*):

San Juan
San Luis
But—
Santo Tomás
Santo Domingo

6. *Ciento* becomes *cien* before a noun:

cien dólares	a hundred dollars

16. POSITION OF ADJECTIVES

1. Descriptive adjectives usually follow the noun:

un libro blanco	a white book
una casa blanca	a white house
mi sombrero nuevo	my new hat
dinero español	Spanish money
un hombre inteligente	an intelligent man
huevos frescos	fresh eggs

2. Exceptions are adjectives which describe an inherent quality:

la blanca nieve	the white snow

3. Articles, numerals, possessives, and quantitatives usually precede the noun:

un muchacho	a boy
cuatro huevos	four eggs
mi hermano	my brother
muchas personas	many persons
poca gente	few people

4. Some descriptive adjectives can come either before or after the noun:

una niña pequeña or *una pequeña niña*	a little girl
un día hermoso or *un hermoso día*	a nice (beautiful) day
una linda muchacha or *una muchacha linda*	a pretty girl

Other common adjectives used this way are *bueno* "good," *malo* "bad," and *bonito* "pretty."

5. A few adjectives have one meaning when they come before a noun and another when they follow:

un hombre pobre	a poor man
¡Pobre hombre!	Poor man!
un hombre grande	a large (tall) man
un gran hombre	a great (important) man
un libro nuevo	a new (recent) book
un nuevo hombre	a different man
una cierta noticia	a certain (particular) piece of news
una noticia cierta	a true piece of news

17. COMPARISON

1. Regular comparison

fácil	easy
más fácil	easier
menos fácil	less easy
el más fácil	the easiest
el menos fácil	the least easy

2. Irregular comparison

bueno	good	*mejor*	better, best
malo	bad	*peor*	worse, worst
mucho	much	*más*	more, most
poco	little	*menos*	less, least

grande	great	{ *mayor* / *más grande*
pequeño	small	{ *menor* / *más pequeño*

Más grande means "larger," "bigger"; *mayor* means "older":

Esta mesa es más grande que aquélla.	This table is larger than that one.
Pedro es mayor que Juan.	Pedro is older than Juan.

Similarly, *más pequeño* means "smaller"; *menor* means "younger."

3. "More (less) . . . than . . ." = *más* (*menos*) . . . que . . .

El español es más fácil que el inglés.	Spanish is easier than English.
Es más inteligente de lo que parece.	He's more intelligent than he seems.

4. "As . . . as . . ." = *tan . . . como . . .* or *tanto . . . como . . .*

a. before an adjective or adverb:

Tan fácil como . . .	As easy as . . .
El habla español tan bien como yo.	He speaks Spanish as well as I do.

b. before a noun:

Tiene tanto dinero como Ud.	He has as much money as you.

5. "The more (less) . . . the more (less) . . ." = *cuanto más* (*menos*) . . . *tanto más* (*menos*) . . .

Cuanto más le trate tanto más le agradará.	The more you get to know him (deal with him) the more you like him.

6. "Most" = *ísimo*

Es muy útil.	It's very useful.
Es utilísimo.	It's most useful.

The *-ísimo* form (called the "absolute superlative") always stands by itself (that is, it never modifies another word).

18. PRONOUNS

Pronouns have different forms depending on whether they are:

1. the subject of a verb
2. used after a preposition
3. used as direct objects
4. used as indirect objects
5. used with reflexive verbs

1. Pronouns as the subject of a verb:

SINGULAR	
yo	I
tú	you (*familiar*)
él	he
ella	she
usted	you (*polite*)

PLURAL	
nosotros	we (*masc.*)
nosotras	we (*fem.*)
vosotros	you (*masc.*)
vosotras	you (*fem.*)
ellos	they (*masc.*)
ellas	they (*fem.*)
ustedes	you (*polite*)

The personal pronouns *yo, tú,* etc., are not ordinarily used since the ending of the verb indicates the subject. "I speak" is just *hablo,* "we speak" *hablamos,* etc. They are used for emphasis or clearness (*usted habla* "you speak" and *él habla* "he speaks"), especially when there are contrasting subjects in the same sentence: *Yo compro la comida y tú traes la cerveza.* I'll buy the food and you bring the beer.

2. Pronouns used after prepositions:

para mí	for me
para ti	for you (*fam.*)
para él	for him
para ella	for her
para usted	for you (*polite*)
para nosotros	for us (*masc.*)
para nosotras	for us (*fem.*)
para vosotros	for you (*masc.*)
para vosotras	for you (*fem.*)
para ellos	for them (*masc.*)
para ellas	for them (*fem.*)
para ustedes	for you (*polite*)

Notice that the form of the pronoun used after a preposition is the same as the form of the pronoun used as a subject, except for *mí* "me" and *ti* "you" (*fam.*)

There is a special form for "with me," "with you," and "with him": *conmigo* "with me," *contigo* "with you," and *consigo* "with him, "with her," "with you."

3. Pronouns as direct objects:

me	me
te	you (*fam.*)
lo	him, it, you (*Ud.*)
la	her, it, you (*Ud.*)
nos	us
os	you (*vosotros/as*)
los	them, you (*Uds.*)
las	them, you (*Uds.*) (*fem.*)

The preposition *a* and the appropriate prepositional pronoun may be added for emphasis.

Los miré a ellos.	I saw them.

4. Pronouns as indirect objects:

me	to me
te	to you (*fam.*)
le	to him, her, it, you (*Ud.*)
nos	to us
os	to you (*vosotros/as*)
les	to them (*masc.* and *fem.*) to you (*masc.* and *fem.*) (*Uds.*)

The preposition *a* and the prepositional forms *él, ella, usted* and *ellos, ellas, ustedes* are often added for clarity.

SHORT FORM

le doy =	I give to him I give to her I give to you

les doy =	I give to them (*masc.*) I give to them (*fem.*) I give to you

FULL FORM

le doy a él	I give (to) him
le doy a ella	I give (to) her
le doy a usted	I give (to) you
les doy a ellos	I give (to) them
les doy a ellas	I give (to) them
les doy a ustedes	I give (to) you

This double construction is also used when the object is a noun:

Le escribí a María ayer.	I wrote to María yesterday.

1. Reflexive pronouns:
   Reflextive pronouns are used when a person (or thing) does something to himself or herself (or itself): e.g.. "I wash myself."

me	myself
te	yourself (fam.)
se	himself, herself, yourself, itself (*Ud.*)
nos	ourselves
os	yourselves (*vosotros/as*)
se	themselves, yourselves (*Uds.*)

Me lavo.	I wash myself.
Ella se habla.	She talks to herself.

19. POSITION OF PRONOUNS

1. When there are both direct and indirect object pronouns in a sentence ("he gives it to me"), the Spanish order is the following:

Me lo da.	He gives it to me.
Nos lo dan.	They give it to us.

That is, the indirect pronoun precedes the direct. If both begin with *l,* the indirect (*le, les*) becomes *se:*

Se lo diré (instead of *le lo diré*).	I will tell it to him (to her, to you, etc.).

1. When *se* is present it comes before the other pronouns. It denotes:

a. an impersonal action:

Se dice.	It is said.
Se la trató bien.	She was treated well.

b. a personal object (may or may not be reflexive):

Se lo dice.	He says it to him (her)/ He says it to himself.

2. If *se* is not present, the first pronoun of the group has the meaning of an indirect object and the second that of a direct object:

Me lo da.	He gives it to me.

3. Object pronouns come before conjugated verbs:

Lo veo.	I see him.
Se lo da.	He gives it to him.

They come after an infinitive or present participle:

Tenerlo.	To have it.
Dárselo.	To give it to him.
Quiero verlo.	I want to see him.
Voy a verlo.	I'm going to see him.
Teniéndolo.	Having it.
Diciéndolo.	Saying it.
Estoy mirándolo.	I am looking at him.

Object pronouns follow affirmative commands:

Tómalo.	Take it.
Dígamelo Ud.	Tell it to me.

They come before negative commands (these are always in the subjunctive):

No me lo diga Ud.	Don't tell me (it).

20. CONJUNCTIONS

y	and
o	or
pero	but
mas	but
sino	but (rather)
que	that
pues	since, as
si	if
por que	why
porque	because
ni . . . ni	neither . . . nor

NOTES

1. *y* "and"

Roberto y Juan son hermanos.	Roberto and Juan are brothers.

e is used instead of *y* before a word beginning with *i-* or *hi-:*

María e Isabel son primas.	María and Isabel are cousins.
Madre e hija.	Mother and daughter.

2. *o* "or"

Voy con mi hermano o con mi hermana.	I'm going with my brother or with my sister.
Cinco o seis pesos.[1]	Five or six pesos.

u is used instead of *o* before a word beginning with *o-* or *ho-:*

Siete u ocho horas.	Seven or eight hours.
Cinco u ocho meses.	Five or eight months.

3. *pero* "but"

Quiero venir pero no puedo.	I want to come but I can't.

4. *mas* "but" is more formal and literary:

Pensé que vendría mas no pudo.	I thought he would come but he wasn't able to.

5. *sino* "but (rather)" is used instead of *pero* after a negative statement:

No es francés sino inglés.	He is not French but English.
No viene hoy sino mañana.	He is not coming today but tomorrow.

1. The letter *o* is accented when used between numbers to distinguish it from zero (e.g., 5 *ó* 6).

21. QUESTION WORDS

1. *¿Qué?*	What?
¿Qué dice usted?	What are you saying?
2. *¿Por qué?*	Why?
¿Por qué dice usted eso?	Why do you say that?
3. *¿Cómo?*	How?
¿Cómo se dice en español esto?	How do you say this in Spanish?
¿Cómo se llama usted?	What's your name?
4. *¿Cuánto?*	How much?
¿Cuánto dinero necesita usted?	How much money do you need?
¿Cuántos libros hay?	How many books are there?
5. *¿Cuál?*	What? Which one?
¿Cuál es su nombre?	What's your name?
¿Cuál quiere usted?	Which one do you want?
6. *¿Quién?*	Who?
¿Quién vino con usted?	Who came with you?
¿Quién tiene eso?	Who has that?
7. *¿Dónde?*	Where?
¿Dónde está su amigo?	Where is your friend?
8. *¿Cuándo?*	When?
¿Cuándo se marcha Ud.?	When are you going (leaving)?
¿Cuándo ocurrió eso?	When did that happen?

Notice that the question words are written with an accent.

22. ADVERBS

1. Spanish *-mente* corresponds to "*-ly*" in English. It is added to the feminine form (whether it differs from the masculine or not) of the adjective:

exclusivamente	exclusively
normalmente	normally

When there are two adverbs, the ending *-mente* is added only to the last one:

clara y concisamente	clearly and concisely

Adverbs can be compared like adjectives.

POSITIVE	*alegremente*	cheerfully
COMPARATIVE	*más alegremente*	more cheerfully

They can also be used with *-ísimo:*

alegrísimamente	very/most cheerfully

2. Irregular comparatives:

POSITIVE		COMPARATIVE	
bien	well	*mejor*	better, best
mal	badly	*peor*	worse, worst
mucho	much	*más*	more, most
poco	little	*menos*	less, least

3. Adverbs as prepositions or conjunctions:
   Many adverbs act as prepositions when *de* is added.

ADVERB:	*después*	afterwards
PREPOSITION:	*después de las cinco*	after five o'clock
ADVERB:	*además*	besides
PREPOSITION:	*además de*	besides

When *que* is added they act as conjunctions:

después de que venga	after he comes

Other words which act similarly: *antes* "before"; *cerca* "near"; *delante* "before," "in front of"; *enfrente* "opposite."

4. Adverbs of time and manner:

hoy	today
ayer	yesterday
mañana	tomorrow
temprano	early
tarde	late
a menudo	often
siempre	always
nunca	never
jamás	never
luego	afterward
aprisa	quickly
despacio	slowly
antes	before
después	afterward

5. Adverbs of place:

aquí	here
acá	here (motion)
ahí	there
allí	there (farther away)
allá	there (motion)
adelante	forward, on
atrás	behind
dentro	inside
arriba	up, above
(*a*) *fuera*	outside
abajo	down, below
cerca	near
lejos	far

6. Adverbs of quantity:

muy	very
mucho	much
poco	little
más	more
menos	less
además	besides
cuan	how much
cuanto	how much
tan	so much
tanto	so much
demasiado	too much
apenas	scarcely, hardly

7. Adverbs expressing affirmation:

sí	yes
verdaderamente	truly
(*por*) *cierto*	certainly
ciertamente	certainly
claro	of course
desde luego	of course
por supuesto	of course

8. Adverbs expressing negation:

no	no, not
nunca	never
jamás	never
nunca jamás	never (more emphatic)
ya no	no more, not now
todavía no	not yet
tampoco	neither, either
no tal	no indeed
ni	nor
ni . . . ni	neither . . . nor
ni siquiera	not even

9. Here and there:
   Aquí "here" refers to something near the speaker:

   Tengo aquí los libros.
   I have the books here.

Ahí "there" refers to something near the person spoken to:

¿Qué tiene Ud. ahí?	What do you have there
¿Está Ud. ahí?	Are you there?

Acá "here" expresses motion toward the speaker:

¡Venga Ud. acá!	Come here!

Allá "there" indicates motion away/distance from the speaker:

¡Vaya Ud. allá!	Go there!
Va allá.	He's going there.

Allí "there" refers to something remote from both:

Vienen de allí.	They come from there.
Viví en América del Sur por varios años. ¿Ha estado Ud. allí?	I've lived in South America for several years. Have you ever been there?

23. DIMINUTIVES AND AUGMENTATIVES

The endings *-ito* (*-cito, -ecito*), *-illo* (*-cillo, -ecillo*), *-uelo* (*-zuelo, -ezuelo*) imply smallness. In addition, *-ito* often implies attractiveness or admiration, *-illo* and *-uelo* unattractiveness or depreciation. (They should be used with care.)

chico	boy	*chiquillo*	little boy
señora	lady, Mrs.	*señorita*	young lady, Miss

un poco	a little	*un poquito*	a little bit
pedazo	piece	*pedacito*	a little piece
gato	cat	*gatito*	kitten
papá	papa	*papacito*	daddy
cuchara	tablespoon	*cucharita*	teaspoon
cigarro	cigar	*cigarrillo*	cigarette
autor	author	*autorcillo*	unimportant author

The endings *-ón* (*-ona*) and *-ote* indicate largeness (often awkwardness and unattractiveness as well):

tonto	foolish, silly fool	*tontón*	big fool
silla	chair	*sillón*	big chair
cuchara	spoon	*cucharón*	a ladle
hombre	man	*hombrón*	he-man

24. DEMONSTRATIVES

1. Demonstrative adjectives:

MASCULINE	FEMININE	
este	*esta*	this
ese	*esa*	that
aquel	*aquella*	that (farther removed)
estos	*estas*	these
esos	*esas*	those
aquellos	*aquellas*	those (farther removed)

a. Spanish demonstrative adjectives usually precede the nouns they modify and always agree in gender and number:

este muchacho	this boy
aquellos vecinos	those neighbors

b. *Ese* and *aquel* both mean "that." *Aquel* points out a thing removed in space or time from the speaker or from the person spoken to:

Esa señora es muy amable.	That lady is very kind.
Aquel señor que llegó el mes pasado.	That gentleman who arrived last month.

2. Demonstrative pronouns:

MASCULINE	FEMININE	
éste	*ésta*	this (one)
ése	*ésa*	that (one)
aquél	*aquélla*	that (one)
éstos	*éstas*	these
ésos	*ésas*	those
aquéllos	*aquéllas*	those

NEUTER	
esto	this (one)
eso	that (one)
aquello	that (one)

The same difference exists between the pronouns *ése* and *aquél* as between the adjectives *ese* and *aquel:*

No quería éste sino aquél.	I didn't want this one but rather the one over there.

Este and *aquél* also mean "the latter" and "the former":

Acaban de llegar el embajador y su secretario.	The ambassador and his secretary just arrived.
Este es joven y aquél es viejo.	The former is old and the latter is young.

Notice that the Spanish order is the opposite of the English: *éste . . . aquél* ("the latter . . . the former").

The neuter demonstrative pronouns *esto, eso,* and *aquello* refer to an idea previously stated and not to a specific thing:

Me dijo que aquello fue horrible.	He told me that that was horrible.

25. INDEFINITE ADJECTIVES AND PRONOUNS

todos	all
tal	such
ni uno	not one
otro	other
alguien	someone
nadie	nobody
algo	something, anything
ninguno	no one, none
alguno	someone, some
varios	several
nada	nothing
cualquiera	whatever, whoever
quienquiera	whoever
dondequiera	wherever

26. NEGATION

1. *No* "not" comes before the verb:

No veo.	I don't see.
El no habla.	He isn't speaking.

2. There are two forms for "nothing," "never," "no one," etc.—one with and one without *no:*

No veo nada.	I see nothing.
No voy nunca.	I never go.

No viene nadie.	No one comes.
Or—	
Nada veo.	I see nothing.
Nunca voy.	I never go.
Nadie viene.	No one comes.

27. WORD ORDER

1. The usual order is subject—verb—adverb—object:

Juan vió allí a sus amigos.	Juan saw his friends there.

This order is flexible, however. For example, the subject may follow the verb, as in: *Llegó Juan.* Juan arrived.

2. As in English, questions sometimes have the same order as statements but with the question intonation (that is, with a rise in pitch at the end):

¿Juan va a ir allí?	Juan is going to go there?

3. However, the more usual way of asking a question is to put the subject after the verb:

¿Va a ir allí Juan?	Is Juan going to go there?
¿Viene su amigo?	Is your friend coming?
¿Ha comido Ud.?	Have you eaten?
¿Habla usted español?	Do you speak Spanish?
¿Tiene usted dinero?	Do you have any money?
¿Por qué volvió Ud.?	Why did you return?
¿Ha recibido Juan mi carta?	Did Juan get my letter?

4. Adjectives come right after *ser:*

¿Es tarde?	Is it late?
¿Es bueno?	Is it good?
¿Es difícil la prueba?	Is the test difficult?
¿Es fácil el problema?	Is the problem easy?

28. THE TENSES OF THE VERB

Spanish verbs are divided into three classes ("conjugations") according to their infinitives:

Class I:	*-ar*	(*hablar*)
Class II:	*-er*	(*comer*)
Class III:	*-ir*	(*vivir*)

1. The present:

I	II	III
-o	*-o*	*-o*
-as	*-es*	*-es*
-a	*-e*	*-e*
-amos	*-emos*	*-imos*
-áis	*-éis*	*-ís*
-an	*-en*	*-en*

hablar to speak	*comer* to eat	*vivir* to live
hablo	*como*	*vivo*
hablas	*comes*	*vives*
habla	*come*	*vive*
hablamos	*comemos*	*vivimos*
habláis	*coméis*	*vivís*
hablan	*comen*	*viven*

The following verbs insert *g* in the first person singular of the present indicative:

tener—tengo	I have
venir—vengo	I come
traer—traigo	I bring
poner—pongo	I put
hacer—hago	I do, make
decir—digo	I say
salir—salgo	I leave

The present can be translated in several ways:

Hablo español.	I speak Spanish. I am speaking Spanish. I do speak Spanish.

2. The imperfect:

I	II AND III
-aba	*-ía*
-abas	*-ías*
-aba	*-ía*
- ábamos	*-íamos*
-abais	*-íais*
-aban	*-ían*

a. The imperfect is used:
to indicate continued or customary actions in the past:

Cuando yo estaba en Madrid, siempre visitaba los teatros.	When I was in Madrid, I always used to visit the theaters.
Lo encontraba todos los días.	I used to meet him every day.

to indicate what was happening when something else happened:

El escribía cuando ella entró.	He was writing when she entered.

Irregular verbs in the imperfect:
The following are the only Spanish verbs which are irregular in the imperfect:
ser—era, eras, era, éramos, erais, eran
ir—iba, ibas, iba, íbamos, ibais, iban
ver—veía, veías, veía, veíamos, veíais, veían

3. The future:
   The future of regular verbs is formed by adding the following endings to the infinitive: *-é, -ás, -á, -emos, -éis, -án:*

hablar to speak	*comer* to eat	*vivir* to live
hablaré	*comeré*	*viviré*
hablarás	*comerás*	*vivirás*
hablará	*comerá*	*vivirá*
hablaremos	*comeremos*	*viviremos*
hablaréis	*comeréis*	*viviréis*
hablarán	*comerán*	*vivirán*

The future generally expresses a future action:

Lo compraré.	I'll buy it.
Iré mañana.	I'll go tomorrow.

Sometimes it expresses probability or conjecture:

¿Qué hora será?	What time can it be? What time do you think it must be?
Será la una.	It must be one.
Estará comiendo ahora.	He's probably eating now.

4. The preterite:
There are two sets of regular preterite endings:

1. One set is used with the stem of Conjugation I (*-ar*):	2. The other set is used with the stem of Conjugation II (*-er*) and Conjugation III (*-ir*):
-é	*-í*
-aste	*-iste*
-ó	*-ió*
-amos	*-imos*
-asteis	*-isteis*
-aron	*-ieron*

There are several verbs that are irregular in the preterite. (See verb charts at the end of this section.)

The preterite expresses an action that began in the past and ended in the past:

El lo dijo.	He said it.
Habló conmigo.	He spoke with me.
Fui allí.	I went there.
El nos vio.	He saw us.
Escribí una carta.	I wrote a letter.
Llovió todo el día.	It rained all day.
El tren se paró.	The train stopped.
Pasó tres años allí.	He spent three years there
Lo vi.	I saw him (it).

5. The present perfect:
The present perfect is formed by adding the past participle to the present tense of *haber.* It is used to indicate a past action which continues into the present or which ended only recently:

Ha venido con su amigo.	He has come with his friend.
Nos ha escrito.	He has written to us.

6. The pluperfect:
   The pluperfect is formed by adding the past participle to the imperfect of *haber*. It translates the English past perfect (pluperfect):

Ya habían llegado.	They had already arrived.

7. The future perfect:
   The future perfect is formed by adding the past participle to the future of *haber*. It translates the English future perfect:

Habrán llegado para entonces.	They will have arrived by then.

It also indicates probability:

Habrán llegado ayer.	They probably arrived yesterday.

8. The preterite perfect:
   The preterite perfect, which is rather rare, is formed by adding the past participle to the preterite of *haber*. It is used to indicate that something occurred immediately before some other action in the past:

Apenas hubo oído eso, se marchó.	No sooner had he heard that than he left.

29. THE SUBJUNCTIVE

The indicative simply makes a statement; the subjunctive indicates a certain attitude towards the statement—uncertainty, desire, emotion, etc. The subjunctive is used in subordinate clauses when the statement is unreal, doubtful, indefinite, subject to some condition, or is affected by will, emotion, etc.

1. Forms
   a. The subjunctive endings of the second and third conjugations are the same.

b. The present subjunctive is formed by adding the subjunctive endings to the stem of the first person singular, present indicative; the imperfect and future subjunctive, by adding the endings to the stem of the third person plural, preterite.

The subjunctive endings are as follows:

Conjugation I

PRES. SUBJ.:	*-e, -es, -e, -emos, -éis, -en*
IMPERF. SUBJ.:	*-ara, -aras, -ara,* *-áramos, -arais, -aran* Or— *-ase, -ases, -ase,* *-ásemos, -aseis, -asen*

Conjugations II and III

PRES. SUBJ.:	*-a, -as, -a, -amos, -áis, -an*
IMPERF. SUBJ.:	*-iera, -ieras, -iera,* *-iéramos, -ierais, -ieran* Or— *-iese, -ieses, -iese,* *-iésemos, -ieseis, -iesen*

EXAMPLES

	I	II	III
INFINITIVE:	*hablar*	*comer*	*vivir*
PRES. SUBJ.:	*hable*	*coma*	*viva*
IMP. SUBJ.:	*hablara* (*hablase*)	*comiera* (*comiese*)	*viviera* (*viviese*)

2. Uses

a. The subjunctive is used with verbs of desire, request, suggestion, permission, approval and disapproval, judgment, opinion, uncertainty, emotion, surprise, fear, denial, etc.:

¡Quisiera verlo!	How I'd like to see him!
¡Ojalá que lo haga!	I wish he would do it!
¡Ojalá lo supiera!	I wish I knew it!
Temo que se lo diga él.	I'm afraid he may tell it to him.
No creo que él lo haya visto.	I don't believe he's seen him.
Niega que lo haya visto.	He denies that he's seen him.
Me sorprende mucho que él no lo haya hecho.	I'm greatly surprised that he hasn't done it.
Espero que no venga.	I hope he doesn't come.
Me alegro de que Ud. esté aquí.	I'm glad you're here!
Temo que esté enfermo.	I'm afraid he's sick.
Temo que no llegue a tiempo.	I'm afraid he won't (may not) come in time.
Duda que lo hagamos.	He doubts that we'll do it.
Dudo que sea verdad.	I doubt that it's true.
Dudo que sea posible.	I doubt it's possible.
No creo que lo sepa.	I don't think he knows it.
Se lo digo para que lo sepa.	I'm telling you so you'll know it.

b. The subjunctive is used in commands:

1. Affirmative and negative commands in the polite (*usted/ustedes*) forms[1]:

1. In Latin America, *ustedes* is both familiar and polite.

¡Abra usted la ventana!	Open the window!
¡No hablen ustedes ahora!	Don't talk now!

2. Negative commands in the familiar forms:

¡No me digas (tú)!	Don't tell me!
¡No habléis ahora!	Don't talk now!

3. Suggestions in which the speaker is included:

¡Leamos!	Let's read!
¡Entremos!	Let's go in!

4. Indirect commands (that is, commands in the third person):

Que vaya él.	Let him go.
¡(Que) Viva España!	Long live Spain!
¡Que vengan!	Let them come!
¡Que entren!	Let them come in!
¡Que no venga!	Let him not come!

c. The subjunctive is used in conditional sentences which are contrary to fact:

Si estaba allí, yo no lo ví.	If he was there, I didn't see him. (*Indicative*)
No iremos si llueve.	If it rains, we won't go. (*Indicative*)

But—

Si fuese él, lo haría.	If I were he, I'd do it.
Si fuera mío esto, lo vendería.	If this were mine, I'd sell it.
Si tuviera el dinero, lo compraría.	If I had the money, I'd buy it.
Aunque hubiese tenido dinero no hubiera ido.	Even if I had had the money I wouldn't have gone.

Si lo hubiera sabido, no habría venido.	If I had known it, I wouldn't have come.
Si hubiese estado aquí, habríamos ido.	If he had been here, we would have gone.
Aunque lo hubiese intentado, no hubiera podido hacerlo.	Even if I had tried, I wouldn't have been able to do it.

d. The subjunctive is used after impersonal verbs which do not express certainty:

Es menester que vengan.	It's necessary for them to come.
Es preciso que estén aquí.	It's necessary for them to be here.
Es necesario que Ud. venga.	It's necessary that you come.
Es posible que lo tenga.	It's possible that he has it.
Fue una lástima que no vinieran.	It was a pity that they didn't come.

e. The subjunctive is used after various conjunctive adverbs:

1. Certain conjunctive adverbs are always followed by the subjunctive because they never introduce statements of accomplished fact:

antes (de) que	before
a condición de	on the condition that
aunque	even if
a (fin de) que	in order that
a menos que	unless
como si	as if
con tal (de) que	provided that, providing
dado que	granted that, given . . .
no obstante que	notwithstanding that
supuesto que	supposing that

2. Other conjunctive adverbs may or may not introduce a statement of accomplished fact. When they do, they take the indicative; otherwise the subjunctive:

a menos que	unless
a pesar de que	in spite of, notwithstanding
así que	as soon as
aunque	although, even though
con tal que	provided (that)
cuando	when
de manera que	so that
de modo que	so that
después (de) que	after
en cuanto	as soon as
hasta que	until
luego que	as soon as
mientras que	as long as, while
para que	in order that, so that
siempre que	provided that, whenever
Aunque él no lo quiera, se lo daré.	I'll give it to him even though he may not want it.
Lo compraré aunque me cueste mucho.	I'll buy it even if it costs me a lot.
Se lo digo para que lo sepa.	I'm telling you so that you will know it.
Aunque llueva mañana . . .	Although it may rain tomorrow . . .
Se fue sin que lo supiésemos.	He went away without our knowing it.
Iré con Ud. con tal que tenga tiempo.	I'll go with you provided I have time.
En caso que llegue . . .	In case he arrives . . .

Compare:

Iremos aunque llueve.	We'll go even though it's raining.
Iremos aunque llueva.	We'll go even if it rains (even if it should rain).

f. The subjunctive is used when the existence of an antecedent limited by an adjective (relative) clause is uncertain:

No hay ningún hombre que entienda esto.	There is no man who understands this.
Busco a alguien que hable español.	I'm looking for someone who speaks Spanish.
No conozco a nadie que pueda hacerlo.	I don't know anyone who can do it (could do it).

g. The subjunctive is used after compounds of *-quiera* "-ever": *quienquiera* "whoever," *dondequiera* "wherever," *cualquier* "whatever," "whichever":

Quienquiera que sea.	Whoever he (it) may be.
El quiere hacer cualquier cosa que ella haga.	He wants to do whatever she does.
El quiere ir donde quiera que ella vaya.	He wants to go wherever she goes.

30. THE CONDITIONAL

1. The present conditional of all verbs is formed by adding the following endings to the infinitive: *ía, ías, ía, íamos, íais, ían.* It translates into English as "would":

I	II	III
hablar to speak	*comer* to eat	*vivir* to live
hablaría	*comería*	*viviría*
hablarías	*comerías*	*vivirías*
hablaría	*comería*	*viviría*
hablaríamos	*comeríamos*	*viviríamos*
hablaríais	*comeríais*	*viviríais*
hablarían	*comerían*	*vivirían*

Sometimes it expresses probability or conjecture:

Serían las dos cuando él llegó.	It was (probably) about two o'clock when he arrived.
¿Qué hora sería?	What time could it have been?

2. The perfect conditional is formed by adding the past participle to the conditional of *haber*. It translates into English as "would have":

Habría hablado.	I would have spoken.
Habría ido.	I would have gone.

3. If a sentence contains a clause beginning with *si* "if," the tense of the verb is determined by the tense of the verb in the main clause.

If the main clause has a verb in the:	The "if" clause has a verb in the:
Present	Present
Future	Present
Imperfect	Imperfect
Preterite	Preterite
Conditional	Past Subjunctive (*-ra* or -se)

Si está aquí, trabaja.	If he is here, he is working.
Si estaba aquí, trabajaba.	If he was here, he was working.
Si está aquí mañana, trabajará.	If he's here tomorrow, he'll be working.
Si estuviera aquí, trabajaría.	If he were here, he'd be working.

A main verb indicating a condition contrary to fact may be in the *-ra* form of the subjunctive.

Si estuviera aquí, trabajara.	If he were here, he'd be working.

31. COMMANDS AND REQUESTS (THE IMPERATIVE)

There are two types of commands, one with *tú* (*vosotros*) and one with *usted* (*ustedes*).

1. Familiar commands (*tú*)
   Familiar commands are used with people to whom you would say *tú.* The singular is the same as the third person singular of the present indicative:

¡Habla (tú)!	Speak!
¡Come (tú)!	Eat!
¡Sube (tú)!	Go up!

The plural is always formed by removing the *-r* of the infinitive and adding *-d:*

I

hablar to speak

SINGULAR:	*¡Habla (tú)!*	Speak!
PLURAL:	*¡Hablad (vosotros, -as)!*	Speak!

II

aprender to learn

SINGULAR:	*¡Aprende (tú)!*	Learn!
PLURAL:	*¡Aprended (vosotros, -as)!*	Learn!

III

escribir to write

PLURAL:	*¡Escribe (tú)!*	Write!
SINGULAR:	*¡Escribid (vosotros, -as)!*	Write!

Common exceptions in the singular (the plural is always regular):

INFINITIVE		IMPERATIVE SINGULAR	IMPERATIVE PLURAL
ser	to be	*sé*	*sed*
decir	to say	*di*	*decid*
ir	to go	*ve*	*id*
hacer	to do	*haz*	*haced*
poner	to put	*pon*	*poned*
tener	to hold	*ten*	*tened*
venir	to come	*ven*	*venid*

Familiar commands in the negative are in the present subjunctive:

SINGULAR

¡No hables!	Don't speak!
¡No me hables!	Don't talk to me!
¡No comas!	Don't eat!

PLURAL

¡No habléis!	Don't speak!
¡No comáis!	Don't eat!

Other examples:

¡Háblame!	Speak to me!
¡Háblales!	Speak to them!
¡No les hables!	Don't speak to them!
¡Hablad!	Speak!
¡No habléis!	Don't speak!
¡Dame!	Give me!
¡No me des!	Don't give me!
¡Dímelo!	Tell it to me!
¡No me lo digas (tú)!	Don't tell it to me!
¡No me digas (tú) eso!	Don't tell me that!
¡Decídnoslo!	Tell it to us!
¡No nos lo digáis!	Don't tell it to us!
¡No estudiéis demasiado!	Don't study too much!

Notice that the object pronouns follow the affirmative imperative (and are attached) and precede the negative imperative.

Note:

- In Latin America, as *vosotros/as* is not used, plural familiar commands are the same as plural polite commands (*Ustedes*). See below.

1. Polite commands (*Usted*)
   Polite commands are used with people to whom you would say *usted* and are in the subjunctive. To make the subjunctive you change the ending of the third person present indicative to *a* if it is *e*, and to *e* if it is *a*.

INDICATIVE		SUBJUNCTIVE	
Habla.	He speaks.	*Hable Ud.*	Speak!
Come.	He eats.	*Coma Ud.*	Eat!

The plural is formed by adding *n* to the singular:

¡Hablen Uds.!	Speak!
¡Coman Uds.!	Eat!
¡Desciendan Uds.!	Go down!

Other examples:

¡Cómalo (Ud.)!	Eat it!
¡Venga (Ud.) a verme!	Come to see me!
¡Tómelo!	Take it!
¡Dígamelo!	Tell it to me!
¡Escríbame (Ud.) una carta!	Write me a letter!
¡Escríbamelo!	Write it to me!
¡Abra (Ud.) la ventana!	Open the window!

NEGATIVE

¡No hable Ud.!	Don't speak!
¡No lo coma Ud.!	Don't eat it!
¡No me lo diga Ud.!	Don't tell me!
¡No me escriba Ud.!	Don't write to me!
¡No hablen Uds. demasiado!	Don't talk too much!

The object pronouns follow the affirmative imperative and are attached to it:

¡Léelo (tú)!	Read it!
¡Habladle!	Speak to him!
¡Véndamelo!	Sell it to me!
¡Díganmelo!	Tell it to me!

3. Indirect commands

   Indirect commands are in the subjunctive and are usually preceded by *que:*

¡Que entren!	Let them come in!
¡Que él lo haga!	Let him do it!
¡Que lo haga Juan!	Let Juan do it!
¡Que le hable María!	Let María talk to him!
¡Que venga!	Let him come!
¡Que vaya él!	Let him go!
¡Que no venga!	Let him not come!
¡(Que) Viva España!	Long live Spain!
¡(Que) Dios guarde a nuestro país!	God keep our country!

4. "Let's" is expressed by the subjunctive:

¡Hablemos un rato!	Let's talk a while!
¡No hablemos!	Let's not talk!
¡Vayamos!	Let's go!
¡Esperemos!	Let's wait!

5. Imperative of reflexive verbs
   The final *-d* of the plural is dropped when *-os* is added; that is, "*sentados*" becomes *sentaos:*

FAMILIAR FORM

SINGULAR

¡Siéntate!	Sit down!
¡Despiértate!	Wake up!
¡No te sientes!	Don't sit down!

PLURAL

¡Sentaos!	Sit down!
¡Despertaos! (*despertad + os*)	Wake up!
¡No os sentéis!	Don't sit down!

POLITE FORM

SINGULAR

¡Siéntese Ud.!	Sit down!
¡No se siente Ud.!	Don't sit down!

PLURAL[1]

¡Siéntense Uds.!	Sit down (*pl.*)!
¡No se sienten!	Don't sit down!
¡Sentémonos! (*sentemos + nos*)	Let's sit down!

32. THE PARTICIPLE

1. The present participle (also called the "gerund") of Conjugation I is formed by dropping the *-ar* of the infinitive and adding *-ando;* the present participle of Conjugations II and III is formed by dropping the *-er* (*-ir*) and adding *-iendo:*

I		II	
hablar	to speak	*comer*	to eat
hablando	speaking	*comiendo*	eating

III	
vivir	to live
viviendo	living

Pronoun objects are attached to the present participle (in such cases the verb has a written accent):

comprándolos	buying them
vendiéndomelo	selling it to me
dándoselo	giving it to him

The present participle is often used absolutely, describing some action or state of being of the subject of the sentence:

Por estar durmiendo, no me oyeron.	Since they were sleeping, they didn't hear me. (They didn't hear me because they were sleeping.)

1. Familiar and polite in Latin America.

Estando cansados, dormían.	Being tired, they were sleeping. (They were sleeping because they were tired.)

2. The past participle is formed by adding *-ado* to the stem of *-ar* verbs (that is, the infinitive minus *-ar*) and *-ido* to the stem of *-er* and *-ir* verbs:

I		II	
hablar	to speak	*comer*	to eat
hablado	spoken	*comido*	eaten

III	
vivir	to live
vivido	lived

3. Irregular participles
The following are some of the most common verbs with irregular present and past participles:

INFINITIVE		IRREGULAR PAST PARTICIPLE	IRREGULAR PRESENT PARTICIPLE
abrir	to open	*abierto*	
caer	to fall	*caído*	*cayendo*
creer	to believe	*creído*	*creyendo*
cubrir	to cover	*cubierto*	
decir	to say	*dicho*	*diciendo*
despedirse	to take leave of		*despidiéndose*
dormir	to sleep		*durmiendo*
escribir	to write	*escrito*	
hacer	to do, make	*hecho*	
ir	to go		*yendo*
leer	to read	*leído*	*leyendo*
morir	to die	*muerto*	*muriendo*

oír	to hear	*oído*	*oyendo*
pedir	to ask for		*pidiendo*
poder	to be able to		*pudiendo*
poner	to put	*puesto*	
romper	to break	*roto*	
seguir	to follow		*siguiendo*
sentir	to feel		*sintiendo*
traer	to bring	*traído*	*trayendo*
venir	to come		*viniendo*
ver	to see	*visto*	
volver	to return	*vuelto*	

33. PROGRESSIVE TENSES

The Spanish progressive tenses are made up of the forms of *estar* plus the present participle. As in English, they denote a continuing action (that is, they describe the action as ongoing):

Estoy trabajando aquí.	I'm working here.
Estábamos leyendo un periódico.	We were reading a newspaper.
Estoy divirtiéndome.	I'm having a good time.
Está hablando.	He's speaking.
Estaba esperándome.	He was waiting for me.

34. PASSIVE VOICE

The passive voice is made up of the forms of *ser* plus the past participle:

La carta fue escrita por ella.	The letter was written by her.

The passive is used as in English. Very often, however, Spanish uses the reflexive where English uses the passive:

Aquí se habla inglés.	English is spoken here.

35. TO BE

There are two words in Spanish for "to be": *ser* and *estar.* In general *ser* indicates a permanent state (I'm an American), and *estar* a temporary one (I'm tired).

SER	ESTAR	
yo soy	*yo estoy*	I am
tú eres	*tú estás*	you are
usted es	*usted está*	you are
él es	*él está*	he is
ella es	*ella está*	she is
ello es	*ello está*	it is
nosotros somos	*nosotros estamos*	we are
nosotras somos	*nosotras estamos*	we are
vosotros sois	*vosotros estáis*	you are
vosotras sois	*vosotras estáis*	you are
ustedes son	*ustedes están*	you are
ellos son	*ellos están*	they are
ellas son	*ellas están*	they are

SER

1. indicates a permanent condition or state:

Mi hermano es alto.	My brother is tall.

2. is used with a predicate noun, in which case it links two equal things:

El es médico.	He is a doctor.
Es escritor.	He's a writer.
Es español.	He's a Spaniard.

3. is used with an adjective to indicate an inherent quality.

El libro es rojo.	The book is red.
Ella es joven.	She is young.
El hielo es frío.	Ice is cold.
Es inteligente.	He's intelligent.
Es encantadora.	She's charming.

4. is used with pronouns:

Soy yo.	It is I.

5. indicates origin, source, or material:

¿De dónde es Ud.?	Where are you from?
Soy de España.	I'm from Spain.
Es de madera.	It's made of wood.
Es de plata.	It's silver.

6. indicates possession:

¿De quién es esto?	Whose is this?
Los libros son del señor Díaz.	The books belong to Mr. Díaz.

7. is used in telling time:

Es la una.	It's one o'clock.
Son las dos.	It's two o'clock.
Son las nueve y diez.	It's ten past nine.

8. is used to indicate cost:

Son a quince centavos la docena.	They are fifteen cents a dozen.
Son a nueve dólares cada uno.	They are nine dollars each.

9. is used in impersonal constructions:

Es tarde.	It's late.
Es temprano.	It's early.
Es necesario.	It's necessary.
Es lástima.	It's a pity.
¿No es verdad?	Isn't it?

ESTAR

1. expresses position or location:

Está allí.	He's over there.
Está en México.	He's in Mexico.
Nueva York está en los Estados Unidos.	New York is in the United States.
Los Andes están en Sudamérica.	The Andes are in South America.
El Canal está en Panamá.	The Canal is in Panama.
¿Dónde está el libro?	Where's the book?
Está sobre la mesa.	It's on the table.

2. indicates a temporary quality or characteristic:

Ella está contenta.	She's pleased.
Estoy cansado.	I'm tired.
Estoy listo.	I'm ready.
El café está frío.	The coffee's cold.
Está claro.	It's clear.
Le ventana está abierta (cerrada).	The window's open (shut).

3. is used to form the present progressive tense:

Están hablando.	They are talking.
Están caminando.	They are walking. They keep (on) walking.

4. is used in the expression "How are you?" etc.:

¿Cómo está Ud.?	How are you?
¿Cómo están ellos?	How are they?

Some adjectives may be used with either *ser* or *estar* with a difference in meaning.

El es malo.	He is bad.
El está malo.	He is sick.
Es pálida.	She has a pale complexion.
Está pálida.	She is pale (at this moment).

	With *ser*	With *estar*
bueno	good	well, in good health
listo	clever	ready, prepared
cansado	tiresome	tired

THE FORMS OF THE REGULAR VERBS
A. CONJUGATIONS I, II, III

INDICATIVE AND CONDITIONAL

infinitive	pres. & past participles	present indicative	imperfect	preterite	future	conditional	present perfect	pluperfect	preterite perfect
I. *-ar* ending	hablando	hablo	hablaba	hablé	hablaré	hablaría	he	había	hube
hablar	hablado	hablas	hablabas	hablaste	hablarás	hablarías	has	habías	hubiste
to speak		habla	hablaba	habló	hablará	hablaría	ha + hablado	había + hablado	hubo + hablado
		hablamos	hablábamos	hablamos	hablaremos	hablaríamos	hemos	habíamos	hubimos
		hablaís	hablabais	hablaréis	hablaréis	hablaríais	habéis	habíais	hubisteis
		hablan	hablaban	hablaron	hablarán	hablarían	han	habían	hubieron
II. *-er* ending	comiendo	como	comía	comí	comeré	comería	he	había	hube
comer	comido	comes	comías	comiste	comerás	comerías	has	habías	hubiste
to eat		come	comía	comió	comerá	comería	ha + comido	había + comido	hubo + comido
		comemos	comíamos	comimos	comeremos	comeríamos	hemos	habíamos	hubimos
		coméis	comíais	comisteis	comeréis	comeríais	habéis	habíais	hubisteis
		comen	comían	comieron	comerán	comerían	han	habían	hubieron
III. *-ir* ending	viviendo	vivo	vivía	viví	viviré	viviría	he	había	hube
vivir	vivido	vives	vivías	viviste	vivirás	vivirías	has	habías	hubiste
to live		vive	vivía	vivió	vivirá	viviría	ha + vivido	había + vivido	hubo + vivido
		vivimos	vivíamos	vivimos	viviremos	viviríamos	hemos	habíamos	hubimos
		vivís	vivíais	vivisteis	viviréis	vivirías	habéis	habíais	hubisteis
		viven	vivían	vivieron	vivirán	vivirían	han	habían	hubieron

		SUBJUNCTIVE						
future perfect	**conditional perfect**	**present**	**imperfect (-*r*-)**	**imperfect (-*s*-)**	**present perfect**	**pluperfect (-*r*-)**	**pluperfect (-*s*-)**	**affirm. imperative**
habré	habría	hable	hablara	hablase	haya	hubiera	hubiese	¡Habla (tú)!
habrás	habrías	hables	hablaras	hablases	hayas	hubieras	hubieses	¡Hable (Ud.)!
habrá + hablado	habría + hablado	hable	hablara	hablase	haya + hablado	hubiera + hablado	hubiese + hablado	¡Hablemos (nosotros)!
habremos	habríamos	hablemos	habláramos	hablásemos	hayamos	hubiéramos	hubiésemos	¡Hablad (vosotros)!
habréis	habríais	habléis	hablarais	hablaseis	hayáis	hubierais	hubieseis	¡Hablen (Uds.)!
habrán	habrían	hablen	hablaran	hablasen	hayan	hubieran	hubiesen	
habré	habría	coma	comiera	comiese	haya	hubiera	hubiese	¡Come (tú)!
habrás	habrías	comas	comieras	comieses	hayas	hubieras	hubieses	¡Coma (Ud.)!
habrá + comido	habría + comido	coma	comiera	comiese	haya + comido	hubiera + comido	hubiese + comido	¡Comamos (nosotros)!
habremos	habríamos	comamos	comiéramos	comiésemos	hayamos	hubiéramos	hubiésemos	¡Comed (vosotros)!
habréis	habríais	comáis	comierais	comieseis	hayáis	hubierais	hubieseis	¡Coman (Uds.)!
habrán	habrían	coman	comieran	comiesen	hayan	hubieran	hubiesen	
habré	habría	viva	viviera	viviese	haya	hubiera	hubiese	¡Vive (tú)!
habrás	habrías	vivas	vivieras	vivieses	hayas	hubieras	hubieses	¡Viva (Ud.)!
habrá + vivido	habría + vivido	viva	viviera	viviese	haya + vivido	hubiera + vivido	hubiese + vivido	¡Vivamos (nosotros)!
habremos	habríamos	vivamos	viviéramos	viviésemos	hayamos	hubiéramos	hubiésemos	¡Vivid (vosotros)!
habréis	habríais	viváis	vivierais	vivieseis	hayáis	hubierais	hubieseis	¡Vivan (Uds.)!
habrán	habrían	vivan	vivieran	viviesen	hayan	hubieran	hubiesen	

B. STEM-CHANGING VERBS

1. GROUP I: *-AR* AND *-ER* VERBS ONLY

a) Change the *o* to *ue* when the stress falls on the root (ex.: *contar, volver*).
b) Change the *e* to *ie* when the stress falls on the root (ex.: *pensar, perder*).

infinitive*	present indicative	present subjunctive	affirm. imperative	similarly conjugated verbs		
contar (*ue*)	cuento	cuente	cuenta	acordar	avergonzar	probar
to count	cuentas	cuentes	cuente	acordarse	avergonzarse	recordar
	cuenta	cuente	contemos	arostarse	colgar	recordarse
	contamos	contemos	contad	almorzar	costar	sonar
	contáis	contéis	cuenten	apostar	encontrar	soñar
	cuentan	cuenten		aprobar	jugar (*u* to *ue*)	volar
volver (*ue*)	vuelvo	vuelva	vuelve	devolver	oler	
to return	vuelves	vuelvas	vuelva	doler	soler	
	vuelve	vuelva	volvamos	dolerse		
	volvemos	volvamos	volved	llover		
	volvéis	volváis	vuelvan	morder		
	vuelven	vuelvan		mover		
pensar (*ie*)	pienso	piense	piensa	acertar	empezar	temblar
to think	piensas	pienses	piense	apretar	encerrar	tentar
	piensa	piense	pensemos	calentar	gobernar	
	pensamos	pensemos	pensad	cerrar	plegar	
	pensáis	penséis	piensen	confesar	quebrar	
	piensan	piensen		despertar	sentarse	
perder (*ie*)	pierdo	pierda	pierde	ascender	extender	
to lose	pierdes	pierdas	pierda	atender	tender	
	pierde	pierda	perdamos	defender		
	perdemos	perdamos	perded	descender		
	perdéis	perdáis	pierdan	encender		
	pierden	pierdan		entender		

* In all the other tenses, these verbs are conjugated like all other regular verbs.

2. GROUP II: *-IR* VERBS ONLY

a) Change *o* to *ue* when stress falls on root (ex.: *dormir); Change o* to *u* when stress falls on ending in the third person preterite forms, the *nosotros/vosotros* forms of the present subjunctive, all forms of the imperfect subjunctive, and the present participle.

b) Change *e* to *ie* when stress falls on root (ex.: *sentir*); Change *e* to *i* when stress falls on ending in the third person preterite forms, the *nosotros/vosotros* forms of the present subjunctive, all forms of the imperfect subjunctive, and the present participle (ex.: *sentir*).

infinitive*	present participle	present indicative	preterite	present subjunctive	imperfect subjunctive (*-r-*)	imperfect subjunctive (*-s-*)	affirm. imperative	similarly conjugated verbs
dormir to sleep	durmiendo	duermo duermes duerme dormimos dormís duermen	dormí dormiste durmió dormimos dormisteis durmieron	duerma duermas duerma durmamos durmáis duerman	durmiera durmieras durmiera durmiéramos durmierais durmieran	durmiese durmieses durmiese durmiésemos durmieseis durmiesen	duerme duerma durmamos dormid duerman	morir (past parti.: *muerto*)
sentir to feel	sintiendo	siento sientes siente sentimos sentís sienten	sentí sentiste sintió sentimos sentisteis sintieron	sienta sientas sienta sintamos sintáis sientan	sintiera sintieras sintiera sintiéramos sintierais sintieran	sintiese sintieses sintiese sintiésemos sintieseis sintiesen	siente sienta sintamos sentid sientan	advertir, herir arrepentirse, mentir consentir, preferir convertir, presentir diferir, referir divertir, sugerir

* In all the other tenses, these verbs are conjugated like all other regular verbs.

3. GROUP III: *-IR* VERBS ONLY

Change *e* to *i* in all persons of the present indicative except the first and second persons plural, all persons of the present and imperfect subjunctive, the third person preterite forms, the imperative forms (except for *vosotros*), and the present participle (ex.: *pedir*).

infinitive†	present participle	present indicative	preterite indicative	present subjunctive	imperfect subjunctive	affirm. imperative	similarly conjugated verbs	
pedir	pidiendo	pido	pedí	pida	pidiera (se)	pide	competir	expedir
to ask		pides	pediste	pidas	pidieras (ses)	pida	conseguir	reír
		pide	pidió	pida	pidiera (se)	pidamos	corregir	repetir
		pedimos	pedimos	pidamos	pidiéramos (semos)	pedid	despedir	seguir
		pedís	pedisteis	pidáis	pidierais (seis)	pidan	despedirse	servir
		piden	pidieron	pidan	pidieran (sen)		elegir	vestir

† In all the other tenses, these verbs are conjugated like all other regular verbs.

C. REGULAR VERBS WITH SPELLING CHANGES

1. VERBS ENDING IN -*CAR*

Example: *buscar* to look for

C changes to *qu* when followed by *e*. This occurs in:

1. the first person singular of the preterite indicative
2. all persons of the present subjunctive

PRETERITE INDICATIVE	PRESENT SUBJUNCTIVE
busqué	*busque*
buscaste	*busques*
buscó	*busque*
buscamos	*busquemos*
buscasteis	*busquéis*
buscaron	*busquen*

Verbs conjugated like *buscar:*

acercar	to place near	*sacrificar*	to sacrifice
educar	to educate	*secar*	to dry
explicar	to explain	*significar*	to signify, mean
fabricar	to manufacture	*tocar*	to touch, play (music)
indicar	to indicate		
pecar	to sin	*verificar*	to verify
sacar	to take out		

2. VERBS ENDING IN -*GAR*

Example: *pagar* to pay

G changes to *gu* when followed by *e*. This occurs in:

1. the first person singular of the preterite indicative

2. all persons of the present subjunctive

PRETERITE INDICATIVE	PRESENT SUBJUNCTIVE
pagué	*pague*
pagaste	*pagues*
pagó	*pague*
pagamos	*paguemos*
pagasteis	*paguéis*
pagaron	*paguen*

Verbs conjugated like *pagar:*

ahogar	to drown	*investigar*	to investigate
apagar	to extinguish	*juzgar*	to judge
arriesgar	to risk	*llegar*	to arrive
cargar	to load	*obligar*	to compel
castigar	to punish	*otorgar*	to grant
congregar	to congregate	*pegar*	to hit
entregar	to deliver	*tragar*	to swallow

3. VERBS ENDING IN *-GUAR*

Example: *averiguar* to ascertain, investigate

Gu changes to *gü* when followed by *e*. This occurs in:

1. the first person singular of the preterite indicative
2. all persons of the present subjunctive

PRETERITE INDICATIVE	PRESENT SUBJUNCTIVE
averigüé	*averigüe*
averiguaste	*averigües*
averiguó	*averigüe*
averiguamos	*averigüemos*
averiguasteis	*averigüéis*
averiguaron	*averigüen*

Verbs conjugated like *averiguar:*

aguar	to water, dilute
atestiguar	to attest

4. VERBS ENDING IN *-ZAR*

Example: *gozar* to enjoy

Z changes to *c* when followed by *e*. This occurs in:

1. the first person singular of the preterite indicative
2. all persons of the present subjunctive

PRETERITE INDICATIVE	PRESENT SUBJUNCTIVE
gocé	*goce*
gozaste	*goces*
gozó	*goce*
gozamos	*gocemos*
gozasteis	*gocéis*
gozaron	*gocen*

Verbs conjugated like *gozar:*

abrazar	to embrace	*organizar*	to organize
alcanzar	to reach	*rechazar*	to reach
cruzar	to cross	*rezar*	to pray
enlazar	to join	*utilizar*	to utilize

5. VERBS ENDING IN *-GER*

Example: *escoger* to choose

G changes to *j* when followed by *o* or *a*. This occurs in:

1. the first person singular of the present indicative
2. all persons of the present subjunctive

PRESENT INDICATIVE	PRESENT SUBJUNCTIVE
escojo	*escoja*
escoges	*escojas*
escoge	*escoja*

escogemos	*escojamos*
escogéis	*escojáis*
escogen	*escojan*

Verbs conjugated like *escoger:*

acoger	to welcome	*recoger*	to gather
proteger	to protect		

6. VERBS ENDING IN *-GIR*

Example: *dirigir* to direct

G changes to *j* when followed by *o* or *a.* This occurs in:

1. the first person singular of the present indicative
2. all persons of the present subjunctive

dirijo	*dirija*
diriges	*dirijas*
dirige	*dirija*
dirigimos	*dirijamos*
dirigís	*dirijáis*
dirigen	*dirijan*

Verbs conjugated like *dirigir:*

afligir	to afflict	*rugir*	to roar
erigir	to erect	*surgir*	to come forth
exigir	to demand		

7. VERBS ENDING IN *-GUIR*

Example: *distinguir* to distinguish

Gu changes to *g* when followed by *o* or *a.* This occurs in:

1. the first person singular of the present indicative
2. all persons of the present subjunctive

PRESENT INDICATIVE	PRESENT SUBJUNCTIVE
distingo	*distinga*
distingues	*distingas*
distingue	*distinga*

distinguimos	*distingamos*
distinguís	*distingáis*
distinguen	*distingan*

Verbs conjugated like *distinguir:*

conseguir	to get, obtain	*perseguir*	to persecute
extinguir	to extinguish	*seguir*	to follow

8. VERBS ENDING IN *-CER, -CIR* (PRECEDED BY A VOWEL)

Examples: *conocer* to know *lucir* to shine

Some verbs ending in *-cer, -cir,* preceded by a vowel, change *c* to *zc* before *o* or *a.* This occurs in:

1. the first person singular of the present indicative
2. all persons of the present subjunctive

conozco	*conozca*	*luzco*	*luzca*
conoces	*conozcas*	*luces*	*luzcas*
conoce	*conozca*	*luce*	*luzca*
conocemos	*conozcamos*	*lucimos*	*luzcamos*
conocéis	*conozcáis*	*lucís*	*luzcáis*
conocen	*conozcan*	*lucen*	*luzcan*

Verbs conjugated like *conocer/lucir:*

aborrecer	to hate	*desaparecer*	to disappear
acaecer	to happen	*desobedecer*	to disobey
acontecer	to happen	*desvanecer*	to vanish
agradecer	to be grateful	*embellecer*	to embellish
amanecer	to dawn	*envejecer*	to grow old
anochecer	to get dark	*fallecer*	to die
aparecer	to appear	*favorecer*	to favor
carecer	to lack	*merecer*	to merit
compadecer	to pity	*nacer*	to be born
complacer	to please	*obedecer*	to obey

conducir	to drive	*ofrecer*	to offer
crecer	to grow	*oscurecer*	to grow dark
padecer	to suffer	*placer*	to please
parecer	to seem	*reconocer*	to recognize
permanecer	to last	*traducir*	to translate
pertenecer	to belong to		

9. VERBS ENDING IN *-CER*
(Preceded by a consonant)
Example: *vencer* to conquer

C changes to *z* when followed by *o* or *a*. This occurs in:

1. the first person singular of the present indicative
2. all persons of the present subjunctive

PRESENT INDICATIVE	PRESENT SUBJUNCTIVE
venzo	*venza*
vences	*venzas*
vence	*venza*
vencemos	*venzamos*
vencéis	*venzáis*
vencen	*venzan*

Verbs conjugated like *vencer:*

convencer	to convince	*ejercer*	to exercise

10. VERBS ENDING IN *-UIR* (BUT NOT *-GUIR* AND *-QUIR*)
Example: *construir* to build

Verbs ending in *-uir*, except those ending in *-guir* or *quir*, add *y* to the stem of the verb before *a, e, o*. This occurs in:

1. all persons of the present indicative (except the first and second familiar persons plural)
2. all persons of the present and imperfect subjunctive

3. the familiar imperative singular (*tú*)
4. third person singular and plural of the preterite

PRESENT INDICATIVE	PRESENT SUBJUNCTIVE
construyo	*construya*
construyes	*construyas*
construye	*construya*
construimos	*construyamos*
construís	*construyáis*
construyen	*construyan*

(*i* between two other vowels changes to *y*)

PRETERITE INDICATIVE	IMPERFECT SUBJUNCTIVE
construí	*construyera* (*se*)
construiste	*construyeras* (*ses*)
construyó	*construyera* (*se*)
construimos	*construyéramos* (*semos*)
construisteis	*construyerais* (*seis*)
construyeron	*construyeran* (*sen*)

IMPERATIVE

construye
construid

Verbs conjugated like *construir:*

atribuir	to attribute	*huir*	to flee
constituir	to constitute	*influir*	to influence
contribuir	to contribute	*instruir*	to instruct
destituir	to deprive	*reconstruir*	to rebuild
destruir	to destroy	*restituir*	to restore
distribuir	to distribute	*substituir*	to substitute
excluir	to exclude		

11. VERBS LIKE *CREER*

Creer to believe

In verbs whose stem ends in *e,* the *i* of the regular endings beginning with *-ie, ió,* becomes *y.* This occurs in:

1. the present participle (*creyendo*)
2. the third person singular and plural of the preterite indicative
3. both forms of the imperfect subjunctive

PRETERITE INDICATIVE	IMPERFECT SUBJUNCTIVE
creí	*creyera* (*se*)
creíste	*creyeras* (*ses*)
creyó	*creyera* (*se*)
creímos	*creyéramos* (*semos*)
creísteis	*creyerais* (*seis*)
creyeron	*creyeran* (*sen*)

Verbs conjugated like *creer:*

caer	to fall (irregular)	*leer*	to read
		poseer	to possess

12. VERBS LIKE *REIR*

Reír to laugh (also stem-changing, group III, *e* to *i*)

In verbs whose stem ends in *i,* the *i* of the regular endings beginning with *-ie, -ió* is dropped to avoid two *i's.* This occurs in:

1. the present participle (*riendo*)
2. the third person singular and plural of the preterite indicative
3. all persons of both forms of the imperfect subjunctive

PRETERITE INDICATIVE	IMPERFECT SUBJUNCTIVE
reí	*riera (se)*
reíste	*rieras (ses)*
rió	*riera (se)*
reímos	*riéramos (semos)*
reísteis	*rierais (seis)*
rieron	*rieran (sen)*

Verbs conjugated like *reír: sonreír* to smile.

13. VERBS ENDING IN *-LLER, -LLIR, -ÑER, -ÑIR*

Example: *tañer* to toll

In *-er* and *-ir* verbs whose stem ends in *ll* or *ñ*, the *i* of the regular endings beginning with *-ie, -ió* is dropped. This occurs in:

1. the present participle (*tañendo*)
2. the third person singular and plural of the preterite indicative
3. all persons of both forms of the imperfect subjunctive

PRETERITE INDICATIVE	IMPERFECT SUBJUNCTIVE
tañí	*tañera (se)*
tañiste	*tañeras (ses)*
tañó	*tañera (se)*
tañimos	*tañéramos (semos)*
tañisteis	*tañerais (seis)*
tañeron	*tañeran (sen)*

Verbs conjugated like *tañer:*

bullir	to boil	*gruñir*	to growl

14. VERBS ENDING IN *-IAR, -UAR*

Examples: *enviar* to send *continuar* to continue

Some verbs ending in *-iar* or *-uar* take a written accent over the *i* or the *u* of the stem. There is no definite rule. This occurs:

1. in all persons of the present indicative (except the first plural and second plural familiar).
2. in all persons of the present subjunctive (except the first plural and second plural familiar).
3. in the singular of the familiar imperative (*tú*).

PRES. IND.	PRES. SUBJ.	PRES. IND.	PRES. SUBJ.
envío	*envíe*	*continúo*	*continúe*
envías	*envíes*	*continúas*	*continúes*
envía	*envíe*	*continúa*	*continúe*
enviamos	*enviemos*	*continuamos*	*continuemos*
enviáis	*enviéis*	*continuáis*	*continuéis*
envían	*envíen*	*continúan*	*continúen*

IMPERATIVE

envía	*continúa*
enviad	*continuad*

Verbs conjugated like *enviar:*

confiar	to trust	*desconfiar*	to distrust
criar	to bring up	*fiar*	to give credit
desafiar	to challenge	*guiar*	to guide

Verbs conjugated like *continuar:*

actuar	to act	*evaluar*	to evaluate
efectuar	to carry out	*perpetuar*	to perpetuate

THE FORMS OF THE IRREGULAR VERBS

infinitive, present and past participles	present indicative	present subjunctive	imperfect	preterite	future	conditional	affirm. imperative
andar "to walk" *andando* *andado*	ando andas anda andamos andáis andan	ande andes ande andemos andéis anden	andaba andabas andaba andábamos andabais andaban	anduve anduviste anduvo anduvimos anduvisteis anduvieron	andaré andarás andará andaremos andaréis andarán	andaría andarías andaría andaríamos andaríais andarían	anda ande andemos andad anden
caber "to fit," "to be contained in" *cabiendo* *cabido*	quepo cabes cabe cabemos cabéis caben	quepa quepas quepa quepamos quepáis quepan	cabía cabías cabía cabíamos cabíais cabían	cupe cupiste cupo cupimos cupisteis cupieron	cabré cabrás cabrá cabremos cabréis cabrán	cabría cabrías cabría cabríamos cabríais cabrían	cabe quepa quepamos cabed quepan
caer "to fall" *cayendo* *caido*	caigo caes cae caemos caéis caen	caiga caigas caiga caigamos caigáis caigan	caía caías caía caíamos caíais caían	caí caíste cayó caímos caísteis cayeron	caeré caerás caerá caeremos caerís caerán	caería caerías caería caeríamos caeríais caerían	cae caiga caigamos caed caigan
conducir "to lead," "to drive" *conduciendo* *conducido*	conduzco conduces conduce conducimos conducís conducen	conduzca conduzcas conduzca conduzcamos conduzcáis conduzcan	conducía conducías conducía conducíamos conducíais conducían	conduje condujiste condujo condujimos condujisteis condujeron	conduciré conducirás conducirá conduciremos conduciréis conducirán	conduciría conducirías conduciría conduciríamos conduciríais conducirían	conduce conduzca conduzcamos conducid conduzcan

dar "to give" *dando* *dado*	doy das da damos dais dan	dé des dé demos deis den	daba dabas daba dábamos dabais daban	di diste dio dimos disteis dieron	daré darás dará daremos daréis darán	daría darías daría daríamos daríais darían	da dé demos dad den
decir "to say," "to tell" *diciendo* *dicho*	digo dices dice decimos decís dicen	diga digas diga digamos digáis digan	decía decías decía decíamos decíais decían	dije dijiste dijo dijimos dijisteis dijeron	diré dirás dirá diremos diréis dirán	diría dirías diría diríamos diríais dirían	di diga digamos decid digan
estar "to be" *estando* *estado*	estoy estás está estamos estáis están	esté estés esté estemos estéis estén	estaba estabas estaba estábamos estábais estaban	estuve estuviste estuvo estuvimos estuvisteis estuvieron	estaré estarás estará estaremos estaréis estarán	estaría estarías estaría estaríamos estaríais estarían	está esté estemos estad estén
haber "to have" (auxiliary) *habiendo* *habido*	he has ha hemos habéis han	haya hayas haya hayamos hayáis hayan	había habías había habíamos habíais habían	hube hubiste hubo hubimos hubisteis hubieron	habré habrás habrá habremos habréis habrán	habría habrías habría habríamos habríais habrían	

* To form compound tenses, use the appropriate form of *haber* together with the past participle of the irregular verb.

THE FORMS OF THE IRREGULAR VERBS

infinitive, present and past participles	present indicative	present subjunctive	imperfect	preterite	future	conditional	affirm. imperative
hacer	hago	haga	hacía	hice	haré	haría	haz
"to do,"	haces	hagas	hacías	hiciste	harás	harías	haga
"to make"	hace	haga	hacía	hizo	hará	haría	hagamos
haciendo	hacemos	hagamos	hacíamos	hicimos	haremos	haríamos	haced
hecho	hacéis	hagáis	hacíais	hicisteis	haréis	haríais	hagan
	hacen	hagan	hacían	hicieron	harán	harían	
ir "to go"	voy	vaya	iba	fui	iré	iría	ve
yendo	vas	vayas	ibas	fuiste	irás	irías	vaya
ido	va	vaya	iba	fue	irá	iría	vayamos
	vamos	vayamos	ibamos	fuimos	iremos	iríamos	id
	vais	vayáis	ibais	fuisteis	iréis	iríais	vayan
	van	vayan	iban	fueron	irán	irían	
oír "to hear"	oigo	oiga	oía	oí	oiré	oiría	oye
oyendo	oyes	oigas	oías	oíste	oirás	oirías	oiga
oído	oye	oiga	oía	oyó	oirá	oiría	oigamos
	oímos	oigamos	oíamos	oímos	oiremos	oiríamos	oíd
	oís	oigáis	oíais	oísteis	oiréis	oiríais	oigan
	oyen	oigan	oían	oyeron	oirán	oirían	
poder	puedo	pueda	podía	pude	podré	podría	puede
"to be able,"	puedes	puedas	podías	pudiste	podrás	podrías	pueda
"can"	puede	pueda	podía	pudo	podrá	podría	podamos
pudiendo	podemos	podamos	podíamos	pudimos	podremos	podríamos	poded
podido	podéis	podáis	podíais	pudisteis	podréis	podríais	puedan
	pueden	puedan	podían	pudieron	podrán	podrían	

poner "to put," "to place" *poniendo* *puesto*	pongo pones pone ponemos ponéis ponen	ponga pongas ponga pongamos pongáis pongan	ponía ponías ponía poníamos poníais ponían	puse pusiste puso pusimos pusisteis pusieron	pondré pondrás pondrá pondremos pondréis pondrán	pondría pondrías pondría pondríamos pondríais pondrían	pon ponga pongamos poned pongan
querer "to want," "to love" *quieriendo* *querido*	quiero quieres quiere queremos queréis quieren	quiera quieras quiera queramos queráis quieran	quería querías quería queríamos queríais querían	quise quisiste quiso quisimos quisisteis quisieron	querré querrás querrá querremos querréis querrán	querría querrías querría querríamos querríais querrían	quiere quiera queramos quered quieran
reír "to laugh" *riendo* *reído*	río ríes ríe reímos reís ríen	ría rías ría riamos riáis rían	reía reías reía reíamos reíais reían	reí reíste rió reímos reísteis rieron	reiré reirás reirá reiremos reiréis reirán	reiría reirías reiría reiríamos reiríais reirían	ríe ría riamos reíd rían
saber "to know" *sabiendo* *sabido*	sé sabes sabe sabemos sabéis saben	sepa sepas sepa sepamos sepáis sepan	sabía sabías sabía sabíamos sabíais sabían	supe supiste supo supimos supisteis supieron	sabré sabrás sabra sabremos sabréis sabrán	sabría sabrías sabría sabríamos sabríais sabrían	sabe sepa sepamos sabed sepan

THE FORMS OF THE IRREGULAR VERBS

infinitive, present and past participles	present indicative	present subjunctive	imperfect	preterite	future	conditional	affirm. imperative
salir "to go out," "to leave" *saliendo* *salido*	salgo sales sale salimos salís salen	salga salgas salga salgamos salgáis salgan	salía salías salía salíamos salíais salían	salí saliste salió salimos salisteis salieron	saldré saldrás saldrá saldremos saldréis saldrán	saldría saldrías saldría saldríamos saldríais saldrían	sal salga salgamos salid salgan
ser "to be" *siendo* *sido*	soy eres es somos sois son	sea seas sea seamos seáis sean	era eras era éramos erais eran	same as preterite of *ir*	seré serás será seremos seréis serán	sería serías sería seríamos seríais serían	sé sea seamos sed sean
tener "to have" *teniendo* *tenido*	tengo tienes tiene tenemos tenéis tienen	tenga tengas tenga tengamos tengáis tengan	tenía tenías tenía teníamos teníais tenían	tuve tuviste tuvo tuvimos tuvisteis tuvieron	tendré tendrás tendrá tendremos tendréis tendrán	tendría tendrías tendría tendríamos tendríais tendrían	ten tenga tengamos tened tengan

traer "to bring" *trayendo* *traído*	traigo traes trae traemos traéis traen	traiga traigas traiga traigamos traigáis traigan	traía traías traía traíamos traíais traían	traje trajiste trajo trajimos trajisteis trajeron	traeré traerás traerá traeremos traeréis traerán	traería traerías traería traeríamos traeríais traerían	trae traiga traigamos traed traigan
valer "to be worth" *valiendo* *valido*	valgo vales vale valemos valéis valen	valga valgas valga valgamos valgáis valgan	valía valías valía valíamos valíais valían	valí valiste valió valimos valisteis valieron	valdré valdrás valdrá valdremos valdréis valdrán	valdría valdrías valdría valdríamos valdríais valdrían	val valga valgamos valed valgan
venir "to come" *viviendo* *venido*	vengo vienes viene venimos venís vienen	venga vengas venga vengamos vengáis vengan	venía venías venía veníamos veníais venían	vine viniste vino vinimos vinisteis vinieron	vendré vendrás vendrá vendremos vendréis vendrán	vendría vendrías vendría vendríamos vendríais vendrían	ven venga vengamos venid vengan
ver "to see" *viendo* *visto*	veo ves ve vemos veis ven	vea veas vea veamos veáis vean	veía veías veía veíamos veíais veían	vi viste vio vimos visteis vieron	veré verás verá veremos veréis verán	vería verías vería veríamos veríais verían	ve vea veamos ved vean

LETTER WRITING

FORMAL INVITATIONS AND RESPONSES

Invitations

Marzo de 1996

Jorge Fernández y Sra. tienen el gusto de participar a Ud. y familia el próximo enlace matrimonial de su hija Carmen con el Sr. Juan García, y los invitan a la Ceremonia que se realizará en la Iglesia de Nuestra Señora de la Merced, el día 6 de los corrientes, a las 6 de la tarde. A continuación tendrá lugar una recepción en la casa de los padres de la novia en honor de los contrayentes.

March 1996

Mr. and Mrs. George Fernández take pleasure in announcing the wedding of their daughter Carmen to Mr. Juan García, and invite you to the ceremony that will take place at the Church of Nuestra Señora de la Merced, on the 6th of this month and year at 6 P.M. There will be a reception for the newlyweds afterward at the residence of the bride's parents.

Los señores Suárez ofrecen sus respectos a los señores García y les ruegen que les honren viniendo a comer con ellos el lunes próximo, a las ocho.

Mr. and Mrs. Suárez send their respects to Mr. and Mrs. García and would be honored to have their company at dinner next Monday at 8 o'clock.

Los señores Suárez y Navarro saludan afectuosamente a los señores Del Vayo y les ruegan que les honren asistiendo a la recepción que darán en honor de su hija María, el domingo 19 de marzo, a las nueve de la noche.

Mr. and Mrs. Suárez y Navarro greet Mr. and Mrs. Del Vayo cordially and request the honor of their presence at the party given in honor of their daughter María, on Sunday evening, March 19, at nine o'clock.

Responses

Los señores Del Vayo les agradecen infinito la invitación que se han dignado hacerles y tendrán el honor de asistir a la recepción del domingo 19 de marzo.

Thank you for your kind invitation. We shall be honored to attend the reception on March 19th.

Los señores García tendrán el honor de acudir al convite de los señores Suárez y entretanto les saludan cordialmente.

Mr. and Mrs. García will be honored to have dinner with Mrs. and Mrs. Suárez. With kindest regards.

Los señores García ruegan a los señores Suárez se sirvan recibir las gracias por su amable invitación y la expresión de su sentimiento al no poder aceptarla por hallarse comprometidos con anterioridad.

Mr. and Mrs. García thank Mr. and Mrs. Suárez for their kind invitation and regret that they are unable to come owing to a previous engagement.

THANK-YOU NOTES

5 de marzo de 1996

Querida Anita,

La presente es con el fin de saludarte y darte las gracias por el precioso florero que me has enviado de regalo. Lo he colocado encima del piano y no te imaginas el lindo efecto que hace.

Espero verte pasado mañana en la fiesta que da Carmen, la cual parece que va a ser muy animada.

Deseo que estés bien en compañía de los tuyos. Nosotros sin novedad. Te saluda cariñosamente, tu amiga.

Lolita

March 5, 1996

Dear Anita,

This is just to say hello and also to let you know that I received the beautiful vase you sent me as a gift. I've put it on the piano and you can't imagine the beautiful effect.

I hope to see you at Carmen's party tomorrow. I think it's going to be a very lively affair.

I hope your family is all well. Everyone here is fine.

Lolita

BUSINESS LETTERS

Aranjo y Cía
Paseo de Gracia, 125
Barcelona, España

2 de abril de 1996

Sres. González e hijos
Madrid, España

Muy señores nuestros:

Nos es grato presentarles al portador de la presente, Sr. Carlos de la Fuente, nuestro viajante, quien está visitando las principales ciudades de esa región. No necisitamos decirles que cualquier atención que le dispensen la consideraremos como un favor personal. Anticipándoles las gracias, nos es grato reiterarnos de Uds. como siempre,

Sus Attos. y. Ss.Ss.
Aranjo y Cía

____
Presidente.

Aranjo & Co., Inc.
125 Paseo de Gracia
Barcelona—Spain

April 2, 1996

González & Sons
Madrid
Spain

Gentlemen:

We have the pleasure of introducing to you the bearer of this letter, Mr. Carlos de la Fuente, one of our salesmen, who is visiting the major cities of your region. Needless to say, we shall greatly appreciate any courtesy you extend to him. (''It is needless to say to you that we shall consider any courtesy you extend him as a personal favor.'') Thanking you in advance, we remain

Very truly yours,

Aranjo & Co., Inc.

____
President

Panamá. 3 de marzo de 1996.

Sr. Julián Pérez
Buenos Aires, 90, Apdo. 22
Córdoba, Argentina

Muy señor mío:

Sírvase encontrar adjunto un cheque de $15 por un año de subscripción a la revista de su digna dirección.

Atentamente,

María Pérez de Perera
Apartado 98
Panamá, Rep. de Panamá

March 3, 1996

Mr. Julián Pérez
Buenos Aires, 90
P.O. Box 22
Córdoba, Argentina

Dear Sir:

Enclosed please find a check for $15.00 for a year's subscription to your magazine.

Very truly yours,

Mrs. María Perera
P.O. Box 98
Panama, Republic of Panama

INFORMAL LETTERS

Mi querido Pepe:

Me ha sido sumamente grato recibir tu última carta. Ante todo déjame darte la gran noticia. He decidido por fin hacer un viaje a Madrid, donde pienso pasar todo el mes de mayo.

Lolita viene conmigo. A ella le encanta la idea de conoceros.

Los negocios marchan bien por ahora y confío en que continuará la buena racha. El otro día estuve con Antonio y me preguntó por ti.

Procura reservarnos una habitación en el Nacional, que te lo agradeceré mucho.

Escríbeme pronto. Da mis recuerdos a Elena y tú recibe un abrazo de tu amigo,

Juan

Dear Pepe,

I was very happy to get your last letter. First of all, let me give you the big news. I have finally decided to make a trip to Madrid, where I expect to spend all of May.

Lolita is coming with me. She is extremely happy to be able to meet the two of you at last.

Business is good now and I hope will keep up that way ("that the good wind will continue"). I saw Antonio the other day and he asked me about you.

I'd appreciate your trying to reserve a room for us at the National.

Write soon. Give my regards to Elena.

Yours,
Juan

FORMS OF SALUTATIONS AND COMPLIMENTARY CLOSINGS

A. Salutations:

FORMAL

Señor:	Sir:
Señora:	Madam:
Señorita:	Miss:
Muy señor mío:	Dear Sir:
Muy señores míos:	Gentlemen:
Estimada señora:	Dear Madam:
De mi consideración:	Dear Sir/Madam:
Muy distinguida señora:	Dear Madam:
Muy señor nuestro:	Dear Sir:
Muy señores nuestros:	Gentlemen:
Señora profesora:	My dear Professor:
Excelentísimo señor:	Dear Sir: ("Your Excellency:")
Estimado amigo:	Dear Friend:
Querida amiga:	Dear Friend:

INFORMAL

Don Antonio (Aguilera):	My dear Mr. Aguilera:
Doña María (de Suárez):	My dear Mrs. Suárez:
Señorita Lolita (Suárez):	My dear Miss Suárez:
Antonio:	Anthony:
Querida Lolita:	Dear Lolita:
Mi querida Lolita:	My dear Lolita:
Amado mío:	My beloved:
Querida mía:	My dear: My beloved:

B. COMPLIMENTARY CLOSINGS:

FORMAL

The following are equivalent to our "Very sincerely yours":

Su atto. y S.S. (Su atento y seguro servidor)
Sus Attos. y Ss. Ss. (Sus atentos y seguros servidores)
S.S.S. (Su seguro servidor)
Ss. Ss. Ss. (Sus seguros servidores)

INFORMAL

Cariñosamente,	Affectionately yours,
Atentamente,	Sincerely yours,
Sinceramente,	Sincerely yours,
Afectuosamente,	Affectionately yours,
Quien mucho le aprecia,	Affectionately,
De quien te estima,	Affectionately,
De su amigo que le quiere,	Affectionately,
De tu querida hija,	Your loving daughter,

Besos y abrazos
De todo corazón.
De quien la adora.
} With love,

C. FORM OF THE LETTER:

FORMAL

Estimado señor:
or *Muy señor mío:*
(Dear Sir:)

Atto. y S.S.[1]
(Yours truly,)

INFORMAL

Querido Juan:
(Dear John,)

Cariñosamente,
(Affectionately,)
or
Afectuosamente,
(Affectionately,)

1. *Atto. y S.S.* stands for *atento y seguro servidor.*

D. COMMON FORMULAS:

Beginning a letter—

1. *Me es grato acusar recibo de su atenta del 8 del corriente. Tengo el agrado de* . . . This is to acknowledge receipt of your letter of the 8th of this month. I am glad to . . .

2. *Obra en mi poder su apreciable carta de fecha 10 de marzo* . . . I have received your letter of March 10th.

3. *En contestación a su atenta carta de* . . . In answer to your letter of . . .

4. *De conformidad con su carta del* . . . In accordance with your letter of . . .

5. *Con referencia a su anuncio en "La Nación" de hoy* . . . In reference to your ad in today's issue of "The Nation" . . .

6. *Por la presente me dirijo a Ud. para* . . . This letter is to . . .

7. *Nos es grato anunciarle que* . . . We are pleased to announce that . . .

8. *Me es grato recomendar a Ud. al Sr.* . . . I take pleasure in recommending to you Mr. . . .

9. *La presente tiene por objeto confirmarle nuestra conversación telefónica de esta mañana* . . . This is to confirm our telephone conversation of this morning . . .

Ending a letter—

1. *Anticipándole las gracias, saludo a Ud. atentamente,*
   Thanking you in advance, I am,
   Sincerely yours,

2. *Anticipándoles las más expresivas gracias, quedamos de Uds.*
   Attos. y. SS.SS.
   Thanking you in advance, We are.
   Sincerely yours,

3. *Quedamos de Ud. atentos y Ss. Ss.*
   We remain
   Sincerely yours,

4. *En espera de sus gratas noticias, me repito de Ud.*
   Atento y S.S.
   Hoping to hear from you, I am
   Sincerely yours,

5. *Esperando su grata y pronta contestación, quedo,*
   Su atento y S.S.
   Hoping to hear from you at your earliest convenience, I remain
   Sincerely yours,

   The following are often used when beginning a business correspondence:

6. *Aprovecho esta ocasión para ofrecerme su atento y S.S.*
   I am taking advantage of this opportunity to introduce myself.

7. *Aprovechamos esta ocasión para suscribirnos,*
   Sus atentos y SS.SS.
   We are taking this opportunity to introduce ourselves.

FORM OF THE ENVELOPE

Félix Valbuena y Cía.
Calle de Zurbarán, 6
Madrid

Señor Don
Ricardo Fitó,
Apartado 5042,
Barcelona

M. Navarro Suárez
San Martín Vía Aérea 820
Buenos Aires, Argentina

Señores
M. Suárez y Coello,
Paseo de la Castellana, 84
28002 Madrid, España

Señorita
Lolita Navarro,
Gran Vía de Germanías, 63
Valencia

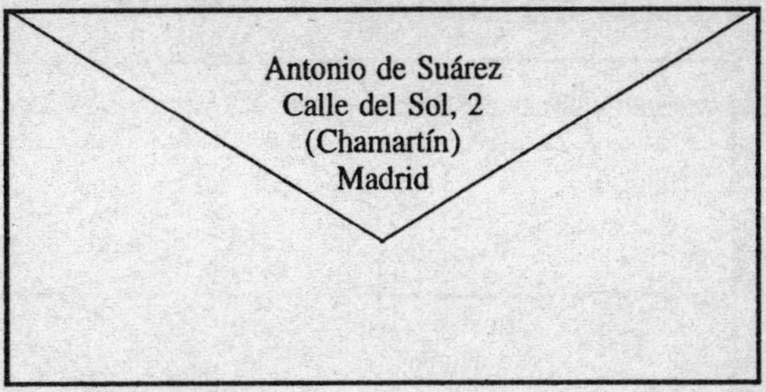

OTHER EXAMPLES

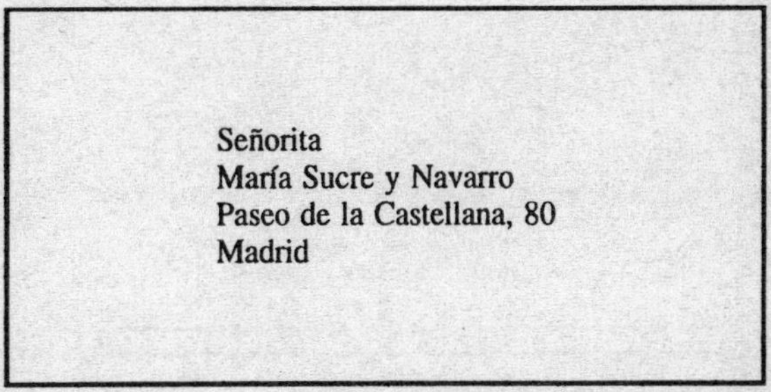

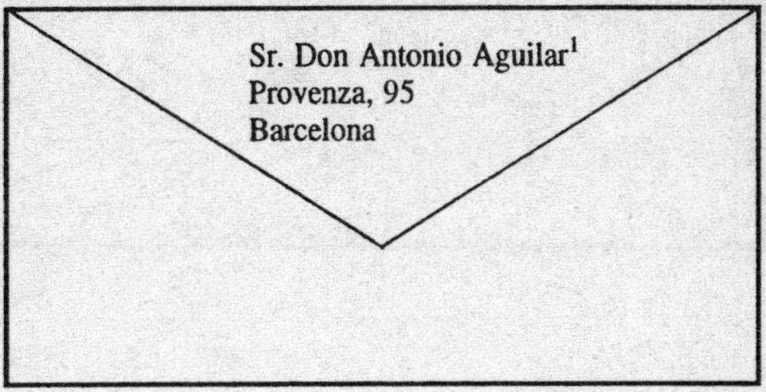

1. To a doctor: *Sr. Dr. Antonio Aguilar.*
To an engineer: *Sr. Ing. Don Antonio Aguilar.*

ANSWERS

TO EXERCISES

ANSWERS

LESSON 1

Exercises

B. 1. *Acabamos de llegar.*
We have just arrived.
2. *Los niños tienen ganas de comer.*
The children want to eat.
3. *Ustedes pueden hacerlo.*
You can do it.
4. *Las muchachas están contentas de verlos.*
The girls are happy to see them.
5. *Lo podemos hacer ahora.*
We can do it now.

C. 1. *El acaba de entrar.*
2. *Ella acaba de comer.*
3. *Tenemos ganas de ir al cine.*
4. *Tengo ganas de bailar.*
5. *Puedo hacerlo ahora.*
6. *Podemos verla mañana.*
7. *Ellos podrán ir allá.*
8. *Estoy contento de verle a usted.*
9. *Estamos sorprendidos de oírlo.*
10. *Están contentos de saberlo.*

D. 1. *¿Quién habla?*
Who's speaking?
2. *¡Qué gusto!*
What a pleasure!
3. *¡Qué manera más agradable de empezar el día!*
What a pleasant way to begin the day!
4. *Espero que hayan tenido buen viaje.*
I hope that you have had a good trip.
5. *Vimos a Miguel en el Café Gijón.*
We saw Miguel at the Café Gijón.

6. *Estábamos aquí todo el día.*
   We were here all day.
7. *Hay muchos monumentos en Madrid.*
   There are many monuments in Madrid.
8. *¿Quiere usted sentarse aquí?*
   Do you want to sit down here?
9. *El señor tiene tanto dinero.*
   The man has so much money.
10. *Acabamos de llegar.*
    We have just arrived.

LESSON 2

Exercises

B. 1. *Ellos saben bailar.*
   They know how to dance.
2. *Ustedes conocerán a los señores Pérez.*
   You will meet Mr. and Mrs. Pérez.
3. *Hay unas clases por la tarde.*
   There are some classes in the afternoon.
4. *Me hacen falta unas pesetas.*
   I need some pesetas.
5. *¿Quiénes son los médicos?*
   Who are the doctors?

C. 1. *¿Sabe usted el número?*
2. *Ellos saben bailar.*
3. *Había muchos desfiles.*
4. *¿Cuál de estos libros quiere usted?*
5. *¿Quiénes son esos hombres en la esquina?*
6. *¿Qué necesita usted? ¿Qué le hace falta a usted?*
7. *¿Saben la dirección?*
8. *¿Quién conoce a María?*
9. *Les hacen falta muchas clases. Necesitan muchas clases.*
10. *Nos hace falta más tiempo. Necesitamos más tiempo.*

D. 1. *Estoy seguro de que ellos conocen a María.*
   I'm sure they know María.
2. *Me dijeron que ellos sabían el título del libro.*
   They told me that they knew the title of the book.

3. *Me hace falta un libro nuevo.*
   I need a new book.
4. *Hay una revista muy buena que sale el lunes.*
   There is a very good magazine which comes out on Monday.
5. *No me dijo cuál de estas novelas es mejor.*
   He didn't tell me which one of these novels is better.
6. *En este lado hay muchos periódicos extranjeros.*
   On this side there are many foreign newspapers.
7. *Esta revista alemana es interesante.*
   This German magazine is interesting.
8. *Este librito debe ser lo que quieren ustedes.*
   This little book should be what you want.
9. *Ellos tienen ganas de ir a la fiesta.*
   They feel like going to the party.
10. *Este libro le da a usted muchos informes.*
   This book gives you a great deal of information.

LESSON 3

Exercises

B. 1. *No me lo diga.*
   Don't say it to me.
2. *No te vayas.*
   Don't go away.
3. *No se lo ponga.*
   Don't put it on.
4. *No te lo quites.*
   Don't take it off.
5. *No me lo compres.*
   Don't buy it for me.

C. 1. *Trabajo más que Juan.*
2. *Viajarán más de tres horas hoy.*
3. *Tenemos más de diez páginas que leer.*
4. *Van a comprar un coche nuevo.*
5. *Va a descansar mañana.*
6. *Ibamos a vender la casa.*
7. *¿Quiere usted ver al médico?*

8. *Quiere darme el libro.*
9. *No se lo mande (a él).*
10. *Ellos no quieren marcharse.*

D. 1. *Usted encontrará la guía telefónica allí.*
You will find the telephone book there.
2. *Tenemos más dinero que ellos.*
We have more money than they do.
3. *Quieren mandarle el libro.*
They want to send the book to him.
4. *Tenía que entrar en la cabina.*
He had to go into the cabin.
5. *Dígale que estoy en Madrid.*
Tell him that I am in Madrid.
6. *Puedo hacer una llamada de larga distancia a Madrid.*
I can make a long-distance call to Madrid.
7. *¿Sabe usted el número?*
Do you know the number?
8. *No se lo diga.*
Don't tell it to him.
9. *Mándenoslo usted mañana.*
Send it to us tomorrow.
10. *Ellos quieren mandarlos en seguida.*
They want to send them at once.

LESSON 4

Exercises

B. 1. *Ellos tienen que verlo mañana.*
They have to see it (or him) tomorrow.
2. *Nosotros tendremos que levantarnos temprano.*
We will have to get up early.
3. *Ellas están lavando los platos.*
They are washing the dishes.
4. *Vosotros tenéis que leer las novelas.*
You have to read the novels.
5. *Ustedes me dieron dos mil pesetas por los libros.*
You gave me two thousand pesetas for the books.

C. 1. *Juan compró el coche para su esposa.*
2. *Pagaron dos mil pesetas por los billetes.*
3. *Tenemos que marcharnos en seguida.*
4. *Están escribiendo cartas ahora.*
5. *¿Cuánto quiere usted por el traje?*
6. *Tiene que pasar por el parque para llegar al museo.*
7. *Le dieron doscientas mil pesetas para pagar el viaje.*
8. *Estaban esuchando la radio cuando llegué.*
9. *Para ver bien, hay que estar en la primera fila.*
10. *Miguel tiene que comprar un libro nuevo.*

D. 1. *Juan cree que tenemos que ir al banco.*
Juan thinks that we have to go to the bank.
2. *Paco pagó el billete.*
Paco paid for the ticket.
3. *Hace cuarenta kilómetros por hora.*
It does forty kilometers per hour.
4. *Los vimos andando por la calle.*
We saw them walking along the street.
5. *Nosotros estábamos sentados en la terraza.*
We were sitting (seated) on the terrace.
6. *Juan está leyendo el periódico.*
Juan is reading the newspaper.
7. *Esta propina es para el camarero.*
This tip is for the waiter.
8. *Ella tiene que comprar el traje.*
She has to buy the suit.
9. *No sé lo que quieren.*
I don't know what they want.
10. *Ellos van a los mismos sitios que nosotros.*
They are going to the same places we are.

LESSON 5

Exercises

B. 1. *Usted no se acuerda de María.*
You don't remember María.
2. *Hace una semana que Juan no está aquí.*
Juan hasn't been here for a week.

3. *Teresa no tiene que llamar al médico.*
   Teresa doesn't have to call the doctor.
4. *No se come bien en este restaurante.*
   The food isn't any good in this restaurant.
5. *Ellos no se acuerdan del viaje.*
   They don't remember the trip.

C. 1. *Hace un mes que están aquí.*
2. *Tiene que llamar al médico.*
3. *Me acuerdo muy bien de usted.*
4. *Hace dos horas que duermo.*
5. *Se come bien en este restaurante.*
6. *No veo a María.*
7. *Podemos sentarnos a descansar un rato.*
8. *Tenemos ganas de andar.*
9. *Tiene que doblar a la derecha.*
10. *Vamos a visitar el museo.*

D. 1. *Estoy aquí hace dos años.*
   I have been here for two years.
2. *Ellos viven en Madrid hace tres meses.*
   They have been living in Madrid for three months.
3. *¿Cuánto tiempo hace que está usted aquí?*
   How long have you been here?
4. *Aquí se habla ruso.*
   Russian is spoken here.
5. *Se encuentran muchos anuncios en el periódico.*
   One finds many ads in the newspaper.
6. *Creo que ellos se acuerdan de la fecha.*
   I think that they remember the date.
7. *Esta es una fiesta en la que se conoce a mucha gente simpática.*
   This is a party where one meets many nice people.
8. *¿Conoce usted a mi amigo?*
   Do you know my friend?
9. *Hace tres años que están en Nueva York.*
   They have been in New York for three years.
10. *Hace una hora que espero.*
   I have been waiting for an hour.

LESSON 6

Exercises

B. 1. *Ella va a comprárselo.*
She is going to buy it for him.
2. *Ellos quieren mandárselo* (*a él*).
They want to send it to him.
3. *Nosotros podemos regalárselos* (*a ella*).
We can give them to her.
4. *Tú prefieres pedírselo (a él).*
You prefer to ask him for it.
5. *Tenéis que enviárselo* (*a ellos*).
You have to send it to them.

C. 1. *Quieren dármelo.*
2. *Usted tendrá que pedírselo a él.*
3. *Queremos mandárselo a ellos.*
4. *Tendrá que ponérselo.*
5. *Nos gusta viajar por España.*
6. *Aquí los tiene usted. Aquí están.*
7. *Te gusta el helado.*
8. *Voy a buscárselo.*
9. *¿Quiere usted llevar el paquete?*
10. *Podemos mandárselo, si quiere.*

D. 1. *Aquí los tiene usted.*
Here they are.
2. *Quiere dármelos ahora.*
He/She wants to give them to me now.
3. *Dámelo.*
Give it to me.
4. *Los tenemos de todas clases.*
We have them in all styles.
5. *Aquí lo tiene usted.*
Here it is.
6. *Voy a buscarle el paquete.*
I am going to look for the package for you.
7. *Quiero comprar un vestido de seda.*
I want to buy a silk dress.

8. *¿Es demasiado caro? Creo que sí lo es.*
   Is it too expensive? I think it is.
9. *Aquí lo tiene usted.*
   Here it is. (Here you are.)
10. *¿Quiere usted mandármelas?*
   Do you want to send them to me?

LESSON 7

Exercises

B. 1. *Se lo digo al volver.*
   I'll tell it to you when you return.
2. *Juan me lo da.*
   Juan gives it to me.
3. *Usted tiene razón.*
   You are right.
4. *Vengo por la mañana.*
   I am coming in the morning.
5. *Ellos pueden dártelo.*
   They can give it to you.

C. 1. *¿Dónde estarán los billetes?*
2. *Habrán ido a casa.*
3. *Al entrar, él nos saludó. El nos saludó al entrar.*
4. *Usted puede pagarlo al salir.*
5. *Creo que él tiene razón.*
6. *Se lo doy a usted mañana.*
7. *¡Qué guapo estás!*
8. *Le hace falta un corte de pelo.*
9. *Iba a buscarte.*
10. *¿Le gusta el color?*

D. 1. *Será difícil.*
   It must be difficult. (It will be difficult.)
2. *Usted puede dármelo al salir.*
   You can give it to me when you leave.
3. *Creo que siempre tienes razón.*
   I think you are always right.
4. *¿Quién será?*
   Who can it be?

5. *Le señora está aquí al lado en la peluquería.*
   The lady is right next door in the beauty shop.
6. *Creo que voy mañana.*
   I think that I'm going tomorrow.
7. *Claro que usted empezó antes que yo.*
   Of course you began an hour before I did.
8. *Le gusta tener razón siempre.*
   You always like to be right.
9. *Nos saludamos al llegar al hotel.*
   We said hello upon arriving at the hotel.
10. *¿Hay algo más?*
    Is there anything else?

LESSON 8

Exercises

B. 1. *Nosotros somos actores.*
   We are actors.
2. *Ellos están en los Estados Unidos.*
   They are in the United States.
3. *Ustedes son de México.*
   You are from Mexico.
4. *Vosotros estáis cansados.*
   You are tired.
5. *Ellas están en la sala.*
   They are in the living room.

C. 1. *¿A qué hora empieza la función?*
2. *¡Qué gusto de verle otra vez!*
3. *Acabo de comprar este vestido.*
4. *Es una comedia muy divertida.*
5. *Vi una película el miércoles pasado.*
6. *No me acuerdo del título.*
7. *Va a volver a empezar. Va a empezar otra vez.*
8. *Un amigo mío fue a ver la comedia.*
9. *Le gustó a ella.*
10. *Vamos a entrar en seguida.*

D. 1. *¡Qué hermosa es la vida!*
   How beautiful life is!
2. *Usted encuentra las cosas siempre.*
   You always find things.

3. *Ellos dicen que pueden ir mañana.*
   They say that they can go tomorrow.
4. *¡Qué día más agradable!*
   What a pleasant day!
5. *Parece que él es un hombre muy importante.*
   It seems that he is a very important man.
6. *Yo lo entiendo todo.*
   I understand it all.
7. *Juana les cuenta una historia todos los días.*
   Juana tells them a story every day.
8. *¿Dónde estará el libro?*
   Where can the book be?
9. *El hermano de Juan era el héroe.*
   Juan's brother was the hero.
10. *¡Qué placer me da verles aquí!*
    What a pleasure it is for me (gives me) to see you here!

LESSON 9

Exercises

B. 1. *No escribo a nadie nunca.*
   I never write to anyone.
2. *No me escribe nadie.*
   No one writes to me.
3. *No compramos nada nunca.*
   We never buy anything.
4. *Juan y José no van nunca a ninguna parte.*
   Juan and José never go anywhere.
5. *No he visto nunca a tanta gente en el museo.*
   I've never seen so many people in the museum.

C. 1. *Hay tanta gente aquí.*
2. *Lo explicó tan claramente que lo comprendí todo.*
3. *Nunca he estado tan ocupado.*
4. *Usted estará cansado. Usted debe estar cansado.*
5. *Juan y María deben estudiar más.*
6. *No quiero verla nunca. Nunca quiero verla.*
7. *¡Qué alargadas parecen todas las figuras!*
8. *Tenemos que hacer un viaje a Toledo.*

9. *¿Cuándo podemos hacerlo?*
10. *Quiero ver la famosa pintura.*

D. 1. *Es tan difícil comprenderlo.*
It's so difficult to understand it.
2. *No lo veo nunca.*
I don't ever see him.
3. *Creo todo lo que me dice Juan.*
I believe everything that Juan tells me.
4. *Juan ha comprado todos los libros que quería.*
Juan bought all the books that he wanted.
5. *¡Roberto tiene tanto tiempo libre!*
Roberto has so much free time!
6. *No quiero nada ahora.*
I don't want anything now.
7. *Me parece que yo debo levantarme ahora.*
It seems to me that I ought to get up now.
8. *No he tenido nunca tantos problemas.*
I haven't ever had so many problems.
9. *No te debo nada.*
I don't owe you anything.
10. *Nunca ha leído libros tan difíciles.*
He has never read such difficult books.

LESSON 10

Exercises

B. 1. *No pienso nunca en el viaje.*
I don't ever think about the trip.
2. *No vamos al museo el lunes.*
We are not going to the museum on Monday.
3. *No le gusta comprar todo lo que ve.*
He doesn't like to buy everything he sees.
4. *Los niños no comieron todo el helado.*
The children didn't eat all the ice cream.
5. *No es difícil comprenderlo.*
It's not difficult to understand it.

C. 1. *Nos han hablado tanto del museo.*
2. *Se dice que es más divertido los domingos.*
3. *Podemos acompañarte mañana.*

4. *Hay que saber regatear.*
5. *No debes dar la impresión de ser rico.*
6. *Se conoce todo el trabajo de aquella fábrica por el estilo.*
7. *Se lo puedo dejar todo a muy buen precio.*
8. *Eso depende de lo que quiere decir.*
9. *Todos los cuadros son caros.*
10. *Debe tenerlos envueltos ahora.*

D. 1. *Le veo todos los martes.*
I see him every Tuesday.
2. *He pasado toda la tarde en la piscina.*
I spent all afternoon in the swimming pool.
3. *Juan estaba leyendo todo el día.*
Juan was reading all day.
4. *Voy a verle el domingo.*
I am going to see him on Sunday.
5. *Usted cree todo lo que él le dice.*
You believe everything that he says (he tells you).
6. *Normalmente voy a visitarlo todos los sábados.*
Normally I go to visit him every Saturday.
7. *El miércoles vamos a ir de compras.*
On Wednesday, we are going to go shopping.
8. *Nunca pienso en ella ahora.*
I never think about her now.
9. *Siempre oigo todas las noticias por radio.*
I always hear all the news on the radio.
10. *Yo no estaba pensando en comprarlo.*
I wasn't thinking of buying it.

LESSON 11

Exercises

B. 1. *Lo compras para él.*
You are buying it for him.
2. *Los señores Andrade hacen el viaje conmigo.*
Mr. and Mrs. Andrade are making the trip with me.
3. *No le veo jamás contigo.*
I never see him with you.

4. *Ellos me lo regalan a mí.*
   They are giving it to me.
5. *El cuadro es para usted.*
   The picture is for you.

C. 1. *Prefiero comprar aquella máquina en la otra tienda.*
2. *Debemos comprar por los menos dos rollos de película en color.*
3. *Podemos sacar unas fotos maravillosas de aquel parque.*
4. *¿Le gusta la vista con aquel edificio en el fondo?*
5. *Quieren sacarle una foto (de usted).*
6. *No se olvide de quitar la tapa del lente.*
7. *Tenemos que hacer copias para nuestros amigos.*
8. *Querían ir a aquel museo el domingo.*
9. *Tenemos que comprar más película en blanco y negro.*
10. *¿Cree usted que le guste aquel traje?*

D. 1. *Van a ir conmigo.*
   They are going to go with me.
2. *Déselo a él.*
   Give it to him.
3. *No me gustan aquellas lámparas. Déme dos de éstas.*
   I don't like those lamps. Give me two of these.
4. *La novela que más me gusta es ésa que tienes en la mano.*
   The novel that I like best is that one that you have in your hand.
5. *Esta alfombra es muy bonita pero, ¿recuerdas aquélla que vimos ayer?*
   This carpet is very pretty, but do you remember that one that we saw yesterday?
6. *Dicen que hay que estudiar mucho.*
   They say that one must study a great deal.
7. *Tenemos que llevar todos estos papeles a casa.*
   We have to take all of these papers home.
8. *La historia es muy interesante. Pablo no me contó todo eso.*
   The story is very interesting. Pablo didn't tell me all that.

9. *Hay muchas cosas que leer.*
   There are many things to read.
10. *Juan no me explicó todo el problema.*
    Juan didn't explain the whole problem to me.

LESSON 12

Exercises

B. 1. *Ellos no quieren ningún coche.*
   They don't want any car.
2. *Ellas no han comprado ningún regalo.*
   They didn't buy any gift.
3. *Esperamos que Juan llegue a tiempo.*
   We hope that Juan arrives on time.
4. *Ellas quieren que Teresa estudie esta noche.*
   They want Teresa to study tonight.
5. *Preferimos que usted se vaya.*
   We prefer that you go away.

C. 1. *Quieren que veamos la película.*
2. *Deseamos que tengan un buen viaje.*
3. *Juan quiere que usted compre película en color.*
4. *No hay dinero en esta chaqueta.*
5. *Se dice que es un gran hotel.*
6. (*El*) *Era un gran poeta.*
7. *No me dé usted un libro cualquiera.*
8. *¿Quiere usted que ellos lo hagan?*
9. (*El*) *Era un gran amigo.*
10. *Temo que no pueda irse ahora.*

D. 1. *Me alegro de que haga tan buen tiempo.*
   I am happy that the weather is so nice.
2. *¿Ha terminado usted el primer capítulo?*
   Have you finished the first chapter?
3. *Espero que nos veamos algún día.*
   I hope that we see each other some day.
4. *Juan no tiene nada de dinero.*
   Juan doesn't have any money.
5. *Es un hombre muy bueno.*
   He's a very good man.

6. *No me dé usted un libro cualquiera.*
   Don't give me just any book.
7. *Es una gran idea.*
   It's a great idea.
8. *Espero que te gusten las habitaciones.*
   I hope that you like the rooms.
9. *Prefieren que nosotros lo hagamos ahora.*
   They prefer that we do it now.
10. *Juan quiere que vayamos.*
    Juan wants us to go.

LESSON 13

Exercises

B. 1. *Se lo pedimos cuando lleguen.*
   We are going to ask them for it when they arrive.
2. *Me cobran trescientas pesetas por hora.*
   They are charging me 300 pesetas per hour.
3. *Ellos me lo dan para que lo estudie.*
   They are giving it to me so that I will study it.
4. *No hay fiesta mañana.*
   There is no fiesta tomorrow.
5. *Juan lo compra para dármelo.*
   John is buying it to give it to me.

C. 1. *Le recomiendo que vaya a buscar el coche a la fábrica.*
2. *En cuanto al dinero, se lo daré (a él) cuando venga.*
3. *Cuando lleguen, Juan se lo dirá.*
4. *María puede marcharse cuando quiera.*
5. *Incluirán un porta-equipajes.*
6. *¿Cuánto cuesta el litro de gasolina?*
7. *Llévese todos los folletos que quiera.*
8. *Cuando haya escogido el modelo que quiere, vaya a la fábrica.*
9. *No hay impuestos sobre los precios de fábrica, ¿verdad?*
10. *¿Quiere usted conocer a un gran amigo mío?*

D. 1. *En cuanto a la gasolina, hay suficiente.*
As for the gasoline, there is enough.
2. *Cuando lleguen, vamos a darles el regalo.*
When they arrive, we are going to give them the gift.
3. *Usted puede hacerlo cuando quiera.*
You can do it whenever you want.
4. *Hace ciento veinte kilómetros por hora.*
It does 120 kilometers per hour.
5. *Voy a decirle el número a Juan, para que lo sepa.*
I am going to tell the number to Juan so that he'll know it.
6. *Hay que decírselo para que vengan pronto.*
One must tell it to them so that they will come at once.
7. *Escríbale los detalles para que lo comprenda bien.*
Write him the details so that he will understand it well.
8. *Hay que anunciarles el examen para que estudien.*
One must announce the examination to them so they will study.
9. *Dásela a María para que la lea.*
Give it to María so she will read it.
10. *Yo siempre les trato bien cuando están aquí.*
I always treat them well whenever they are here.

LESSON 14

Exercises

B. 1. *No me quedan ningunas pesetas.*
I don't have any pesetas left.
2. *¿No quiere usted algunos periódicos?*
Don't you want any newspapers?
3. *Ellos no tienen ningunas dificultades.*
They don't have any difficulties.
4. *No queríamos comprar ningunas revistas.*
We didn't want to buy any magazines.
5. *No me dieron ningunos papeles.*
They didn't give me any papers.

C. 1. *Creo que dejé unas cuantas cartas allí.*
2. *El oyó unos ruidos raros.*
3. *Eche un poco de agua en el radiador.*
4. *Acabo de comprar algunos sellos (postales).*
5. *¿Quiere usted volver a las cinco?*
6. *Haga usted sólo lo necesario.*
7. *Haremos todo lo que podamos.*
8. *Lo bueno es que llegamos temprano.*
9. *Estoy seguro que le gustará el coche.*
10. *Lo malo del asunto es que ellos no nos comprenden.*

D. 1. *Les voy a enviar unos programas del concierto.*
I am going to send them some programs of the concert.
2. *No me ha dado nada de dinero.*
He didn't give me any money.
3. *Me gustan las novelas románticas. ¿Tiene usted algunas?*
I like romantic novels. Do you have any?
4. *Voy a decírselo algún día.*
I am going to tell it to him someday.
5. *Eso precisamente es lo imposible del caso.*
That is precisely the impossible part of the matter.
6. *No se lo ha dicho a ninguno de sus amigos.*
He didn't tell it to any of his friends.
7. *Querían vender unos cuantos vestidos.*
They wanted to sell some dresses.
8. *Me gustó la comedia. Las primeras escenas fueron lo mejor de la obra.*
I liked the comedy. The first scenes were the best (thing) in the play.
9. *¿Le ha dado algo de dinero?*
Did you give him any money?
10. *Les he explicado lo más difícil.*
I have explained the most difficult part to them.

LESSON 15

Exercises

B. 1. *Ellos vinieron hace un año.*
They came a year ago.
2. *Ella me escribió hace un mes.*
She wrote me a month ago.
3. *Jorge se casó hace dos días.*
Jorge got married two days ago.
4. *Hoy es el quince de agosto. María se marchó hace tres días.*
Today is the fifteenth of August. María left three days ago.
5. *Me mandaron el libro hace un año.*
They sent me the book a year ago.

C. 1. *Hay tantos turistas que pasan por Port Bou.*
2. *¿Van a quedarse en Francia mucho tiempo?*
3. *Creía que sería mejor el martes.*
4. *No hay que abrir las maletas.*
5. *Todos los papeles están en orden.*
6. *Dígale que espere un momento.*
7. *Espero verle en el viaje de vuelta.*
8. *Fue mucho más rápido que la última vez.*
9. *El vino hace un año.*
10. *Estamos en camino a Montecarlo.*

D. 1. *Juan llamó hace una hora.*
Juan called an hour ago.
2. *Nuestros amigos llegaron hace unas horas.*
Our friends arrived a few hours ago.
3. *Dígale que espere.*
Tell her to wait.
4. *El dice que lo puede hacer fácilmente.*
He says that he can do it easily.
5. *Lo hizo Juan hace mucho tiempo.*
Juan did it a long time ago.
6. *Dígales que vengan.*
Tell them to come.

7. *Los señores Andrade llegaron hace unos días.*
   Mr. and Mrs. Andrade arrived a few days ago.
8. *El jefe me lo dijo claramente.*
   The boss told it to me clearly.
9. *Dígale a María que escriba.*
   Tell María to write.
10. *¿Tienen ustedes algo que declarar?*
    Do you have anything to declare?

LESSON 16

Exercises

B. 1. *¿Se saludan Juan y José siempre que se vean?*
   Do Juan and José say hello whenever they see each other?
2. *¿Está buscando Rafael una secretaria que hable inglés?*
   Is Rafael looking for a secretary who speaks English?
3. *¿Van ellos a esperar hasta que lleguemos?*
   Are they going to wait until we arrive?
4. *¿Conoce usted a alguien que trabaje rápidamente?*
   Do you know anyone who works fast?
5. *¿Lo dirá María en cuanto lo sepa?*
   Will María say it as soon as she knows it?

C. 1. *Voy a buscar un libro que me guste.*
2. *No conocen a nadie que escriba poesía.*
3. *Juan esperará hasta que lleguemos.*
4. *¿Se ven siempre ustedes en París?*
5. *¿Me escribirá usted cuando llegue a Nueva York?*
6. *Dudo que estén aquí.*
7. *No creemos que Juan lo sepa.*
8. *Juan no cree que María venga.*
9. *El busca un banco que tenga sucursal en Madrid.*
10. *En cuanto lo compre, se lo enseñaré.*

D. 1. *No creo que María esté aquí.*
   I don't think María is here.
2. *Es imposible que ellos hagan tal cosa.*
   It's impossible for them to do such a thing.

3. *No hay ninguno que pueda hacerlo.*
   There is no one who can do it.
4. *Quiero encontrar una casa que tenga siete habitaciones.*
   I want to find a house that has seven rooms.
5. *Es imposible que ella crea la historia.*
   It's impossible for her to believe the story.
6. *Niegan que sea verdad.*
   They deny that it's true.
7. *Tenemos que esperar hasta que Juan hable.*
   We have to wait until Juan speaks.
8. *En cuanto ellos lo tengan, se lo mandarán a usted.*
   As soon as they have it, they will send it to you.
9. *Nos vemos todos los días.*
   We see each other every day.
10. *Busco una bolsa que sea bastante grande.*
    I am looking for a purse that is large enough.

LESSON 17

Exercises

B. 1. *Acostémonos.*
   Let's go to bed.
2. *Comprémoslo.*
   Let's buy it.
3. *No lo digamos.*
   Let's not say it.
4. *Lleguemos a tiempo.*
   Let's arrive on time.
5. *Estudiémoslo.*
   Let's study it.

C. 1. *Si Juan estuviera aquí, le daría el libro.*
2. *Si ellos tuvieran tiempo, irían a Barcelona.*
3. *Si María estuviera en París, compraría el vestido.*
4. *Si llueve, no iremos al teatro.*
5. *Si ellos nos ven, les hablaremos.*
6. *Si usted tuviera el coche, llegaríamos a tiempo.*
7. *Vamos a ir a la tienda.*
8. *No nos levantemos temprano mañana.*

9. *Busquemos el libro la semana que viene.*
10. *No se lo demos a Juan.*

D. 1. *Si yo fuera usted, no lo haría.*
If I were you, I wouldn't do it.
2. *Juan ganaría mucho más si trabajara más.*
Juan would earn a lot more if he worked harder.
3. *Yo se lo daría a los señores Andrade si estuvieran aquí.*
I would give it to Mr. and Mrs. Andrade if they were here.
4. *Si ellos leyeran el periódico, sabrían lo que ha pasado.*
If they read the newspaper, they would know what has happened.
5. *Levantémonos temprano mañana.*
Let's get up early tomorrow.
6. *No leamos el periódico esta mañana.*
Let's not read the newspaper this morning.
7. *No les decimos nada si llegan tarde.*
We won't say anything to them if they arrive late.
8. *No queremos ir al campo si llueve.*
We don't want to go to the country if it rains.
9. *Hablemos de lo que tenemos que hacer.*
Let's talk about what we have to do.
10. *Permítame contar las palabras.*
Let me count the words.

LESSON 18

Exercises

B. 1. *No tengo más que tres hermanos.*
I only have three brothers.
2. *No me cobraron más que cien pesetas.*
They charged me only 100 pesetas.
3. *No hay más que cinco sastres.*
They are only five tailors.
4. *No compraron más que cinco maletas.*
They only bought five suitcases.

5. *No murieron más que veinte soldados.*
   Only twenty soldiers died.

C. 1. *Tienen un coche mejor.*
2. *Somos mayores que ellos.*
3. *Este vestido es más caro.*
4. *Este jabón lava mejor.*
5. *La tela que compré es más suave.*
6. *Juana es la muchacha más bonita de la clase.*
7. *El es mi hijo menor.*
8. *Es la mejor revista del mundo.*
9. *No puedo escribir más.*
10. *El es más inteligente que su hermano mayor.*

D. 1. *No quiero estudiar más.*
   I don't want to study anymore.
2. *Juan es mucho más fuerte que José.*
   Juan is much stronger than José.
3. *Este edificio es bastante más grande.*
   This building is quite a bit bigger.
4. *Es el edificio más grande de la ciudad.*
   It's the biggest building in the city.
5. *No creo que tenga más de veinte pesetas.*
   I don't think I have more than twenty pesetas.
6. *No me dieron más que treinta dólares.*
   They didn't give me more than (only gave me) thirty dollars.
7. *Esta lección es más fácil que la otra.*
   This lesson is easier than the other one.
8. *Ella es más inteligente que su hermana.*
   She is more intelligent than her sister.
9. *El profesor les dijo que hablaran más fuerte.*
   The professor told them that they should speak louder (more loudly).
10. *Es mi hermana menor.*
    She is my younger sister.

LESSON 19

Exercises

B. 1. *Ellos siempre mandan los mismos periódicos.*
They always send the same newspapers.
2. *El compra la misma crema de afeitar que Juan.*
He buys the same shaving cream as Juan.
3. *Tú recibes el mismo premio que yo.*
You receive the same prize as I do.
4. *Cuando mi padre recibe su máquina de escribir nueva, me da la vieja.*
When my father receives a new typewriter, he gives me the old one.
5. *Juan no escucha el mismo programa que yo.*
Juan isn't listening to the same program as I am.

C. 1. *Me gusta tu coche pero el mío es mejor.*
2. *Compramos el mismo disco que María.*
3. *Juan siempre va a la misma escuela que su hermano.*
4. *Cuando perdió su libro le di el mío.*
5. *Compraron entradas en la misma fila que las nuestras.*
6. *Juan y yo fuimos al mismo teatro que tú.*
7. *Yo tenía mi paraguas pero Juan perdió el suyo.*
8. *Compré unos dulces. ¿Quieres algunos?*
9. *¿Quiere usted darme algunas pesetas?*
10. *¿Dónde están las suyas?*

D. 1. *Estos discos son los mismos que tengo yo.*
These records are the same ones that I have.
2. *Me gusta este coche más que el mío.*
I like this car better than mine.
3. *Esta es mi pluma. ¿Dónde está la tuya?*
This is my pen. Where is yours?
4. *Me gusta esta casa. La nuestra es más pequeña.*
I like this house. Ours is smaller.
5. *Me pidió el libro porque había perdido el suyo.*
He asked me for the book because he had lost his.

6. *Puedes llevar estos lápices aunque me quedan muy pocos.*
   You can take these pencils, although I have very few left.
7. *Veo que hay muchas revistas. Voy a comprar algunas.*
   I see that there are many magazines. I am going to buy some.
8. *Tengo las mismas preocupaciones que tú.*
   I have the same worries as you.
9. *Aquí están mis maletas. ¿Dónde están las tuyas?*
   Here are my suitcases. Where are yours?
10. *Tu sombrero es muy bonito y me gusta el suyo también.*
    Your hat is very pretty, and I like hers, too.

LESSON 20

Exercises

B. 1. *Era posible que vinieran Juan y José.*
   It was possible that Juan and José came.
2. *Lo dijo para que lo supiéramos.*
   He said it so that we would know it.
3. *Esperaba que lo hicieran inmediatamente.*
   I hoped that they would do it immediately.
4. *Dudaba que Juan lo oyera.*
   I doubted that Juan heard it.
5. *María sentía que ellos lo creyeran.*
   María was sorry that they believed it.

C. 1. *Siento que él esté aquí.*
2. *El sintió que yo lo hiciera.*
3. *¡Ojalá él estuviera aquí!*
4. *¡Que lo hagan ellos!*
5. *El más informado nos habló.*
6. *Lo dijeron para que él lo supiera.*
7. *Es imposible que ellos lo crean.*
8. *El dudaba que lo supiéramos.*
9. *Ellos querían que compráramos el libro.*

10. *El jefe me dijo que lo hiciera.* (*El jefe me mandó hacerlo.*)

D. 1. *Me gustaría hablar con la más informada.*
I would like to talk to the best-informed girl.
2. *Tenían que ayudar a los heridos.*
They had to help the wounded.
3. *Que él lo escriba.*
Have him write it.
4. *Fue imposible que ellos vendieran el coche.*
It was impossible for them to sell the car.
5. *Sentía que Juan no pudiera venir a la boda.*
I was sorry that Juan couldn't come to the wedding.
6. *Quería que ellos fueran al cine.*
I wanted them to go to the movies.
7. *Que lo haga Juan.*
Let Juan do it.
8. *De todos los empleados, Rafael es el preferido.*
Of all the employees, Rafael is the preferred man.
9. *Querían que el jefe lo dijera.*
They wanted the boss to say it.
10. *Dicen que soy muy inteligente. ¡Ojalá!*
They say that I am very intelligent. I hope so!